WOMEN: BODY AND CULTURE

WOMEN: Body and Culture

Essays on the Sexuality of Women
in a Changing Society

Edited, and with Introductions, by
SIGNE HAMMER

PERENNIAL LIBRARY
Harper & Row, Publishers
New York, Evanston, San Francisco, London

First PERENNIAL LIBRARY edition published 1975
LIBRARY OF CONGRESS CATALOG CARD NUMBER: 74–9136
STANDARD BOOK NUMBER: 06–080337–1

75 76 77 78 10 9 8 7 6 5 4 3 2 1

CONTENTS

III: THE MENSTRUAL CYCLE:
MENSTRUATION AND MENOPAUSE

Introduction

IV: PREGNANCY, BIRTH, AND CHILD CARE

Introduction

ACKNOWLEDGMENTS

My thanks to Dr. Marjorie Taggart White for her support and encouragement; to Elisabeth Jakab and Corona Machamer of Harper & Row for editorial help and advice; to Mrs. Phyllis Rubinton, former librarian at the New York Psychoanalytic Institute, for help with research; and to all my friends, past and present, in the Women's Liberation movement.

INTRODUCTION

Feminism, femaleness, femininity; body and culture. The word "female" can be a statement of simple biological fact, referring to the body, but it is loaded with overtones of what it means to be a female in a particular culture. "Femininity" suggests the attributes a female person is expected to have in a culture; female persons should be "feminine," otherwise they are considered "masculine." "Feminism" implies a critique of the cultural values of "femininity" and, often, of the meaning of "femaleness." Body and culture are inextricably related in our perception of the meaning of all these terms; the essays in this anthology explore, in different ways and from different points of view, some of the ways in which body and culture affect, separately or together, the sexual life of women in our society. Sexuality was chosen as a focus because, despite the controversy surrounding it in recent years, it remains poorly understood, and because it remains central to every person's experience of herself. A woman experiences her sexuality as a child, when she must integrate the information given to her by her body and her culture into an identity as a female person. This process continues throughout the age of menstruation, which includes puberty, the repetition of cycles throughout adulthood, and their cessation at menopause. As a child, adolescent, and adult, a woman uses her experience of her own body and of her culture in encompassing or retreating from sexual arousal and orgasm, whether through masturbation, heterosexual intercourse, or homosexual activity. In pregnancy, abortion, birth, and child care she again experiences the activity of her body in a social context.

All of the work in this anthology is by professionals in various fields: psychoanalysis, psychology, anthropology,

and sex research. Some of the writers are feminists,
others are not. The book is personal and, perhaps,
idiosyncratic; it represents one result of two years of research and several years of thought by a nonprofessional
who has been deeply involved both in feminism and in
psychoanalysis, where I found myself—bewilderingly—
increasingly more conscious of the validity of my own
identity as a person than I was able to feel through the
ever more militant ideology of radical feminism. My interest in psychology sent me into research; my experience
as an editor made it natural to compile an anthology,
because I felt that my personal experience could be illuminated by knowledge as well as by insight, that knowledge
can lead to insight, and that much work by professionals
is more accessible than seems immediately apparent from
the formidable titles of professional articles or the sometimes forbidding jargon or statistics in which much professional work is written. Feminism became for me not
an answer, but a question aimed at the nature of identity
itself. The essays in this collection are not meant to provide answers, only to provide form and context for some
of the questions.

Psychology has been responding to feminism as more
and more professionals have themselves been writing and
thinking as feminists, but it is still important to understand that even nonfeminists have dealt with important
and valid issues. Feminism did not form in a vacuum.
While women have been questioning the information
produced by professionals, the professionals have become
increasingly aware of the influence of society and environment in the formation of identity, the structuring of
sexual roles, and the maintenance of traditional sexual
attitudes. In psychoanalysis such consciousness began as
early as the twenties and thirties, when a debate on the
nature of female sexuality was the burning issue in the
sedate *International Journal of Psycho-Analysis*, with
Karen Horney in Europe and then America and Melanie

Klein and the "London School" pitted—if that is not too strong a word to use in this context—against the reiterations of Freudian theory by Freud himself and his disciples. Karen Horney's work was itself informed by her consciousness of her own experiences as a woman and by her explorations in other sciences, such as sociology. Margaret Mead has been examining the lives of women for almost as many years; her book *Male and Female*, published in 1949, remains an invaluable source for those wishing to examine the structure of identity in a social context.

When I began this book I was concerned only about women. It now seems odd to me that I ever thought of examining femininity separately from masculinity. Freud was right; the two sexes exist in dialectic from the beginning. Nevertheless, I think the principle of this book remains valid. Its purpose is to put together essays from many disciplines that speak to issues in female sexuality —issues that persist despite all attempts at resolving them once and for all. In some of the essays the dialectic between feminine and masculine is explored; in others, only the feminine experience is considered.

With the rise of modern feminism an inquiry into the nature of women was undertaken, for the first time, by women themselves. It is no wonder that we cannot agree on what we find. As soon as we stopped seeing ourselves as Freud saw us, as people who do not possess penises, disagreement began. Is a female one-who-possesses-a-uterus? No! scream the radical feminists. Is it one-who-possesses-a-vagina? Mixed denials and affirmations. Well, then, is it one-who-possesses-a-clitoris? Radicals cheer, moderates question—still no agreement. Much muttering from various camps. The functions of the body may be autonomous, but they occur in a social context; and our minds, responding to both our bodies and society, structure our feelings about the value or appropriateness of the activity of our bodies. Unfortunately, body and culture are frequently at odds; throughout our lives we are subject to insights, fears, fantasies, and demands that are often mutually contradictory and confusing.

When modern feminism began to express itself, we women, always confined to our bodies as the sole context of our identity, began naturally at the point where we felt the greatest strain. But in the ensuing ferment many of us went so far as to deny the necessity of any separately definable female sexuality at all. Utopians such as Shulamith Firestone and Phyllis Chesler advocated the abolition of all biologically specific activity, with extrauterine birth and power redistribution patterned after Marx or the myths of the Amazons, who are said to have mated anonymously and to have crippled their boy children. A fierce desire for sexual independence manifested itself first in the litany of "man hating" and then, increasingly, in a cry for independence from sexuality itself. But sexuality persists, and as I found the proliferation of personal statements in consciousness raising, books, and articles echoing but not necessarily illuminating my own predicaments, I turned to research as another way of acquiring information to define the questions raised by feminism. Personal statement may be invaluable, but in the absence of information it can degenerate into mere assertion.

Some of the old ideological fiats of feminism have begun to seem quaint and simplistic now, as the rigid dichotomies of the sex war have come to sound as forced and unproductive coming from feminists as they do from militant traditionalists. Some radical feminists have retreated into the ultimate cul-de-sac of lesbianism as a defense against the necessity of continuing to exist in the same world as men. The absolute equation of personal struggle with political struggle has begun to sound naive, as many people realize that their personal lives are more complex than allowed for by ideology. None of us will ever be quite so sanguine about isolating "personal pathology" from its social context as we were before feminism and other forms of social and personal consciousness grew within us, but we know now that personal solutions are political only in the broadest possible sense of that word, and that political ideology can provide a mere refuge into which we carry all the unresolved questions of our own identities. The attempt to discover more flexible terms than some feminist ideology allows was one of the motivating factors in the compilation of this anthology.

Once we get beyond penis envy and attempt to discover what has been found out about femininity as a positive identity rather than a negative condition, we discover that the work has really only begun. How does a woman arrive at a comfortable relationship with her own body and with herself as a person relating to the world? In a way, these two questions are the same, because relating to the world directly has for so long been seen as an essential factor of masculine identity, and much literature has been devoted to explaining how this comes irresistably out of the very nature of masculine sexuality—full of drives, aggressions, and so on. The fact that most aspects of women's sexuality relate to her ability to bear children has made it equally easy to see her identity as inextricably linked with her maternal role, defined as necessarily separate from the activity of the "world." Freud's views have been reinforced by contemporary writers such as Lionel Tiger and others, who manage to find in prehistory and the animal world all sorts of evidence pointing to the essential nature of the sexual and social status quo. Others have argued the tenuous nature of such connections. On the psychological level, the phallocentric view has been well castigated for seeing women in a framework in which penis superiority was bound to produce penis envy and female inferiority. Books have been written on the implications of such a view in terms of deeper masculine feelings of inferiority about the birth process and the primacy of the mother. Men, it has been argued, have seen women as securely grounded in a sexuality that, because it seemed part of her very being rather than being dependent on anything she did, aroused envy, hatred, and sometimes imitation among men who felt their own identities more tenuously linked to activities and rituals whose main function has always appeared to be to keep women out. The topsy-turvy nature of this business, in which the conscious mind erects social structures to compensate for the shortcomings of life as seen from the eye of the unconscious, is certainly ironic on a grand scale.

Feminism has been largely concerned with the impact of these structures on the everyday lives of women, and on the way in which, finally, the patriarchal compensations deprived women of opportunities to affirm their being. The fantasies of the nursery evolve into the myths of an age, and so, when Betty Friedan, writing *The Feminine Mystique*, discovered that housewives were suffering from a sense of devaluation so powerful as to be paralyzing, male novelists were at the same time evoking the powerful image of Mom, the castrating female who rendered them impotent both sexually and, in the larger sense, socially and politically. On the face of it, it seems nothing short of incredible that men have been so opposed to the liberation of Mom from the nurseries of their minds. One answer, of course, lies in the human tendency to equate woman-power with Mother-power, and man-power with Father-power. This is too vast a subject to explore here, but it does suggest the magnitude of the problem.

What is taken up by some of the essays that follow is the way in which our rigid dichotomization of sex roles into masculine-appropriate and feminine-appropriate has created difficulties for women who wish to do things considered appropriate only for men. The unquestioning acceptance of social norms, and the equation of sex roles with identity, has undoubtedly been destructive to women. Once one questions this equation, a whole new range of questions opens up about the real nature of identity in a culture. No one has yet satisfactorily explained why these divisive sex roles—a kind of shorthand, really, in which the full range of human potential is curtailed in both sexes—seem to be so pervasive in our thinking. Appeals to biology or evolution offer no real explanation, because if the identification of the sexes according to their roles really came "naturally," there would be no need for the continued reinforcement of roles through social means such as disapproval and even censorship of those who cross role boundaries. The existence of such sanctions suggests, rather, some fundamental insecurity in sexual identity that can find relief only through the identification with a role.

Anthropology has shown us the importance, among many primitive peoples, of adolescent puberty rituals, in which males are "reborn" into the masculine culture after their initial identification with the feminine world of the mother. One could interpret Freud's view of the Oedipal complex in the same terms, which then suggests that the need to see women as inferior arises from the male's deep anxiety about the wish to identify with the mother. It seems likely that such anxiety is greatest in a culture in which masculine and feminine sex roles are sharply defined and mutually exclusive (or "complementary," as many social scientists put it). The difficulties of integrating identification with both the father and the mother may be at the root of the traditional insistence on the importance of sex roles as a way of distinguishing one sex from the other.

The problem is complicated by the fact that small children and early adolescents tend to see masculine and feminine identity in very simplistic terms; mothers have babies and clean house, fathers go to work, and so on. Young adolescents, who are struggling to integrate and resolve revived Oedipal fantasies into newly emerging adult personality structures, may retain rigid stereotypes in the face of all evidence to the contrary, as I found when teaching a class of exceptionally bright, upper-middle-class twelve-year-olds at a private school. When

asked to describe "a man" and "a woman," without exception they came up with stereotypes of women as
mothers, who were very involved with housecleaning and
cooking. In discussion, however, it became clear that
nearly half the mothers of these children were working
full time, many at professional careers. One boy said that
his father, a writer, stayed home all day and did the
shopping, cleaning, and laundry as well, because his
mother worked at her career outside the home. Yet his
portrait involved the same stereotypes as the others. It
may be that stereotypical thinking is necessary for small
children and young adolescents, as a protection against
confusion and anxiety in defining their own identities; we
need to discover, however, whether the carry-over of
rigid sex-role definitions into adulthood does not represent simply a perpetuation of childhood and adolescent
thinking.

Feminism has increasingly been concerning itself with
issues of achievement and activity in the world, which
seems to be a more useful approach than ideological
struggles, essential as they may have been to create some
terms with which to begin. And it is becoming clear that
drives for autonomy, mastery, competence, and achievement are not sex-linked, but exist in every person. But
every woman must come to terms with herself as a sexual
being as well, and it is perhaps on this level that her
deepest sense of identity—or the lack of it—is formed.
Certainly it is on this level that clashes with conventional
ideas about autonomy and femininity affect her feeling
about herself as a sexual being and simply as a person.
As we have suggested, the sense of identity is provided by
both the body and the culture.

One point that several of the essays in this collection
make is that a woman who feels herself to be a whole
person as a female does better in the world than one who
is confused and anxious about her sexual identity. Of
course, this holds true for men as well, and in both sexes
overcompensation for presumed inferiorities can provide

motivation for achievement. But the processes of identity formation, of puberty, menstruation, and menopause, of sexual arousal, and of childbirth must be dealt with in one way or another by all women—even if they decide not to have children, or to avoid heterosexual involvement, or to take the pill every day of the month and so suppress even the breakthrough bleeding that poses as menstruation when one is taking the pill. In the realm of the psychological, the social and physiological events of sexuality meet to shape a woman's experience of her body and her relationship to the world, and this experience profoundly influences her sense of herself.

I

HOW DOES A GIRL KNOW SHE'S A GIRL?

Introduction

The process of identity formation, in which a girl learns to know herself as a female person, remains something of a mystery. In the overreaction to Freudian theory, it has become fashionable among feminists to see identity almost entirely in terms of sex roles and social conditioning. But body and culture surely interact most profoundly in the psyche of the infant and young child, and the essays in this section explore some of the ways in which that interaction occurs.

The role of the vagina in the development of feminine identity has never been satisfactorily explained. Freud held that the vagina remains undiscovered until puberty, and that little girls see themselves essentially as little boys until knowledge of their "castrated" condition forces them into passivity and femininity. But a number of analysts, among them Karen Horney and Melanie Klein, have observed that knowledge of the vagina, however unconscious, plays a vital part in the evolution of a girl's sense of identity. In "The Denial of the Vagina," Karen Horney suggests that at some point in a little girl's development it is essential for her sense of security to deny the existence of her vagina. This is an extremely interesting question because of the new light shed on the physiology of female sexuality by Masters and Johnson and other sex researchers. Masters and Johnson show indisputably that the primary sensory focus of female sexuality lies in the clitoris; they also show that the vagina functions in sexual arousal, and that vaginal response always accompanies full sexual arousal and orgasm. The emphasis of

radical feminists on clitoral, as opposed to vaginal, sexuality seems, ironically, to be something of a mirror
image of the Freudian division of "infantile, masculine"
clitoral sexuality and "adult" vaginal sexuality. Many
feminists appear to have absorbed Freud's dictum and to
have reversed it to suggest that, in order for women to
operate successfully in the world, they must deny their
vaginal, or heterosexually oriented, sexuality in favor of
clitoral sexuality, whether in masturbation or lesbianism.
The source of anxiety about vaginal or heterosexual sex
has been located directly by feminists in the traditional
sex-role dichotomies. If femininity is equated with femaleness, and women have felt oppressed in their feminine roles, one answer has been to give up heterosexual-
ity. The all-too-common equation of heterosexual sex
with rape—as expressed by both feminist writers and by
many male writers of fantasy and of gynecological textbooks—may be partially illuminated by Horney who,
writing forty years ago, recognized rape fantasies as
common among preadolescent girls. She takes the persistence of such fantasies to indicate that the vagina is
involved in female sexuality and in a girl's awareness of
her own body from an early age. (The persistence of the
rape theory among men must, of course, have its antecedents in masculine personality structure and will not be
considered here.)

As a psychoanalyst, Horney is deeply concerned with
the child's subjective relationship to her body. All the
talk about clitoral sex has hardly obscured the simple fact
that women do possess a vagina, that it necessarily enters
into our fantasies about ourselves from infancy on, and
that our awareness of this entrance to our bodies can be
accompanied by great anxiety. It is important to realize,
however, that Horney was also concerned about women
as achievers in the adult world, and that she was one of
the first psychoanalysts to take social factors into account in her work on the development of identity. When
Horney talks about a girl's "assent to her feminine role,"

she is referring only to the acceptance of vaginal sexuality, and to the feminine role in heterosexual sex. Her strong case for the influence of the vagina in a girl's development is made to refute Freud's concept of the girl as a sort of boy *manqué*. Horney thus anticipated the concern of contemporary feminists with the existence of an independent female sexual development. She differs from many feminists, however, in recognizing that no realistic picture of female sexual identity can leave out the vagina.

Lois Wladis Hoffman, in "Early Childhood Experiences and Women's Achievement Motives," examines some of the factors in early development that can motivate women for achievement in adulthood. She examines the interplay between constitutional factors and the expectations of the environment, as communicated by parents to the child. Girls at an early age seem to work more for love than for achievement, are more verbal than boys, and also more anxious. Hoffman suggests that these aspects of a girl's personality are rooted in her earliest experience, when she is given insufficient encouragement for mastery, competence, and achievement. Also, the girl has a harder time separating herself from her mother because she is of the same sex. Boys, possibly because they are more physically impulsive, have more conflicts with the mother, and this also helps them achieve a sense of a separate self. At the same time, boys are perhaps pushed too fast into competence, with a resulting loss in the capacity for love. The balance between these factors is complicated and delicate, and our understanding of them is still very limited. Mothers react to the real demands of their infants, some of which must be innate, or constitutional; but the ways in which they react to infants of different sexes are rooted in their own unconscious expectations of different behavior for boys and girls.

Some of the ways in which sex role expectations can operate to make a girl or woman who crosses sex-role boundaries unsure of her feminine identity are explored in a perceptive article by Betty J. Kronsky, a psychotherapist who has worked with women having problems in dealing with their own assertiveness. In our culture assertiveness is considered to be a masculine trait, so that girls may have to identify with their fathers in order to incorporate assertiveness into their own sense of identity. The desire to be a man, then, rather than being penis envy in any literal sense, may simply be evidence of the only terms available to the girl in which to see herself as assertive. The fact that sex roles and identity need not be the same—that women can perform "masculine" activities and still identify themselves as "feminine," as suggested by Kronsky—opens up a whole range of questions about the real nature of identity and the necessity for rigid sex role boundaries.

The problem of identification with both parents is further explored by Joyce McDougall, a psychoanalyst, in an excerpt from "Homosexuality in Women." Little girls must sort out a number of aims in relation to both parents, among them the desire to possess the mother completely and the desire to be the father. Girls who manage successfully to integrate their homosexual and heterosexual aims may identify with the father in a number of ways, without identifying with him completely in his sexual role. McDougall feels that homosexual impulses, integrated into the adult woman's identity, enrich her capacities for work and for heterosexual love, in which she can empathize with her sexual partner. Both "masculine" women—those who feel that everyone of both sexes dislikes women—and homosexuals have, for whatever reasons, been unable to integrate their identifications with their father and mother into a self-accepting, independent female identity. These are loaded issues, and it is important to note that McDougall does not equate homosexuality with immaturity; she sees it as one solution to the problem of ego identity. She does believe, however, that it is a precarious solution because it blocks off the integration of identification with both parents into the personality structure.

Relatively little attention has been paid in the literature to the father's role in defining the sexual and social identity of his daughter. In an excerpt from her thesis of nearly twenty years ago, Evelyn Goodenough Pitcher shows how fathers seem more actively concerned about their daughters' "feminine" behavior—in terms of flirtatiousness, affection, and so on—than do mothers. Mothers, in fact, seem to be less concerned with sex typing in both sexes than do fathers. The implications of this study are extremely interesting when considered in terms of the increasing evidence that males achieve their identity to a large extent in opposition to femaleness or femininity, while girls must achieve identification with the mother— the same person from whom they must also separate themselves to become independent persons. It appears that the father is very concerned about teaching the girl her role in opposition to his masculine role, and this certainly is an important function in terms of a child's necessary development of awareness of sexual differentiation. It may even be that the father's role is essential in helping a girl to achieve a sense of separation from her mother, by relating to him—a suggestion made by Erich Neumann in his perceptive study of the myth of Amor and Psyche. The problem, of course, is that girls must also integrate "masculine" aims and identifications if they are to grow up as whole persons. Dr. Hoffman suggests that girls who identify with passive mothers will grow up with passive aims for themselves; but certainly a father who is insecure about his own masculine differentiation could overcompensate by imposing rather rigid standards of appropriate feminine behavior on his daughter. Again, we are left with the fact that the process of identification is complex and remains poorly understood.

The relationship between innate and environmental factors in producing psychosexual differentiation—the differentiation of male and female gender identity in human beings—is explored by John Money, professor of medical psychology at The Johns Hopkins Hospital, in "Psychosexual Differentiation." Money shows how the foundations for the development of both male and female internal sex organs are present in every embryo, while external sex organs develop from a single foundation. Furthermore, an embryo develops into a male only through the influence of androgen. As Money so graphically expresses it, "mammalian masculine anatomy . . . is brought about by something added, failing which the more basic disposition of the embryo toward the feminine asserts itself." Here is a factor that can truly be called innate, and Money "wonders whether to look for a parallel in human psychosexual differentiation."

Money also points out that the environment has an extraordinarily strong effect on the continuing process of differentiation after birth; a person can actually be "assigned" a gender in opposition to hormones, genes, and even physiological appearance. But hormones can also influence behavior. Women who, as embryos, received "an excess of adrenal androgens" were aroused by erotic art and stories to the point of" masturbation; Money cites "hormonal correction with cortisone" as a way of raising their threshold of erotic response to a more "appropriate" level. A few researchers have recently begun to show, however, that many "normal" women are aroused by erotic art and stories, and the idea that this response is peculiar to men has begun to be questioned.

Money shows that the evidence on the complex relationship between "nature" and "nurture" in the process of psychosexual differentiation is by no means all in; the important point is that neither can be held completely responsible. One question that remains unanswered is the relationship of sex-role stereotypes to the process of gender differentiation. In his recent book, *Man and Woman, Boy and Girl*, Money states that the bottom line of differentiation between the two sexes is in terms of their respective roles in reproduction; if these are clearly conveyed, it does not matter whether purely social sex roles are reversed, with the father cooking and the mother driving a truck. Yet, as Money says in the article included here, sex-role expectations play an integral part in the development of gender identity, along with information from one's own body. We clearly need a new evaluation of sex roles and a more subtle understanding of ways in which the two sexes can differentiate without the rigid dichotomization into mutually exclusive sex roles that presently tends to work against empathy and understanding between the sexes. The resurgence of interest in bisexuality and homosexuality in the last few years has tended to obscure the fact that there are still two sexes, and that they must find ways of relating as well as differentiating—whether between two people or within the psyche of the individual.

1

The Denial of the Vagina:
A Contribution to the Problem of the Genital
Anxieties Specific to Women

KAREN HORNEY

. . . Freud . . . assumes that the girl's early genital sensations and activities function essentially in the clitoris. He
regards it as very doubtful whether any early vaginal
masturbation takes place and even holds that the vagina
remains altogether "undiscovered."

To decide this very important question we should once
more require extensive and exact observation of normal
children. Josine Müller[1] and I myself, as long ago as
1925, expressed doubts on the subject. Moreover, most
of the information we occasionally get from gynecologists
and children's physicians interested in psychology suggests that, in the early years of childhood, vaginal masturbation is at least as common as clitoral. The various
data that give rise to this impression are: the frequent
observation of signs of vaginal irritation, such as redden-
ing and discharge, the relatively frequent occurrence of
the introduction of foreign bodies into the vagina, and
finally, the fairly common complaints by mothers that

[1] Josine Müller, "The Problem of Libidinal Development of the
Genital Phase in Girls," *Int. J. Psycho-Anal.*, Vol. XIII (1932).

SOURCE: From "Die Verleugnung der Vagina. Ein Beitrag zur
Frage der spezifisch weiblichen Genitalangst," *Internationale
Zeitschrift für Psychoanalyse*, XIX (1933), pp. 372–384; *Inter-
national Journal of Psycho-Analysis*, 14 (1933), pp. 57–70.
Reprinted by permission of the *International Journal of
Psychoanalysis* and the Association for the Advancement of
Psychoanalysis of the Karen Horney Psychoanalytic Institute
and Center.

their children put their fingers into the vagina. The well-known gynecologist Wilhelm Liepmann has stated[2] that his experience has led him to believe that in early child-hood and even in the first years of infancy, vaginal mas-turbation is much more common than clitoral, and that only in the later years of childhood are the relations re-versed in favor of clitoral masturbation.

These general impressions cannot take the place of systematic observations, nor therefore can they lead to a final conclusion. But they do show that the exceptions Freud himself admits seem to be of frequent occurrence.

Our most natural course would be to try to throw light upon this question from our analyses, but this is difficult. At very best, the material of the patient's conscious recol-lections or the memories that emerge in analysis cannot be treated as unequivocal evidence, because here as ev-erywhere else, we must also take into account the work of repression. In other words, the patient may have good reason for not remembering vaginal sensations or mas-turbation, just as, conversely, we must feel sceptical about her ignorance of clitoral sensations.[3]

A further difficulty is that the women who come for analysis are just those from whom one cannot expect even an average naturalness about vaginal processes. For they are always women whose sexual development has departed somehow from the normal and whose *vaginal* sensibility is disturbed in a greater or lesser degree. At the same time it does seem as if even accidental differences in the material play their part. In approximately two-thirds of my cases I have found the following state of affairs:

1. Marked vaginal orgasm produced by manual vagi-nal masturbation prior to any coitus. Frigidity in the

[2] In a private conversation.

[3] In a discussion following the reading of my paper on the phallic phase before the German Psychoanalytical Society in 1931, Boehm cited several cases in which only vaginal sensations and vaginal masturbation were recollected and the clitoris had apparently re-mained undiscovered.

form of vaginismus and defective secretion in coitus. (I have seen only two cases of this sort, which were quite unmistakable.) I think that, in general, preference is shown for the clitoris or the labia in manual genital masturbation.

2. Spontaneous vaginal sensations, for the most part with noticeable secretion, aroused by unconsciously stimulating situations, such as that of listening to music, motoring, swinging, having the hair combed, and certain transference situations. No manual vaginal masturbation; frigidity in coitus.

3. Spontaneous vaginal sensations produced by extra-genital masturbation, e.g., by certain motions of the body, by tight lacing, or by particular sado-masochistic fantasies. No coitus, because of the overpowering anxiety aroused whenever the vagina is about to be touched, whether by a man in coitus, by a physician in a gynecological examination, or by the subject herself in manual masturbation, or in any douching prescribed medically.

For the time being, then, my impressions may be summed up as follows: In manual genital masturbation the clitoris is more commonly selected than the vagina, *but spontaneous genital sensations resulting from general sexual excitation are more frequently located in the vagina.*

From a theoretical standpoint I think that great importance should be attached to this relatively frequent occurrence of spontaneous vaginal excitations even in patients who were ignorant, or had only a very vague knowledge, of the existence of the vagina, and whose subsequent analysis did not bring to light memories or other evidence of any sort of vaginal seduction, nor any recollection of vaginal masturbation. For this phenomenon suggests the question *whether from the very beginning sexual excitations may not have expressed themselves perceptibly in vaginal sensations.*

In order to answer this question we should have to

wait for very much more extensive material than any single analyst can obtain from his own observations. Meanwhile there are a number of considerations that seem to me to favor my view.

In the first place there are the fantasies of rape that occur before coitus has taken place at all, and indeed long before puberty, and are frequent enough to merit wider interest. I can see no possible way of accounting for the origin and content of these fantasies if we are to assume the nonexistence of vaginal sexuality. For these fantasies do not in fact stop short at quite indefinite ideas of an act of violence, through which one gets a child. On the contrary, fantasies, dreams, and anxiety of this type usually betray quite unmistakably an instinctive knowledge of the actual sexual processes. The guises they assume are so numerous that I need only indicate a few of them: criminals who break in through windows or doors; men with guns who threaten to shoot; animals that creep, fly, or run inside some place (e.g., snakes, mice, moths); animals or women stabbed with knives; or trains running into a station or tunnel.

I speak of an "instinctive" knowledge of the sexual processes because we meet typically with ideas of this sort—e.g., in the anxieties and dreams of early childhood —at a period when as yet there is no intellectual knowledge derived from observation or from explanations by others. It may be asked whether such instinctive knowledge of the processes of penetration into the female body necessarily presupposes an instinctive knowledge of the existence of the vagina as the organ of reception. I think that the answer is in the affirmative if we accept Freud's view that "the child's sexual theories are modelled on the child's own sexual constitution." For this can only mean that the path traversed by the sexual theories of children is marked out and determined by spontaneously experienced impulses and organ sensations. If we accept this origin for the sexual theories, which already embody an attempt at rational elaboration, we must all the more admit it in the case of that instinctive knowledge which finds symbolic expression in play, dreams, and various forms of anxiety, and which obviously has not reached the sphere of reasoning and the elaboration which takes place there. In other words, we must assume that both the dread of rape, characteristic of puberty, and the infantile anxieties of little girls are based on vaginal organ sensations (or the instinctual impulses issuing from these), which imply that something ought to penetrate into that part of the body.

I think we have here the answer to an objection which may be raised, namely, that many dreams indicate the idea that an opening was only created when the penis first brutally penetrated the body. For such fantasies would not arise at all but for the previous existence of instincts —and the organ sensations underlying them—having the passive aim of reception. Sometimes the connection in which dreams of this type occur indicates quite clearly the origin of this particular idea. For it occasionally happens that when a general anxiety about the injurious consequences of masturbation makes its appearance, the patient has dreams with the following typical content: she is doing a piece of needlework and all at once a hole appears, of which she feels ashamed; or she is crossing above a river or a chasm on a bridge that suddenly breaks off in the middle; or she is walking along a slippery incline and all at once begins to slide and is in danger of falling over a precipice. From such dreams we may conjecture that when these patients were children and indulged in onanistic play, they were led by vaginal sensations to the discovery of the vagina itself, and that their anxiety took the very form of the dread that they had made a hole where no hole ought to be. I would here emphasize that I have never been wholly convinced by Freud's explanation why girls suppress direct genital masturbation more easily and frequently than boys. As we know, Freud supposes[4] that (clitoral) masturbation becomes odious to little girls because comparison with the penis strikes a blow at their narcissism. When we consider the strength of the drive behind the onanistic impulses, a narcissistic mortification does not seem altogether adequate in weight to produce suppression. On the other hand, the dread that she has done herself an irreparable injury in that region might well be powerful enough to prevent vaginal masturbation, and either to compel the girl to restrict the practice to the clitoris, or else permanently to set her against all manual genital masturbation. I believe that we have further evidence of this early dread of vaginal injury in the envious comparison with the man, which we frequently hear from patients of this type, who say that men are "so nicely closed up" underneath. Similarly, that deepest anxiety which springs out of masturbation for a woman, that dread that it has made her unable to have children, seems to relate to the inside of the body rather than to the clitoris.

This is another point in favor of the existence and the significance of early vaginal excitations. We know that observation of sexual acts has a tremendously exciting effect upon children. If we accept Freud's view we must assume that such excitation produces in little girls in the main the same phallic impulses to penetrate as are evoked in little boys. But then we must ask: Whence comes the anxiety met with almost universally in the analyses of female patients—the dread of the gigantic penis that might pierce her? The origin of the idea of an excessively large penis can surely not be sought anywhere but in childhood, when the father's penis must actually have appeared menacingly large and terrifying. Or again, whence comes that understanding of the female sexual role, evinced in the symbolism of sexual anxiety, in which those early excitations once more vibrate? And how can

[4] Freud, "Some Psychological Consequences of the Anatomical Distinction between the Sexes," *Int. J. Psycho-Anal.*, Vol. VIII (1927).

we account at all for the unbounded jealous fury with the mother, which commonly manifests itself in the analyses of women when memories of the "primal scene" are affectively revived? How does this come about if at that time the subject could only share in the excitations of the father?

Let me bring together the sum total of the above data. We have: reports of powerful vaginal orgasm going with frigidity in subsequent coitus; spontaneous vaginal excitation without local stimulus, but frigidity in intercourse; reflections and questions arising out of the need to understand the whole content of early sexual games, dreams, and anxieties, and later fantasies of rape, as well as reactions to early sexual observations; and finally, certain contents and consequences of the anxiety produced in women by masturbation. If I take all the foregoing data together, I can see only one hypothesis that gives a satisfactory answer to all these questions, the hypothesis, namely, that *from the very beginning the vagina plays its own proper sexual part.*

Closely connected with this train of thought is the problem of frigidity, which to my mind lies *not* in the question how the quality of libidinal sensibility becomes transmitted to the vagina,[5] but rather, how it comes

[5] In reply to Freud's assumption that the libido may adhere so closely to the clitoral zone that it becomes difficult or impossible for sensibility to be transferred to the vagina, may I venture to enlist Freud against Freud? For it was he who showed convincingly how ready we are to snatch at fresh possibilities of pleasure and how even processes that have no sexual quality—e.g., movements of the body, speech, or thought—may be eroticized and that the same is actually true of tormenting or distressing experiences such as pain or anxiety. Are we then to suppose that in coitus, which furnishes the very fullest opportunities for pleasure, the woman recoils from availing herself of them! Since to my thinking this is a problem that really does not arise, I cannot follow H. Deutsch and M. Klein in their conjectures about the transference of the libido from the oral to the genital zone. There can be no doubt that in many cases there is a close connection between the two. The only question is whether we are to regard the libido

about that the vagina, in spite of the sensibility it already possesses, either fails altogether to react or reacts in a disproportionately small degree to the very strong libidinal excitations furnished by all the emotional and local stimuli in coitus? Surely there could be only *one* factor stronger than the will for pleasure, and that factor is anxiety.

We are now immediately confronted by the problem of what is meant by this vaginal anxiety or rather by its infantile conditioning factors. Analysis reveals, first of all, castration impulses against the man, and associated with these, an anxiety whose source is twofold: on the one hand, the subject dreads her own hostile impulses, and on the other, the retribution she anticipates in accordance with the law of talion, namely, that the contents of her body will be destroyed, stolen, or sucked out. Now these impulses in themselves are, as we know, for the most part not of recent origin, but can be traced to infantile feelings of rage and impulses of revenge against the father, feelings called forth by the disappointments and frustrations the little girl has suffered.

Very similar in content to these forms of anxiety is that described by Melanie Klein, which can be traced back to early destructive impulses directed against the body of the mother. Once more it is a question of the dread of retribution, which may take various forms, but its essence is in general that everything which penetrates the body or is already there (food, faeces, children) may become dangerous.

Although at bottom these forms of anxiety are so far analogous to the genital anxiety of boys, they take on a specific character from that proneness to anxiety which is part of the biological make-up of girls. In this and earlier

---

as being "transferred" or whether it is simply inevitable that when an oral attitude has been early established and persists, it should manifest itself in the genital sphere *also*.

papers I have already indicated what are these sources of anxiety and here I need only complete and sum up what has been said before:

1. They proceed first of all from the tremendous difference in size between the father and the little girl, between the genitals of father and child. We need not trouble to decide whether the disparity between penis and vagina is inferred from observation or whether it is instinctively apprehended. The quite comprehensible and indeed inevitable result is that any fantasy of gratifying the tension produced by vaginal sensations (i.e., the craving to take into oneself, to receive) gives rise to anxiety on the part of the ego. As I showed in my paper "The Dread of Woman," I believe that in this biologically determined form of feminine anxiety we have something specifically different from the boy's original genital anxiety in relation to his mother. When he fantasies the fulfillment of genital impulses he is confronted with a fact very wounding to his self-esteem ("my penis is too small for my mother") ; the little girl, on the other hand, is faced with destruction of part of her body. Hence, carried back to its ultimate biological foundations, the man's dread of the woman is genital-narcissistic, while the woman's dread of the man is physical.

2. A second specific source of anxiety, the universality and significance of which is emphasized by Daly,[6] is the little girl's observation of menstruation in adult relatives. Beyond all (secondary!) interpretations of castration she sees demonstrated for the first time the vulnerability of the female body. Similarly, her anxiety is appreciably increased by observations of a miscarriage or parturition by her mother. Since, in the minds of children and (when repression has been at work) in the unconscious of adults, there is a close connection

[6] Daly, "Der Menstruationskomplex," *Imago*, Bd. XIV (1928).

between coitus and parturition, this anxiety may take
the form of a dread not only of parturition but also of
coitus itself.

3. Finally, we have a third specific source of anxiety
in the little girl's reactions (again due to the anatomical
structure of her body) to her early attempts at vaginal
masturbation. I think that the consequences of these
reactions may be more lasting in girls than in boys,
and this for the following reasons: In the first place
she cannot actually ascertain the effect of masturbation.
A boy, when experiencing anxiety about his genital,
can always convince himself anew that it does exist and
is intact.[7] A little girl has no means of proving to herself
that her anxiety has no foundation in reality. On the
contrary, her early attempts at vaginal masturbation
bring home to her once more the fact of her greater
physical vulnerability,[8] for I have found in analysis
that it is by no means uncommon for little girls, when
attempting masturbation or engaging in sexual play
with other children, to incur pain or little injuries, obviously caused by infinitesimal ruptures of the hymen.[9]

Where the general development is favorable—i.e.,
where the object relations of childhood have not become
a fruitful source of conflict—this anxiety is satisfactorily
mastered and the way is then open for the subject to

[7] These real circumstances must most certainly be taken into
account, as well as the strength of unconscious sources of anxiety.
For instance, a man's castration anxiety may be intensified as the
result of phimosis.

[8] It is perhaps not without interest to recall that the gynecologist
Wilhelm Liepmann (whose standpoint is not that of analysis), in
his book *Psychologie der Frau*, says that the "vulnerability" of
women is one of the specific characteristics of their sex.

[9] Such experiences often come to light in analysis, firstly, in the
form of screen memories of injuries to the genital region, sustained
in later life, possibly through a fall. To these recollections patients
react with a terror and shame out of all proportion to the cause.
Secondly, there may be an overwhelming dread lest such an injury
should possibly occur.

assent to her feminine role. That in unfavorable cases the
effect of the anxiety is more persistent with girls than
with boys is, I think, indicated by the fact that, with the
former, it is relatively more frequent for direct genital
masturbation to be given up altogether, or at least it is
confined to the more easily accessible clitoris with its
lesser cathexis of anxiety. Often everything connected
with the vagina—the knowledge of its existence, vaginal
sensations, and instinctual impulses—succumbs to a re-
lentless repression; in short, the fiction is conceived and
long maintained that the vagina does not exist, a fiction
that at the same time determines the little girl's preference for the masculine sexual role.

All these considerations seem to me to be greatly in
favor of the hypothesis that *behind the "failure to discover" the vagina is a denial of its existence.*

It remains to consider the question of what importance
the existence of early vaginal sensations or the "discovery" of the vagina has for our whole conception of early
feminine sexuality. Though Freud does not expressly
state it, it is nonetheless clear that if the vagina remains
originally "undiscovered," this is one of the strongest
arguments in favor of the assumption of a biologically
determined, primary penis envy in little girls or of their
original phallic organization. For if no vaginal sensations
or cravings existed, but the whole libido were concentrated on the clitoris, phallically conceived of, then and
then only could we understand how little girls, for want
of any specific source of pleasure of their own or of any
specific feminine wishes, must be driven to concentrate
their whole attention on the clitoris, to compare it with
the boy's penis, and then, since they are in fact at a
disadvantage in this comparison, to feel themselves definitely slighted.[10] If on the other hand, as I conjecture, a

[10] Helene Deutsch arrives at this basis for penis envy by a process of logical argument. Cf. Deutsch, "The Significance of Masochism in the Mental Life of Women," *Int. J. Psycho-Anal.*, Vol.
XI (1930).

little girl experiences from the very beginning vaginal sensations and corresponding impulses, she must from the outset have a lively sense of this specific character of her own sexual role, and a primary penis envy of the strength postulated by Freud would be hard to account for. . . .

2

Early Childhood Experiences and Women's Achievement Motives

LOIS WLADIS HOFFMAN

The failure of women to fulfill their intellectual potential has been adequately documented. The explanations for this are so plentiful that one is almost tempted to ask why women achieve at all. Their social status is more contingent on whom they marry than what they achieve; their sense of femininity and others' perception of them as feminine is jeopardized by too much academic and professional success; their husband's masculinity, and hence their love relationship as well as their reciprocal sense of femininity, is threatened if they surpass him; discrimination against women in graduate school admittance and the professions puts a limit on what rewards their performance will receive; their roles as wives and mothers take time from their professional efforts and offer alternative sources of self-esteem. Perhaps most important, they have an alternative to professional success and can opt out when the going gets rough. A full scale achievement effort involves painful periods of effort and many a man would drop out if that alternative were as readily available as it is to women. (Indeed, the Vietnam war and the new distrust of the old goals have provided young men with just such an opportunity and many have grabbed it.) But women's underachievement must have roots deeper even than these, for the precursors of the underachieving woman can be seen in the female child.

Source: From "Early Childhood Experiences and Women's Achievement Motives" by Lois Wladis Hoffmann, in *Journal of Social Issues*, 28, no. 2 (1972), pp. 129–155. Reprinted by permission of the *Journal of Social Issues* and the author.

Even at preschool age girls have different orientations toward intellectual tasks than do boys. Little girls want to please; they work for love and approval; if bright, they underestimate their competence. Little boys show more task involvement, more confidence, and are more likely to show IQ increments. Girls have more anxiety than boys and the anxiety they have is more dysfunctional to their performance. There are also differences in the specific skills of each sex: Males excel in spatial perceptions, arithmetical reasoning, general information, and show less set-dependency; girls excel in quick-perception of details, verbal fluency, rote memory, and clerical skills.

Boys and girls enter the world with different constitutional make-ups, and recent studies show that parents treat boys and girls differently even from birth. Social roles are first—and most impressively—communicated through parent-child relations and events in early childhood may have an impact that cannot later be duplicated in effectiveness.

As a result, interest in women's intellectual achievement has led a number of people to look to the child development data for insights. . . .

*   *   *

FEMALE ACHIEVEMENT ORIENTATIONS

There are very few studies that have empirically connected socialization experiences to sex differences in achievement orientations. As a matter of fact, there are few studies of sex differences in child rearing practices in general, and existing data—most of which were originally collected for other purposes—are subject to limitations. . . .

The present paper will focus on . . . the question of motivation for top intellectual performance. There are data that the very brightest women more often than comparable men stop short of operating at their top intellectual level. Terman and Oden (1947) have shown that gifted girls did not as adults fulfill their potential as often as gifted boys. Rossi (1965a, 1965b) has summarized data indicating that even those few women who do go into science and the professions rarely achieve eminence.[1]

These data reflect in part the factors mentioned earlier —alternative choices in life that have been available to women but not to men, barriers to career opportunities that exist because of women's family roles, and discrimination in the professions which limits the rewards obtainable. The concern here is not with these factors, however, but with a deeper, more psychologically-based motivation that occurs in women. The most relevant data come from the work of Horner (1968, 1972) who has demonstrated with a projective story completion measure a "fear of success" among able college women. Furthermore, women who indicate fear of success show poorer performance in a competitive task than when the same task is performed alone. In interpreting her results, Horner suggests that this fear exists in women because their anticipation of success is accompanied by the anticipation of negative consequences in the form of social rejection or loss of femininity.

The idea that the affiliative motive can be dysfunctional to performance is supported by another of Horner's findings. Men who were motivated both to achieve and to affiliate showed a performance decrement when asked to compete with another man. Horner suggests this decrement may have resulted from a conflict of motives since "out-performing a competitor may be antagonistic to making him a friend."

AFFILIATIVE NEEDS AND ACHIEVEMENT

There is a great deal of evidence that females have greater affiliative needs than males (Oetzel, 1966; Wal-

[1] Simon, Clark, and Galway (1970), on the other hand, have reported that the woman PhD who is employed full time publishes as much as her male colleagues.

berg, 1969) and therefore the conflict between affiliation and achievement probably will occur more often for women. It seems that, apart from direct concerns with whether or not their behavior is sufficiently "feminine," academic and professional women frequently allow their concern with affective relationships to interfere with the full use of their cognitive capacities. In group discussion and in intellectual argument, women often seem to sacrifice brilliance for rapport.

However, while the findings of the Horner studies (1972) and our observations of professional women focus attention on the dysfunctions of affiliative motivations for performance, there are data indicating that the desire for love and approval can also have a positive effect. In fact, the Crandalls (V. J. Crandall, 1963; V. C. Crandall, 1964) as well as others (Garai & Scheinfeld, 1968) have suggested that achievement behavior in girls is motivated not by mastery strivings as with boys, but by affiliative motives.

In two very different studies, nursery school and elementary school girls' achievement efforts were motivated by a desire for social approval to a greater extent than were boys'. In the nursery school study the attempt was also made to motivate the children by appeals to mastery strivings; this technique succeeded with boys but failed with girls (Lahtinen, 1964). In the study with elementary school children, achievement motives in boys were related positively to achievement test scores. Among the girls, affiliative motives, not achievement motives, were so related (Sears, 1962, 1963). Other studies with nursery school and elementary school children found affiliative behavior and achievement efforts positively related in girls, but boys showed no such relationship (Tyler, Rafferty, & Tyler, 1962; Crandall, Dewey, Katkovsky, & Preston, 1964). Similarly with adult women, the achievement arousal techniques that are effective with males have failed with females (Veroff, Wilcox, & Atkinson, 1953;

Horner, 1968), but appeals to social acceptability have been successful (Field, 1951).

There are also several studies that indicate that throughout grade school boys are more motivated than girls to master challenging tasks when social approval is not involved. When given the opportunity to perform an easy or more difficult task, to work on a puzzle they had already solved or one they had failed, to pursue further or escape a difficult problem, boys are more likely to choose the more difficult and challenging, girls to choose the task that promises easy success or to leave the scene (Crandall & Rabson, 1960; Moriarty, 1961; McManis, 1965; Veroff, 1969).

From these studies it appears that female achievement behavior even at preschool or early grade school ages is motivated by a desire for love rather than mastery. When achievement goals conflict with affiliative goals, as was the case in Horner's projective responses and in the competitive situation in which her fear-of-success girls showed less competent performance, achievement behavior will be diminished and/or anxiety result. This does not mean that academic performance is lower for females in general since it is often compatible with affiliative motives. In elementary schools, excellence is rewarded with love and approval by parents, teachers, and peers. Even in the lower socioeconomic class, sociometric studies show that academic excellence in girls is rewarded with popularity (Glidewell et al., 1966; Pope, 1953). In college, however, and in professional pursuits, love is less frequently the reward for top performance. Driving a point home, winning an argument, beating others in competition, and attending to the task at hand without being side-tracked by concern with rapport require the subordination of affiliative needs.

In short, the qualities needed for sustained top performance—especially as an adult—are not typically part of a girl's make-up. She wants approval and so she performs well in school. She works for good grades. And indeed throughout grammar school, high school, and college, she obtains higher grades than boys (Oetzel, 1966; Garai & Scheinfeld, 1968). If overachievement is thought of as grades exceeding IQ's, then girls as a group are more overachieving than boys. But girls are less likely to become involved in their task; they are less motivated by strivings for mastery. In McClelland's sense of *achievement* (McClelland, Atkinson, Clark, & Lowell, 1953)— competition with a standard of excellence—they fall short.[2]

This affiliative need may be particularly germane to achievement patterns because it may be rooted in early experiences when the child is learning patterns of effectance. When little boys are expanding their mastery strivings, learning instrumental independence, developing skills in coping with their environment and confidence in this ability, little girls are learning that effectiveness—and even safety—lie in their affectional relationships. The idea expressed by Kagan (1964) that boys try to "figure the task" and girls try to "figure the teacher" seems rooted in early childrearing practices and reinforced by later experiences.

STATEMENT OF THEORY

It is the thesis here that the female child is given inadequate parental encouragement in early independence strivings. Furthermore, the separation of the self from the mother is more delayed or incomplete for the girl because she is the same sex with the same sex role expectations, and because girls have fewer conflicts with their parents. As a result, she does not develop confidence in her ability

---

[2] Women have obtained scores on McClelland's test of achievement motivation under neutral conditions that are as high or higher than those obtained by men under arousal conditions; however, researchers have questioned the validity of the measure for women (see McClelland et al., 1953; and Horner, 1968).

to cope independently with the environment. She retains her infantile fears of abandonment; safety and effectiveness lie in her affective ties. These points will now be elaborated and supportive data brought in where available.

The Development of Independence, Competence, and Self-Confidence

All infants are dependent; as the child matures his independence strivings increase. Observers have often been impressed with what White (1960) calls the *effectance motive*—the child's need to have an effect upon his environment. Thus the child grasps and releases, reaches and pulls, and in the course of doing this he learns about his environment and his ability to manipulate it. He develops cognitive abilities, and he develops a sense of effectiveness—a sense of competence through increasingly successful interaction with his environment.

As the infant matures, the feats he undertakes get scarier. Increasingly they involve separating the self from the mother and leaving the security of that unity. Early independence explorations seem to take place most successfully with the parent present; the child moves toward independence so long as the "safety man" is in sight. As he gains confidence, the parent's presence becomes less and less necessary.

Very likely this period—somewhere between a year and three or four years of age—is critical in the development of independence and competence (Erikson, 1959; Veroff, 1969; White, 1960; Stendler, 1963). By critical, we mean a period when independence and competence orientations are more efficiently learned than at other times. There is a rapid building up of notions about the self and about the world.

Although theories differ as to the exact timing and differential importance of the events occurring in this period, all would probably agree on the minimal requirements for the development of independence and competence. Thus if the infant is deprived of affection, rejected, or prematurely pushed toward independence, he will not have a secure base from which to build true independence. The dependency that results from a short shrift in early affective ties is probably of a distinct kind (Stendler, 1963). We do not think it is more characteristic of girls, nor that it is sufficiently common to the nonpathogenic middle class family to be useful in understanding prevalent female achievement orientations.

Even with an adequate affective base, independent behavior does not happen automatically. It requires not only opportunities for independent behavior but also actual parental encouragement. Evidence for this can be found in Baumrind's research (Baumrind & Black, 1967; Baumrind, 1971) which indicates that competence comes not from permissiveness but from guidance and encouragement. The first steps a child takes are exciting but also frightening, and cues from the mother can greatly influence the subsequent behavior. The mother's delight is part of her independence training; her apprehension constitutes training in dependence.

Further, if the child's early independence behaviors are to be followed by more, these ventures must be reasonably in accord with his abilities. Repeated successes such as these will have the important effect of developing in the child a sense of competence. There may be a delicate timing mechanism—premature independence can backfire; but the parent who withholds independence opportunities too long and indeed does not encourage independent behavior will also fail to produce an independent child. (It is possible that the appropriate timing is different for boys than girls due to differences in abilities and maturation rates.)

The awareness that the mother is a separate person whose wishes are not the same as his serves to increase the child's striving for autonomy and independence. Both Erikson and White see the period between one and three as the battle for autonomy. At this age the child's motoric

explorations often require parental interference. The span
of consecutive action is such that interference can be
frustrating for the child and completions gratifying. Toilet training usually occurs around this time. The child
thus enters into conflict with his mother; out of this conflict, if it does not involve his humiliation and defeat, the
child will emerge with "a lasting sense of autonomy and
pride [Erikson, 1959]" and "a measure of confidence in
his own strength [White, 1960]."

THE EMPIRICAL FINDINGS

Independence Training: Sex Differences

Early exploratory behaviors in which the child inter-
acts effectively with his environment are seen here as
crucial in building up a sense of competence. In this respect males have a number of advantages.

INFANT STUDIES. Studies of neonates suggest a higher
activity level on the part of the male, while females demonstrate greater tactile sensitivity and a lower pain
threshold (Garai & Scheinfeld, 1968). From these predispositions alone we could expect more exploratory behavior on the part of male infants, but to compound the
matter observations of mothers with neonates show that
even controlling for the differences in activity levels,
mothers handle and stimulate males more than females
(Moss, 1967, undated). And a study by Rubenstein
(1967) suggests that such maternal attentiveness facili-
tates exploratory behavior.

Kagan and Lewis and their associates have also reported differences in maternal behavior toward male and
female infants (Kagan, Levine, & Fishman, 1967; Goldberg & Lewis, 1969). Whether the maternal behavior is
primarily a response to infant predispositions or a cause
of the differences is not definitely established, but there is
some evidence that both influences occur. That maternal
behavior is not entirely a response to the infant is indi-

cated by relationships found between the mother's infant
care and her orientations prior to the child's birth. For
example, Moss (1967) reports that mothers were inter-
viewed two years before they gave birth and rated on
their attitudes toward babies. A positive attitude toward
babies was found to relate significantly to the amount of
responsiveness later shown to her 3-week-old infant. This
same investigator also found mutual visual regard—one
of the earliest forms of mother-infant communication—
to be related to maternal attitudes expressed before the
birth (Moss & Robson, 1968). On the other hand, that
maternal behavior is not the sole determinant of the infant's behavior is indicated by the fact that the sex differences in tactile stimulation and pain thresholds mentioned
above have been established for infants less than four
days old and still in the hospital nursery (Garai & Scheinfeld, 1968; Silverman, 1970). An interaction hypothesis
seems most tenable in the light of the present data.

One of Moss's mother-infant interaction findings is
particularly pertinent to the theory presented in this paper
(1967, undated). He reports data on the mother's responsiveness to the infant's cries and notes that this sequence—baby cries and mother responds with the needed
care—is important in shaping the infant's response to the
mother as a supplier of comfort. The more closely the
mother's caretaking behavior is related to the infant's
cries, the more effectively will the child "regard the
mother as having reinforcing properties and respond to
her accordingly [Moss, undated, p. 10]." The correlation
obtained between maternal contact and infant irritability
was statistically significant for females but not for males.
The mothers did not attend to the female infants more
than the male (less, in fact) but their attention was more
closely linked to the infant's state of need as expressed by
crying. This finding if borne out by further research could
be very important for several reasons. First, it could sig-
nify the beginning of a pattern of interaction between
mothers and daughters in which the daughters quickly

learn that the mother is a source of comfort; and the mother's behavior is reinforced by the cessation of crying. The sheer presence of the mother would soon signal the satisfaction of the infant's needs. Second, there is agreement among most investigators that there are critical periods in infancy when learning takes place so efficiently that long range behaviors are effected by simple but pertinently timed events; this might be such a critical period. Third, even if this is not a critical period, the finding may reflect an orientation of mothers toward daughters that is often repeated beyond the infancy period.

In any case, one thing appears certain from this body of research on early mother-infant interaction: There are sex differences in both maternal and infant behavior during the first year of life. That sex role learning is begun so early should not be surprising. Sex is a primary status —the first one announced at birth. The mother is very much aware of it. Her early behaviors toward the infant are not deliberate efforts to teach the child his proper sex role, but she has internalized society's view and acts accordingly. She acts toward her son as though he were sturdy and active and she is more likely to show pleasure when his behavior fits this image. Her daughter is her doll—sweet and delicate and pink. The mother's behavior reflects this perception, and if the child exhibits behavior consistent with the female stereotype, such as dependency, she is not as likely to discourage it as she would with a son.

INDEPENDENCE TRAINING IN CHILDHOOD. Moving from early infancy, we find studies that link independence training and the parent's achievement orientations to the child's competence (Baumrind & Black, 1967) and achievement orientations (Winterbottom, 1958; Rosen & D'Andrade, 1959), but few examining sex differences in the independence and achievement training children receive. It is our view that because of parental attitudes toward male and female children which reflect their cul-

turally assigned roles, males receive more effective independence training and encouragement.

. . . Collard (1964) asked mothers of 4-year-olds to
indicate the ages they thought parents should expect or
permit certain child behaviors. For example, the parents
were asked at what age they believed parents should: (a)
begin to allow their child to use sharp scissors with *no*
adult supervision, (b) begin to allow their child to play
away from home for long periods of time during the day
without first telling his parents where he will be. The
answers to these questions yielded two measures—*independence granting* and *achievement induction*. Mothers
of girls responded with later ages than mothers of boys.
This difference was significant for the independence-
granting items and it was particularly strong in the middle
class. The achievement induction scores were not significantly different for the two sexes, but close inspection of
the data revealed that, for the middle class, mothers of
girls indicated an earlier age for only two of the 18 items
making up the scale. One of the two exceptions was "sharing toys" which may have more to do with inter-personal
relationships than with achievement.

PARENTAL ANXIETY AND PROTECTIVENESS. Still another
difference in the independence training received by boys
and girls may stem from parental ambivalence: Parents
may show more unambivalent pleasure in sons' achievements than in daughters'. The young child's first motoric
adventures can produce anxiety in the mother as well as
the child, just as they produce pleasure for both. It seems
likely that for the parent of a boy there is a particular
pride in the achievement and less of a feeling of the
child's fragility; as a result there is a clearer communication of pleasure in the achievement per se. A beaming
mother when the child takes his first steps may have a
very different effect than the mother who looks anxious
while holding out loving arms. In the former case, the
task itself becomes the source of pleasure (in reinforcement terms the reward is closer to the act). In the latter

case, the mother is saying in effect, "You may break your neck en route, but I will give you love when you get here." The mother's indications of anxiety as the child moves toward independence make the child doubt his own competence, for mothers are still omniscient to the young child.

There is some indirect evidence for this view. Despite the greater maturity and sturdiness of the female infant (Garai & Scheinfeld, 1968), parents think of them as more fragile. Furthermore, behavioral observations of infants have shown that male infants are handled more vigorously (Moss, 1967). The setting of later ages for granting autonomy to girls, as indicated in the Collard (1964) study mentioned earlier, suggests that parents are more protective, if not more anxious, toward girls. For example, parents report allowing boys to cross busy streets by themselves earlier, though they are not motorically more advanced than girls and their greater motoric impulsivity would seem to make this more dangerous. And we do know that infants pick up the subtle attitudes of their caretakers. This was demonstrated in the well known study by Escalona (1945) in which the infant's preference for orange or tomato juice depended heavily on the preference of the nurse who regularly fed him. The infant had no way of knowing his nurse's preference except through sensing her attitude as she fed him.

Another kind of parent behavior that is detrimental to the development of independence might be called *overhelp*. Mastery requires the ability to tolerate frustration. If the parent responds too quickly with aid, the child will not develop such tolerance. This shortcoming—the tendency to withdraw from a difficult task rather than to tackle the problem and tolerate the temporary frustration —seems to characterize females more than males. This has been demonstrated in the test situations mentioned earlier, and Crandall and Rabson (1960) have also found that, in free play, grade school girls are more likely than boys to withdraw from threatening situations and more frequently to seek help from adults and peers. The dysfunctions of this response for the development of skills and a sense of competence are clear. There are no data to indicate that over-help behavior is more characteristic of parents of girls, but such a difference seems likely in view of the greater emphasis placed on the independence training of boys.

Clearly more research is needed to identify differences in the independence and achievement training—and in any overprotection and over-help—that parents provide boys and girls. . . .

Establishing a Separate Self: Sex Differences

SAME SEX PARENT AS PRIMARY CARETAKER. Separation of the self is facilitated when the child is the opposite sex of the primary caretaker. Parsons (1949, 1965) and Lynn (1962, 1969), as well as others, have pointed out that both males and females form their first attachment to the mother. The girl's modeling of the mother and maintaining an identity with her is consistent with her own sex role, but the boy must be trained to identify with his father or to learn some abstract concept of the male role. As a result, the boy's separation from the mother is encouraged; it begins earlier and is more complete. The girl, on the other hand, is encouraged to maintain her identification with the mother; therefore she is not as likely to establish an early and independent sense of self. If the early experiences of coping with the environment independently are crucial in the development of competence and self-confidence, as suggested previously, the delayed and possibly incomplete emergence of the self should mitigate against this development.

There are no studies that directly test this hypothesis. As indirect evidence, however, there are several studies showing that the more identified with her mother and the more feminine the girl is, the less likely she is to be a high achiever and to excel in mathematics, analytic skills, creativity, and game strategies. For example, Plank and

Plank (1954) found that outstanding women mathematicians were more attached to and identified with their fathers than their mothers. Bieri (1960) found that females high on analytical ability also tended to identify with their fathers. Higher masculinity scores for girls are related positively to various achievement measures (Oetzel, 1961; Milton, 1957; Kagan & Kogan, 1970), as are specific masculine traits such as aggressiveness (Sutton-Smith, Crandall, & Roberts, 1964; Kagan & Moss, 1962). The relation between cross-sex identification and cognitive style for both boys and girls is discussed also by Maccoby (1966).

For several reasons the above studies provide only limited support for our view. First, there is some evidence, though less consistent, that "overly masculine" males, like "overly feminine" females, are lower on various achievement-related measures (Maccoby, 1966; Kagan & Kogan, 1970). Second, the definitions and measures of femininity may have a built-in antiachievement bias. Third, the question of the mother's actual characteristics has been ignored; thus the significant factor may not be closeness to the mother and insufficient sense of self, as here proposed. The significant factor may be identifying with a mother who is herself passive and dependent. If the mother were a mathematician, would the daughter's close identification be dysfunctional to top achievement?

Clearly the available data are inadequate and further research is needed to assess the importance of having the same sex as the primary caretaker for personality and cognitive development.

PARENT-CHILD CONFLICT. Establishing the self as separate from the mother is also easier for boys because they have more conflict with the mother than do girls. Studies of neonates suggest, as mentioned above, that males are more motorically active; this has also been observed with older children (Garai & Scheinfeld, 1968; Moss, 1967; Goldberg & Lewis, 1969). Furthermore, sex differences in aggressive behavior are solidly established

(Oetzel, 1966; Kagan, 1964), and there is some evidence
that this is constitutionally based (Bardwick, 1971). Because of these differences, the boy's behavior is more
likely to bring him into conflict with parental authority.
Boys are disciplined more often than girls, and this discipline is more likely to be of a power assertive kind
(Becker, 1964; Sears, Maccoby, & Levin, 1957; Heinstein, 1965). These encounters facilitate a separation of
the self from the parent. (While extremely severe discipline might have a very different effect, this is not common in the middle class.)

One implication of this is that girls need a little maternal rejection if they are to become independently competent and self-confident. And indeed a generalization that
occurs in most recent reviews is that high achieving females had hostile mothers while high achieving males had
warm ones (Bardwick, 1971; Garai & Scheinfeld, 1968;
Maccoby, 1966; Silverman, 1970). This generalization is
based primarily on the findings of the Fels longitudinal
study (Kagan & Moss, 1962). In this study "maternal
hostility" toward the child during his first three years was
related positively to the adult achievement behavior of
girls and negatively to the adult achievement behavior of
boys. Maternal protection, on the other hand, as mentioned earlier, related negatively to girls' achievement and
positively to boys'.

In discussions of these findings "maternal hostility" is
often equated with rejection. There is reason to believe,
however, that it may simply be the absence of "smother
love." First, the sample of cooperating families in the
Fels study is not likely to include extremely rejecting parents. These were primarily middle class parents who co-
operated with a child development study for 25 years.
They were enrolled in the study when the mother was
pregnant, and over the years they tolerated frequent
home visits, each lasting from 3 to 4 hours, as well as
behavioral observations of their children in nursery
school and camp. Second, we have already pointed out

that what is "high hostility" toward girls, might not be so labeled if the same behavior were expressed toward boys. It is interesting to note in this connection that "high hostility" toward girls during these early years is related positively to "acceleration" (i.e., the tendency to push the child's cognitive and motoric development) and negatively to maternal protectiveness. Neither of these relationships is significant for the boys (Kagan & Moss, 1962, p. 207). Further, the mothers who were "hostile" to their daughters were better educated than the "nonhostile." In addition to being achievers, the daughters were "less likely to withdraw from stressful situations" as adults. The authors themselves suggest that the latter "may reflect the mother's early pressure for independence and autonomy [p. 213]."

Our interpretation of these findings then is that many girls experience too much maternal rapport and protection during their early years. Because of this they find themselves as adults unwilling (or unable) to face stress and with inadequate motivation for autonomous achievement. It is significant that the relationships described are strongest when the early years are compared to the adult behavior. Possibly the eagerness to please adults sometimes passes as achievement or maturity during the childhood years.

While excessive rapport between mother and son occurs, it is less common and usually of a different nature. The achievement of boys may be in greater danger from too much conflict with parents—there being little likelihood of too little.

The danger for girls of too much maternal nurturance has been pointed out by Bronfenbrenner (1961a, 1961b) and is consistent with data reported by Crandall, Dewey, Katkovsky, and Preston (1964). The finding that girls who are more impulsive than average have more analytic thinking styles while the reverse pattern holds for boys also fits this interpretation (Sigel, 1965; Kagan, Rosman, Day, Phillips, & Phillips, 1964). That is, impulsive girls

may be brought into more conflict with their mothers, as
in the typical pattern for boys. Maccoby (1966) has suggested that the actual relationship between impulsivity
and analytic thinking is curvilinear: The extreme impulsivity that characterizes the very impulsive boys is
dysfunctional, but the high impulsivity of the girls falls
within the optimal range. In our view, the optimal range
is enough to insure some conflict in the mother-child relationship but not so much as to interfere with the child's
effective performance.

Inadequate Self-Confidence and Dependence on Others

Since the little girl has (a) less encouragement for
independence, (b) more parental protectiveness, (c) less
cognitive and social pressure for establishing an identity
separate from the mother, and (d) less mother-child conflict which highlights this separation, she engages in less
independent exploration of her environment. As a result
she does not develop skills in coping with her environment nor confidence in her ability to do so. She continues
to be dependent upon adults for solving her problems and
because of this she needs her affective ties with adults.
Her mother is not an unvarying supply of love but is
sometimes angry, disapproving, or unavailable. If the
child's own resources are insufficient, being on her own is
frustrating and frightening. Fears of abandonment are
very common in infants and young children even when
the danger is remote. Involvement in mastery explorations and the increasing competence and confidence that
results can help alleviate these fears, but for girls they
may continue even into adulthood. The anticipation of
being alone and unloved then may have a particularly
desperate quality in women. The hypothesis we propose
is that the all-pervasive affiliative need in women results
from this syndrome.

Thus boys learn effectance through mastery, but girls
are effective through eliciting the help and protection of
others. The situations that evoke anxiety in each sex

should be different and their motives should be different.

The theoretical view presented in this paper is speculative but it appears to be consistent with the data. In the preceding sections we have reviewed the research on sex differences in early socialization experiences. The theory would also lead us to expect that owing to these differences females would show less self-confidence and more instrumental dependency than males.

The data on dependency are somewhat unclear largely because the concept has been defined differently in different studies. . . . The balance of the evidence is that females are more dependent, at least as we are using the concept here, and this difference appears early and continues into maturity. . . .

The findings on self-confidence show that girls, and particularly the bright ones, underestimate their own ability. When asked to anticipate their performance on new tasks or on repetition tasks, they give lower estimates than boys and lower estimates than their performance indicates (Brandt, 1958; Sears, 1964; Crandall, Katkovsky, & Preston, 1962; Crandall, 1968). The studies that show the girls' greater suggestibility and tendency to switch perceptual judgments when faced with discrepant opinions are also consistent with their having less self-confidence (Iscoe, Williams, & Harvey, 1963; Allen & Crutchfield, 1963; Nakamura, 1958; Hamm & Hoving, 1969; Stein & Smithells, 1969).[3] Boys set higher standards for themselves (Walter & Marzolf, 1951). As mentioned earlier, difficult tasks are seen as challenging to males, whereas females seek to avoid them (Veroff, 1969; Crandall & Rabson, 1960; Moriarty, 1961; McManis, 1965). Thus the research suggests that girls lack confidence in their own abilities and seek effectance through others (Crandall & Rabson, 1960). Affective re-

---

[3] Girls do not conform more to peer standards which conflict with adult norms (Douvan & Adelson, 1966), even though they conform more when group pressure is in opposition to their own perceptual judgments.

lationships under these conditions would indeed be paramount.

The findings indicating that this is the case—that affective relationships are paramount in females—were summarized earlier in this paper. The data suggest that they have higher affiliative needs and that achievement behavior is motivated by a desire to please. If their achievement behavior comes into conflict with affiliation, achievement is likely to be sacrificed or anxiety may result.

IMPLICATIONS

If further research provides support for the present developmental speculations, many questions will still need answering before childrearing patterns used with girls can be totally condemned. Even from the standpoint of achievement behavior, I would caution that this paper has only dealt with the upper end of the achievement curve. Indices of female performance, like the female IQ scores, cluster closer to the mean and do not show the extremes in either direction that the male indices show. The same qualities that may interfere with top performance at the highest achievement levels seem to have the effect of making the girls conscientious students in the lower grades. Is it possible for the educational system to use the positive motivations of girls to help them more fully develop their intellectual capacities rather than to train them in obedient learning? The educational system that rewards conformity and discourages divergent thinking might be examined for its role in the pattern we have described.

Although childrearing patterns that fail to produce a competent and self-confident child are obviously undesirable, it may be that boys are often prematurely pushed into independence. Because this paper has focused on achievement orientations, it may seem that I have set up the male pattern as ideal. This is not at all intended. The ability to suppress other aspects of the situation in striving for mastery is not necessarily a prerequisite for mental health or a healthy society. The more diffuse achievement needs of women may make for greater flexibility in responding to the various possibilities that life offers at different stages in the life cycle. A richer life may be available to women because they do not single-mindedly pursue academic or professional goals. And from a social standpoint, a preoccupation with achievement goals can blot out consideration of the effect of one's work on the welfare of others and its meaning in the larger social scheme.

A loss in intellectual excellence due to excessive affiliative needs, then, might seem a small price to pay if the alternative is a single-minded striving for mastery. But the present hypothesis suggests that women's affiliative needs are, at least in part, based on an insufficient sense of competence and as such they may have a compelling neurotic quality. While I have not made the very high achievement needs more characteristic of males the focus of this paper, they too may have an unhealthy base. By unraveling the childhood events that lead to these divergent orientations we may gain insights that will help both sexes develop their capacities for love and achievement.

REFERENCES

Allen, V. L., & Crutchfield, R. S. Generalization of experimentally reinforced conformity. *Journal of Abnormal and Social Psychology*, 1963, 67, 326–333.

Bardwick, J. M. *The psychology of women: A study of biosocial conflict.* New York: Harper & Row, 1971.

Baumrind, D. Current patterns of parental authority. *Developmental Psychology Monograph*, 1971, 4 (1, Pt. 2).

Baumrind, D., & Black, A. E. Socialization practices associated with dimensions of competence in preschool boys and girls. *Child Development*, 1967, 38, 291–327.

Becker, W. Consequences of different kinds of parental discipline. In M. L. Hoffman and L. W. Hoffman (Eds.), *Review of child development research.* Vol. 1. New York: Russell Sage, 1964.

Brandt, R. M. The accuracy of self-estimate: A measure of self concept. *Genetic Psychology Monographs*, 1958, 58, 55–99.

Bronfenbrenner, U. Some familial antecedents of responsibility and leadership in adolescents. In L. Petrullo and B. M. Bass (Eds.), *Leadership and interpersonal behavior*. New York: Holt, Rinehart, & Winston, 1961. (a)

Bronfenbrenner, U. Toward a theoretical model for the analysis of parent-child relationships in a social context. In J. Glidewell (Ed.), *Parent attitudes and child behavior*. Springfield, Illinois: Thomas, 1961. (b)

Collard, E. D. Achievement motive in the four-year-old child and its relationship to achievement expectancies of the mother. Unpublished doctoral dissertation, University of Michigan, 1964.

Crandall, V. C. Achievement behavior in young children. *Young Children*, 1964, 20, 77–90.

Crandall, V. C. Sex differences in expectancy of intellectual and academic reinforcement. In C. P. Smith (Ed.), *Achievement-related motives in children*. New York: Russell Sage, 1968.

Crandall, V. J. Achievement. In H. W. Stevenson (Ed.), *Child Psychology: The 62nd Yearbook of the National Society for the Study of Education*. Part I. Chicago: University of Chicago Press, 1963.

Crandall, V. J., Dewey, R., Katkovsky, K., & Preston, A. Parents' attitudes and behaviors and grade school children's academic achievements. *Journal of Genetic Psychology*, 1964, 104, 53–66.

Crandall, V. J., Dewey, R., Katkovsky, W., & Preston, A. and ability determinants of young children's intellectual achievement behaviors. *Child Development*, 1962, 33, 643–661.

Crandall, V. J., & Rabson, A. Children's repetition choices in an intellectual achievement situation following success and failure. *Journal of Genetic Psychology*, 1960, 97, 161–168.

Erikson, E. H. Identity and the life cycle. *Psychological Issues*, 1959, 1, 1–171.

Escalona, S. K. Feeding disturbances in very young children. *American Journal of Orthopsychiatry*, 1945, 15, 76–80.

Field, W. F. The effects of thematic apperception upon certain experimentally aroused needs. Unpublished doctoral dissertation. University of Maryland, 1951.

Garai, J. E., & Scheinfeld, A. Sex differences in mental and behavioral traits. Genetic Psychology Monographs, 1968, 77, 169–299.

Glidewell, J. C., Kantor, M. B., Smith, L. M., & Stringer, L. A. Socialization and social structure in the classroom. In L. W. Hoffman and M. L. Hoffman (Eds.), Review of child development research. Vol. 2. New York: Russell Sage, 1966.

Goldberg, S., & Lewis, M. Play behavior in the year old infant: Early sex differences. Child Development, 1969, 40, 21–31.

Hamm, N. K., & Hoving, K. L. Conformity of children in an ambiguous perceptual situation. Child Development, 1969, 40, 773–784.

Heinstein, M. Child rearing in California. Bureau of Maternal and Child Health, State of California, Department of Public Health, 1965.

Horner, M. S. Sex differences in achievement motivation and performance in competitive and non-competitive situations. Unpublished doctoral dissertation, University of Michigan, 1968.

Horner, M. S. Toward an understanding of achievement related conflicts in women. Journal of Social Issues, 1972, 28 (2).

Iscoe, I., Williams, M., & Harvey, J. Modifications of children's judgements by a simulated group technique: A normative developmental study. Child Development, 1963, 34, 963–978.

Kagan, J. Acquisition and significance of sex-typing and sex-role identity. In M. L. Hoffman and L. W. Hoffman (Eds.), Review of child development research. Vol. 1. New York: Russell Sage, 1964.

Kagan, J., & Kogan, N. Individuality and cognitive performance. In P. H. Mussen (Ed.), Carmichael's manual of child psychology. Vol. 1. New York: Wiley, 1970.

Kagan, J., Levine, J., & Fishman, C. Sex of child and social class as determinants of maternal behavior. Paper presented at the meeting of the Society for Research in Child Development, March 1967.

Kagan, J., & Moss, H. A. *Birth to maturity*. New York: Wiley, 1962.

Kagan, J., Rosman, B. L., Day, D., Phillips, A. J., & Phillips, W. Information processing in the child: Significance of analytic and reflective attitudes. *Psychological Monographs*, 1964, 78, 1.

Lahtinen, P. The effect of failure and rejection on dependency. Unpublished doctoral dissertation, University of Michigan, 1964.

Lynn, D. B. Sex role and parental identification. *Child Development*, 1962, 33, 555–564.

Lynn, D. B. *Parental identification and sex role*. Berkeley: McCutchan, 1969.

Maccoby, E. E. Woman's intellect. In S. M. Farber and R. H. L. Wilson (Eds.), *The potential of woman*. New York: McGraw-Hill, 1963.

Maccoby, E. E. Sex differences in intellectual functioning. In E. E. Maccoby (Ed.), *The development of sex differences*. Stanford, California: Stanford University Press, 1966.

McClelland, D. C., Atkinson, J. W., Clark, R. A., & Lowell, E. L. *The achievement motive*. New York: Appleton-Century-Crofts, 1953.

McManis, D. L. Pursuit-motor performance of normal and retarded children in four verbal-incentive conditions. *Child Development*, 1965, 36, 667–683.

Milton, G. A. The effects of sex-role identification upon problem solving skill. *Journal of Abnormal and Social Psychology*, 1957, 55, 208–212.

Moriarty, A. Coping patterns of preschool children in response to intelligence test demands. *Genetic Psychology Monographs*, 1961, 64, 3–127.

Moss, H. A. Laboratory and field studies of mother-infant interaction. Unpublished manuscript, NIMH, undated.

Moss, H. A. Sex, age, and state as determinants of mother-infant interaction. *Merrill-Palmer Quarterly*, 1967, 13, 19–36.

Moss, H. A., & Robson, K. S. Maternal influences in early social visual behavior. *Child Development*, 1968, 39, 401–408.

Nakamura, C. Y. Conformity and problem solving. *Journal of Abnormal and Social Psychology*, 1958, 56, 315–320.

Oetzel, R. M. The relationship between sex role acceptance and cognitive abilities. Unpublished masters thesis, Stanford University, 1961.

Oetzel, R. M. Annotated bibliography and classified summary of research in sex differences. In E. E. Maccoby (Ed.), *The development of sex differences.* Stanford, California: Stanford University Press, 1966.

Parsons, T. *Essays in sociological theory pure and applied.* Glencoe, Illinois: Free Press, 1949.

Parsons, T. Family structure and the socialization of the child. In T. Parsons and R. F. Bales (Eds.), *Family socialization and interaction process.* Glencoe, Illinois: Free Press, 1965.

Plank, E. H., & Plank, R. Emotional components in arithmetic learning as seen through autobiographies. In R. S. Eissler et al. (Eds.), *The psychoanalytic study of the child.* Vol. 9. New York: International Universities Press, 1954.

Pope, B. Socio-economic contrasts in children's peer culture prestige values. *Genetic Psychology Monographs,* 1953, 48, 157–220.

Rosen, B. C., & D'Andrade, R. The psychosocial origins of achievement motivations. *Sociometry,* 1959, 22, 185–218.

Rossi, A. S. Barriers to the career choice of engineering, medicine, or science among American women. In J. A. Mattfeld and G. G. Van Aken (Eds.), *Women and the scientific professions: Papers presented at the M.I.T. symposium on American Women in Science and Engineering, 1964.* Cambridge, Massachusetts: M.I.T. Press, 1965. (a)

Rossi, A. S. Women in science: Why so few? *Science,* 1965, 148, 1196–1202. (b)

Rubenstein, J. Maternal attentiveness and subsequent exploratory behavior in the infant. *Child Development,* 1967, 38, 1089–1100.

Sears, P. S. Correlates of need achievement and need affiliation and classroom management, self concept, and creativity. Unpublished manuscript, Stanford University, 1962.

Sears, P. S. The effect of classroom conditions on the strength of achievement motive and work output of elementary school children. Final report, cooperative research project No. OE-873, U.S. Dept. of Health, Education, and Welfare, Office of Education, Washington, D. C., 1963.

Sears, P. S. Self-concept in the service of educational goals.

California Journal of Instructional Improvement, 1964, 7, 3–17.

Sears, R. R., Maccoby, E. E., & Levin, H. *Patterns of child rearing*. Evanston, Illinois: Row, Peterson, 1957.

Sigel, I. E. Rationale for separate analyses of male and female samples on cognitive tasks. *Psychological Record*, 1965, 15, 369–376.

Silverman, J. Attentional styles and the study of sex differences. In D. L. Mostofsky (Ed.), *Attention: Contemporary theory and analysis*. New York: Appleton-Century-Crofts, 1970.

Stein, A. H., & Smithells, J. Age and sex differences in children's sex role standards about achievement. *Developmental Psychology*, 1969, 1, 252–259.

Stendler, C. B. Critical periods in socialization. In R. G. Kuhlen and G. G. Thompson (Eds.), *Psychological studies of human development*. New York: Appleton-Century-Crofts, 1963.

Sutton-Smith, B., Crandall, V. J., & Roberts, J. M. Achievement and strategic competence. Paper presented at the meeting of the Eastern Psychological Association, April 1964.

Terman, L. M., & Oden, M. H. *The gifted child grows up*. Stanford, California: Stanford University Press, 1947.

Tyler, F. B., Rafferty, J. E., & Tyler, B. B. Relationships among motivations of parents and their children. *Journal of Genetic Psychology*, 1962, 101, 69–81.

Veroff, J. Social comparison and the development of achievement motivation. In C. P. Smith (Ed.), *Achievement-related motives in children*. New York: Russell Sage, 1969.

Veroff, J., Wilcox, S., & Atkinson, J. W. The achievement motive in high school and college age women. *Journal of Abnormal and Social Psychology*, 1953, 48, 108–119.

Walberg, H. J. Physics, femininity, and creativity. *Developmental Psychology*, 1969, 1, 47–54.

Walter, L. M., & Marzolf, S. S. The relation of sex, age, and school achievement to levels of aspiration. *Journal of Educational Psychology*, 1951, 42, 258–292.

White, R. W. Competence and the psychosexual stages of development. In M. Jones (Ed.), *Nebraska Symposium on Motivation*. Lincoln, Nebraska: University of Nebraska Press, 1960.

Winterbottom, M. R. The relation of need for achievement to learning experiences in independency and mastery. In J. W. Atkinson (Ed.), *Motives in fantasy, action, and society*. Princeton: Van Nostrand, 1958.

3

Feminism and Psychotherapy

BETTY J. KRONSKY

Although the Women's Liberation Movement has had its personal impact on therapists, there have been few attempts in the literature to consider the technical innovations which could emerge from the feminist viewpoint. Perhaps the reason for this is that therapists are so concerned with being scientific at all costs they they do not permit new value-assumptions to reshape therapeutic techniques until a proper time interval has elapsed. At the time of writing this (July, 1970), I know of only two serious articles which discuss the implications of feminism for psychotherapy, and neither of them deals specifically with questions of technique.[1] In this paper, I shall attempt a reformulation of technique in regard to the therapeutic management of assertiveness* in women patients.

DEPARTURE FROM FREUDIAN THEORY

Contrary to the beliefs of many feminists, I do not think it necessary for a feminist-oriented therapist to throw out the entire body of Freudian principles in which he or she

---

* I use the term "assertiveness" rather than "aggression" to avoid the negative implications of the latter term. While in my edition of Webster's Collegiate Dictionary each term is used as a definition of the other, the secondary meaning of assertive is "positive," while the secondary meaning of aggressive is "pushing" or "disposed to attack."

SOURCE: From "Feminism and Psychotherapy" by Betty J. Kronsky, M.S., in Journal of Contemporary Psychotherapy (Forest Hills, N.Y.), 3, no. 2 (1971), pp. 89–98. Reprinted by permission of the Journal of Contemporary Psychotherapy and the author. References have been renumbered.

may have been trained. On the contrary, it seems to me helpful in my daily work with patients to proceed from a Freudian base: that is, with respect for the role of the unconscious in determining human behavior, an awareness of the primacy of childhood in forming the constellation of personality still more or less operative in the adult patient, together with a conviction that careful analysis of transferences and resistances within the analytic situation can lead to a reorganization of the psychic structure.

Where I depart from Freud is in that part of his theory in which he has been influenced by the patriarchal myths of his culture. . . . His most glaring distortion was simply this: that he viewed feminine assertiveness as a neurotic phenomenon. . . .

Freud held that non-neurotic feminine assertiveness could be achieved by women only at the point of their becoming mothers, at which point identification with the active child-rearing activities of their own mothers could lead to assertive behavior within well-defined limits.[2] The logical outcome of this theory has been to view feminine assertiveness in vocational and political areas as being *sine qua non* neurotic manifestations (i.e., determined by masculine identifications or competitiveness with males).

Because we live in much the same patriarchal society as Freud, with many of the same basic assumptions, we are forced to confront the element of truth in his theory that women who are assertive have made masculine identifications. The reasons for this are sociological and cultural, not biological. The young girl who grows up in a patriarchal family in the twentieth century is caught in a web of contradictions. She becomes aware that assertiveness in women is rewarded economically and culturally in select cases, but that it is deplored psychologically. She responds to the latent values of the culture, its Protestant work ethic and its consumerism, in which contexts assertiveness in women is rewarded; but she also becomes aware, even as a small child, of the psychological sanctions against her developing her own assertiveness.

In many cases, in seeking a way out of her confusion, she may identify partially with the father, who is a role model of sanctioned assertiveness. Such identifications often go underground and become unconscious, since women have internalized stringent prohibitions against such identifications. To be feminine at all costs becomes the primary goal for the adolescent girl and young adult, and in the process of growth, her identifications with assertive men (and women, where such models were available) are often repressed wholesale.

Once we dismiss Freud's view of women as biologically deprived creatures, we can be quite clear that women who identify with males or envy males do so because of the social and political advantages which accrue to males in our society, and because of their awareness that males do not have to internalize such painful and inconsistent prohibitions as do females. The concept of "penis envy" can thus be decontaminated of its invidious biological comparisons predicated by Freud; it can then be viewed as any other mechanism in which preoccupation with alleged inferiority is present: e.g., many men's preoccupation with shortness or physical fraility or lack of money. The lack of penis, in brief, has become for some women a symbol of their general feeling of unacceptability and powerlessness.[3]

As Clara Thompson has pointed out in her classic articles on the subject,[4] an actual wish for a penis, based on a traumatic discovery in childhood of the absence of a penis, is present in only a small minority of the patients we see. Such an attitude has usually been nurtured by a family in which the girl child is derogated and the brother is over-valued (a not unusual situation in our society). What is more common, according to Clara Thompson, is that a woman may come to use her lack of a penis as both a symbol of and a rationalization for the perceived disadvantages of being a female.[5] Needless to say, this symbol has also great vitality in the ruminations of male psychologists, to symbolize and rationalize their own fears of loss of power.

The important point that I would like to make here from my clinical experience is that such symbolic "penis envy" in women often vanishes when the woman is enabled to accept her sexuality in her own right and to find a new definition of her possibilities for self-assertion. Where, however, "penis envy" is regarded as central to a woman's problem, and is over-stressed in the therapy as if it were some kind of disease, the woman patient's feelings of guilt and self-loathing are increased. "Penis envy" is thus paradoxically reinforced by the very interpretations which are supposed to lead to its dissolution.

WORKING WITH THE WOMAN PATIENT

In view of the inconsistent super-ego prohibitions which women have internalized, it is small wonder that the most common feature of women patients upon initial contact is their free-floating sense of guilt. This can almost always be traced to a punitive attitude towards their own assertiveness, which has often had to be repressed, and to a vague sense that they are not living up to a concept they have of a truly feminine woman. They come to us blaming themselves for being angry at the limitations of their roles, ashamed of their deep-seated resentments, questioning whether they are feminine enough, whether they have the right kinds of orgasms, the right kinds of feelings. The worst doubt is whether they may after all be "castrating females" or "ballbusters," images which haunt the modern woman and warn her to suppress her natural assertive strivings.

Many of these women have repressed their assertiveness to the point where they present themselves as passive and helpless, commonly phobic to the extent that they have projected onto the environment the repressed rage which they cannot confront in themselves. Some of

them play the role of sex-symbols, glamour girls who
have become promiscuous to convince themselves and
everyone else of their femininity. Both the passive
housewives and the glamour girls are filled with rage,
which they express in hidden ways against the men in
their lives, all the while reassuring themselves that they
are truly feminine.[6]

When such women enter treatment, they are burdened
with such sensitivity to the judgments of others that they
can be expected to read into most remarks of the therapist the negative self-valuations which they most fear.
What they need is a permissive atmosphere in which they
can release their pent-up feelings of rage, helplessness
and inadequacy, and explore their strivings towards
healthier assertiveness which are commingled with feelings of competitiveness, hatred and envy towards men.
They need to be able to sift through the early partial
identifications which they had made with active males
and females and later discarded. It is my impression that
many therapists rush in with premature interpretations
which highlight the masculine identifications and "penis
envy," perhaps due to some unconscious elation at finding evidence of these.

I believe that interpretations or even "mirrorings" of
such negative attitudes can carry implicit normative messages. It is the negative side of her feelings which we
comment upon; this can imply to the already over-sensi-
tive woman patient that there is something neurotic or
unhealthy about such attitudes. Such implicit messages
can also be conveyed by the choice of culturally freighted
words, by tone of voice or even body posture. For instance, when a shy inhibited woman patient begins to
have dreams in which she is a man, it could be frightening to her to have her wish taken literally as a wish for a
penis; to make such an interpretation will probably serve
to discourage her from exploring the rich multiple meanings of her longings for self-assertion. The result may be
a premature halt to the flood of repressed strivings. These

may either be re-repressed in the service of a desire to please the analyst (especially the male analyst) or they may be explored by the patient as if they were merely neurotic manifestations to be made ego-dystonic and worked through. In both instances, the result of therapy will be an inauthentically "feminine" woman.

Such considerations have led me to some simple precautions in dealing with the assertive strivings of women patients. I have learned to avoid interpretations which highlight anger or competitiveness towards men, knowing that these will be experienced as criticisms by the patient. I have instead been careful to communicate an explicit attitude of acceptance of the woman's strivings to be more assertive, viewing these as primary and not as derivative from competition with males. I have refrained from calling special attention to attitudes of "penis envy," hatred of men, and masculine competitiveness, even where these seem to have developed in the wake of the girl's repression of assertiveness.

I have found that almost without exception, the patient herself will get into this area, because she has been groomed by her society to be super-critical of such attitudes in herself. Many of my patients have spontaneously passed through a phase where negative attitudes towards men and feelings of competition were very strong and persistent, but as these were worked through in connection with their efforts to realize their own potentials, the patients gradually moved to a point in which negative attitudes diminished. Even the most intransigent infantile longings to be a man fade away when the patient discovers the broader scope of her existential possibilities as a woman.

CASE ILLUSTRATIONS

CASE OF JOANNE D. Joanne D., a talented 19-year-old art student, entered therapy after she had flunked out of art school in her freshman year. She re-enrolled in school

during the first year of therapy and was confronted by a
severe work-block, which was initially analyzed in terms
of a bitter anal struggle with a compulsive work-oriented
mother. As her school work improved, it became clear
that her conflicts surrounding her identity as an artist
sprang from an early conflict between masculine and
feminine identifications. Her father, a commercial artist,
had chosen Joanne, the elder of two daughters, to be the
artist in the family and had even given her, as she saw it,
one-half of his name (Joseph). Her mother had always
been intolerant of her husband's profession and of his
artistic interests, and had groomed Joanne to be a neat,
inhibited child. She worked as a child model until age
seven. Her initial attempts to be assertive and to run with
the boys in the neighborhood were thwarted by the
mother, as were her first attempts at "messing with" artistic materials.

Upon entering puberty, Joanne developed a fantasy of
becoming a boy; she was convinced that she was changing sex when she discovered some hairs growing from her
developing breasts. Her behavior became increasingly inhibited, passive and childlike as she tried to ward off such
fantasies and retain her mother's approval. When she entered therapy, she seemed the model of a sweet, neat little
girl, passive to the extreme, and unable to respond to the
demands of the art school where women were expected to
be assertive and inventive in their creative work.

In therapy, Joanne became accustomed to revealing her
phallic fantasies, for which she felt guilty and ashamed,
and these were decontaminated by the acceptant attitude
of the therapist. As she could risk acting out some of her
assertive strivings, her excessive passivity diminished and
her paintings improved. She discovered the joys of "action painting," wildly spattering the canvas from a stand-
ing-up position. In the sculpture studio, however, she felt
acutely anxious, until the day she became aware, as she
used the chisel and power drill, that she was having fantasies of having a penis and penetrating the wooden figure

as a man would penetrate a woman. She began to be more comfortable with such fantasies, and the sculpture studio became her favorite work area. She discovered similar conflicts in the workshop where she went to stretch canvases and build frames. Her manual skills improved when she could become conscious of the sexual fantasies evoked by work she had defined as masculine. She was helped to see that such active skills sprang from her own abilities as a creative woman and were acceptable for a woman; that by being strong, she did not have to turn into a man.

Joanne became more adequate in many areas she previously had felt were closed to her. She no longer had to play the helpless doll and get her boyfriend to perform many necessary tasks for her. She gained a sense of pride in being a woman artist, and helped to organize a women's liberation group at her school; she also successfully planned a women artists' group show. She still has further work in sorting out her confusions in identification, but seems to have begun to work out a synthesis of the "feminine" and "masculine" aspects of her own personality. Her relationship with her boyfriend has improved, as she has become less symbiotic and her attitudes towards men have become more friendly.

CASE OF MRS. JENSEN. Mrs. Jensen, a 39-year-old married housewife and former office worker with one daughter, age 9, entered therapy with symptoms of claustrophobia, anxiety and depression. She felt pressured by her husband to have a second child and felt unable to say no to him directly. She viewed having another child with distaste, realizing that it would entail a postponement of her hopes to gain mobility outside the home. She already suffered from guilt for the resentment she felt to her daughter, whom she could not help seeing as an obstacle to her own development as a person. Since her husband had been attending night school for eight years, she had been completely responsible for the care of the home and the child, and she had rarely been able to go out because they could not afford a babysitter. At the time when her daughter was finally occupied in school for the entire day, and Mrs. J. could realistically plan a part-time job, her phobias became more intense and she applied for therapy.

Mrs. J. had been brought up in a Scandinavian country, the oldest of three sisters in a home which was under the absolute domination of a strong authoritarian father. The father made all decisions for everybody, and his wife never questioned him. He kept his philosophical diary open on a table for all his daughters to read, and they were deeply influenced by his opinions and values. As a young adult, Mrs. J. continued to live with her parents, while her two younger sisters managed to marry and move away. She came with her family to the United States when they immigrated, and remained with them until her first sexual affair at the age of 29. Mrs. J. became pregnant out-of-wedlock and married her first lover; an Irish-Catholic who had also come from an authoritarian family, he easily took over the role of dominant father-surrogate. She continued to be passive, childlike, and afraid of disagreeing with her husband. She repressed her hostility, projected it outward onto the world which seemed increasingly dangerous, and she suffered from headaches and crying spells.

In the first months of therapy, after working with the guilt surrounding any expression of hostility, Mrs. J. became aware of her intense hostility towards her husband and her father and of her suppressed desire to revolt from their domination. She felt blocked, as always before, by her fear of displeasing them, and felt incapable of coping with the world without their support. In an early dream, these feelings of inadequacy came into focus. She dreamt that *she was driving alone through a European countryside and suddenly became frightened as she saw busses and cars heading straight towards her. She felt she could not go on or she might have an accident. She stopped at a farmhouse and begged the farmer to keep the car safe for her; it belonged to her father who was in Berlin and*

he would come and pick it up. Instead of focussing on
the patient's competition with the father (symbolized by
her driving *his* car in the dream), the therapist focussed
on her feelings of inadequacy as a woman; when she gets
in the driver's seat (both literally and symbolically) she
feels that she cannot handle the car; she had to find a
man to help her. In actuality, the patient had a strong
desire to learn to drive, since her husband had just bought
a car a few weeks before the dream. The therapist encouraged her to learn to drive, and she was able to gain
her license within a few months. In later dreams, the
theme of her fear of losing control of the car became
more clearly a fear of her own aggressive impulses.

Some months later, Mrs. J. dreamt that *she and her
husband were driving to visit an elderly aunt who was a
paragon of housewifely virtues. Mrs. J. insisted that her
husband stop the car and she announced to him that she
was getting out. She said she felt he only wanted a "yes
woman" and she was tired of being that. She left the car,
found a bicycle, and went riding alone to the park, enjoying every sight and sound. She had a wonderful day,
but towards evening became frightened because she had
nothing to eat. She knew she must go home, but vowed
she would never talk to her husband again.* This dream
was used to help the patient become more aware of her
fears of independent functioning, based on wartime events
in her childhood when she was repeatedly overwhelmed
by experiences of the outside world for which she had
not yet developed the necessary skills. Her hostility towards her husband was not stressed in this context, since
this was viewed as secondary to Mrs. J.'s own fear of
independent functioning. To stress the hostility only increases the guilt in this kind of patient.

As Mrs. J. has been helped to become more assertive,
her negative attitudes toward men have diminished. She
now works half-time in an office, attends movies and
concerts by herself, and has become interested in a voluntary organization dedicated to convincing parents to limit

their number of children because of the threat of over-population.

With Mrs. J., as with Joanne D., the crucial point was to alleviate guilt surrounding assertive strivings and to encourage the appropriate fulfillment of these strivings in real life. With Mrs. J. it was also important to help her acknowledge her own rage and to cease to project this upon the outside world. Her rage was accepted and understood as a natural consequence of her position in the family and of her lifelong pattern of inhibition and suppression.

There are some therapists who see the woman patient solely in terms of her relationships with men, instead of as a whole person functioning in many areas and striving for fulfillment in many directions. I believe that this stance is more common than one would suppose. Perhaps this is due to our realization, as therapists, of the importance of sexual problems. Perhaps it is a reflection of the attitudes of our women patients themselves, who have learned to see themselves through the eyes of men and in terms of their interaction with men. As Karen Horney has written:[7]

> Women have adapted themselves to the wishes of men and felt as if their adaptation were their true nature. That is, they see or saw themselves in the way that their man's wishes demanded of them; unconsciously they yielded to the suggestion of masculine thought.

CASE OF GLORIA Z. Gloria Z., a 22-year-old married recent college graduate, found herself constricted in all her relationships, including those with her individual therapist (female) and her couples group therapist (male). In one year of conjoint therapy, she had become aware of her deep mistrust of women and of men, and from her stilted associations and occasional dreams, it was clear that as an only child adopted by elderly parents and never told anything about her origins, her position in the family had felt precarious. Her relationship with her

mother deteriorated as soon as she had attempted individuation. Her mother was remembered as warm up to the
age of six but thereafter cold and critical, unhappy with
her work, and prone to periods of withdrawal when she
would not talk to anyone in the family for an entire day.
There had been an irrational fear of the father, based not
so much on his aggressive behavior but on a sense the
patient had of the enormous rage which he was sitting
on.

After a year of therapy, during which Gloria had
courted rejection from her individual therapist by missing
appointments and being withholding in her sessions, she
began to feel more trusting and spoke of her wish to drop
her defenses and become more open and involved. She
wished to sit on the couch, although she was still too
fearful to lie on it. At the same time, she moved to the
couch in her therapy group as well; the couch was located
in a more central position in the group therapy room, and
she felt more a part of things than she had felt in her
usual corner chair. She felt that her move was an expression of a wish to become more involved. However, her
group therapist, whom she experienced as a powerful
male authority, noticed her move and analyzed it as a
"come-on" to some of the men in the group. Confronted
with this interpretation, the patient lapsed back into her
usual well-defended hunched-over seating position.

This patient had become interested in Women's Liberation and had spontaneously formed a "consciousness-
raising" group. During the first sessions of her group, she
assumed a leadership role, was more assertive than usual,
and won the respect of the other women in the group. She
brought up some ideas of Women's Liberation in her
therapy group in an appropriate context, with the intention of helping one of the women who was having difficulty in asking her husband to share the responsibility of
their child. The therapist made an interpretation that
Gloria had brought up Women's Liberation because she
wished to provoke the male patients in the group. Again

Gloria was struck dumb by this unwarranted attribution of sex-related motives to her behavior.

By now it may be evident that this couples group is a male-dominated group, in which the wives are docile and the men do the interpreting. When Gloria brought up her feelings of helpless anger when confronted with lewd remarks and obscene gestures of men on the New York streets, the men in the group told Gloria that her problem was that she could not accept her femininity. The women did not support Gloria, although they undoubtedly had experienced the same.

A similar experience was told to me by an acquaintance, Joan R., who had gone through a period of acute depression after the break-up of a love affair. The psychiatrist whom she saw for a year of supportive therapy concentrated almost exclusively on her relations with men, and gave her "pep talks" and helpful hints on how to wear her hair and what kind of clothes she might wear. He tried to help her feel more comfortable and successful in her role as sexual object. When she became interested, for the first time in her adult life, in something other than a man and became involved in acting lessons, he cautioned her that she should not stay up working at her lines until late at night, because she would ruin her looks. She was too grateful to the therapist for his interest in her to feel outraged until years later.

When a patient reports such experiences in dealing with another therapist who has been biased, I think that it is important for the present therapist to reinforce the patient's objection to such treatment. This is one of those situations in which an open human response is useful to counteract the patient's expectation that she will be somehow blamed for her oppositional attitude to the kind of therapy she has experienced. If the therapist is able to put aside a tendency to be loyal to the practice of the entire therapeutic profession, he can be most helpful to the patient in standing by her rejection of false forms of therapy. In the case of Gloria Z., for instance, I shared with her my feelings that her therapist was not being helpful and was being inaccurate and biased in his remarks; she was able to continue in the couples group, which had many benefits for her, but became more outspoken in challenging the therapist when he came in with a facile interpretation.

In summary, then, it is my view that the feminist-oriented therapist will take special precautions in the use of interpretations and will view assertive strivings in women patients as too precious and vulnerable to be subjected to interpretations which stress negative attitudes towards men. This kind of therapist will view partial identifications with father figures as normal and healthy in our male-dominated society, and will try to help the patient overcome feelings of guilt and shame surrounding such identifications. The therapist will concentrate on helping the patient to improve her self-concept and to develop her assertiveness. The therapist will refrain from interpretations which will reinforce the patients' tendencies to be exclusively preoccupied with their relations with men and to see themselves as sexual objects, and will contradict the views of other therapists where warranted. Finally, the feminist-oriented therapist will have a sensitive awareness of what it means subjectively to be a woman in a male-dominated society, to be bewildered by the conflicting stereotypes and hounded by a sense that she's damned if she does (assert herself) and damned if she doesn't. For this, it may well be that the feminist-oriented therapist will have to be a woman herself.

REFERENCES

1. Articles by Judith Brown and Natalie Shainess.
2. For a clear exposition of orthodox Freudian theory on these matters, see the articles by Ruth M. Brunswick and J. Lampl-De Groot.
3. Thompson, Clara, p. 255 and passim.
4. Thompson, Clara, Penis Envy in Women, op. cit., passim.
5. Thompson, Clara, op. cit., p. 247.

6. For a discussion of such types of women, see Karen Horney, The Overvaluation of Love, in op. cit.
7. Horney, Karen, The Flight from Womanhood, in op. cit., pp. 56–57.

BIBLIOGRAPHY

Brown, Judith, Feminism and Its Implications for Therapy, The Radical Therapist, 1:1, pp. 5–6, 1970.

Brunswick, Ruth M., A Supplement to Freud's "History of an Infantile Neurosis," in Fliess (Ed.), The Psychoanalytic Reader, New York: International Universities Press, 1948.

Horney, Karen, Feminine Psychology, ed. by Kelman, New York: Norton, 1967.

Lampl-De Groot, J. The Evolution of the Oedipus Complex in Women, in Fliess (Ed.) The Psychoanalytic Reader, New York: International Universities Press, 1948.

Millett, Kate, Sexual Politics, New York: Doubleday, 1970.

Shainess, Natalie, Images of Woman: Past and Present, Overt and Obscured, American Journal of Psychotherapy, 23:1, 1969.

Thompson, Clara, Interpersonal Psychoanalysis: The Selected Papers of Clara Thompson, ed. by Green, New York: Basic Books, 1964.

4

Homosexuality in Women

JOYCE McDOUGALL

Bisexuality! I am sure you are right about it. I am accustoming myself to regarding every sexual act as an event between four individuals.

Freud to Fliess, 1889

Clinical studies of overt homosexuality are rendered difficult by the fact that only when the delicate balance achieved by manifest homosexuality is threatened or lost will homosexuals of either sex turn to a psychiatrist or analyst for help. I have been fortunate enough to have had in analysis four homosexual women and three others who, while not exclusively homosexual, were dominated by conscious homosexual wishes. My thanks are due to these cases for the clinical material which furnished the basis for this paper. These patients enabled me to recognize a specific form of Oedipal constellation and to appreciate the significance of overt homosexuality in maintaining psychic equilibrium and ego identity in spite of the evident disturbance in sexual identity.

. . . Psychoanalytic theory considers the homosexual

SOURCE: From "Homosexuality in Women" by Joyce McDougall, in *Female Sexuality*, edited by Janine Chasseguet-Smirgel with C.-J. Luquet-Parat, Béla Grunberger, Joyce McDougall, Maria Torok, Christian David (Ann Arbor, The University of Michigan Press, 1970), pp. 171–212. Copyright © by The University of Michigan 1970. All rights reserved. Published in the United States of America by The University of Michigan Press and simultaneously in Don Mills, Canada, by Longmans Canada Limited. First published as *Recherches psychoanalytiques nouvelles sur la sexualité féminine.* © copyright 1964 by Payot, Paris. All rights reserved. Reprinted by permission of The University of Michigan Press.

component of the libido to be an integral part of every
human being's psychic structure, so it is well to define
what we mean by "homosexual libido" and to ask in
what manner this component is cathected and integrated
into the adult personality in people who are not homosexual. Second, since clinical categories notoriously over-
lap . . . it is necessary to differentiate between commonly
disguised expressions of homosexuality and its overt expression in sexual relations. Where do "normal neurotic"
and "psychotic" leave off, and where does "perverse"
begin? Does the term "latent homosexual" really mean
anything? What place do we accord homosexual and perverse fantasy in daydreams and masturbation? What relationship might be found to exist between the overt homosexual woman and the "masculine woman" who feels at
home among men and abhors the company of other
women?

It seems evident that the homosexual component of the
libido implies two distinct aims, depending on the object;
in the little girl one of these instinctual aims corresponds
to a desire for total *possession of the mother* in a world
without men; while the other represents *a desire to be the
father* and, therefore, masculine. Expanding this we
might say that in every small girl's relation to her mother
(both the real mother and her internal representation)
her homosexual attachment will express itself in positive
feelings toward the mother as a sexual object and in defenses against these wishes. In relation to the real and
internalized father, homosexual libido is expressed in a
desire to be like, or *be*, the father—which may or may
not include identification with him in his sexual role.
However, to say that the little girl must make either an
object-choice or an identification oversimplifies the problem. It goes without saying that she must achieve various
identifications with her mother if she is to function har-
moniously as an adult woman; but her equally essential
identifications with her father raise a number of important questions for the understanding of female sexuality

and ego identity. For example, is she trying to become her father in order to be an object of desire and love for the mother? Or, on the contrary, is she trying to camouflage her Oedipal wishes by saying in effect: "See, I don't want to take daddy from my mother. I don't even want to be a girl!" To say that the little girl wants a penis still leaves open the question of why she wants one. What significance has she given to her father's possession of the penis? Does it represent a purely narcissistic enhancement to be desired as such? Or does it stand for the object of the mother's desire? Or a symbol of power? Or protection? The two latter meanings arise frequently from the period of pregenital conflicts before the Oedipal significance of sexual differences is acknowledged; that is, the father (or his penis) comes to represent a protection from the all-controlling "anal" mother or from being engulfed by a devouring "oral" mother, protection therefore against the primitive anxieties associated with these images. Any or all of these fantasies may play a dynamic role in the structure of the unconscious. Then again, fragmented "penis identifications" are also common, for example, the wish to fulfill the role of a penis for the mother. This may be conceived of as a way of repairing her, of tying oneself up to her, of remaining the constant object of her desire and preoccupation, etc.

We clearly cannot advance too far on the basis of fantasy alone. Certain reality experiences leave their imprint. Children, caught in the nets of their parents' unconscious desires, weave their fantasies out of an amalgam of primitive instinctual drives organized around what they have decoded of their parents' wishes and around what they believe they represent to their parents. Of such stuff is ego identity made.

Before trying to understand why certain women create a homosexual identity, we might first of all attempt to see how homosexual libido (in its double aspect) is integrated in women who do not become overtly homosexual. To my mind, this complex instinctual component finds three main expressions in the adult woman. First, it enriches and makes possible sublimated object relations with friends of her own sex. Second, although it is only in her relation to a man that a woman feels herself to be sexually a woman and complementary to her mate, nevertheless her ability to identify with him in the sex act enriches her love life in all its aspects. (The same is, of course, true for the man.) Freud's statement, quoted at the beginning of this paper, already suggests this double identification. Thus, her ability to identify sexually with the father eventually contributes an important element to her feeling of feminine identity. Finally, much homosexual libido is expressed in her various ego activities, particularly in creative and professional work and in the activity of motherhood. Her normal homosexual demands on both parents find manifold sublimated satisfactions when she herself becomes a parent; as regards work capacity, unconscious identification with the opposite sex allows both sexes to bring forth—parthenogenetically, so to speak—their self-created brain children. Failure to accept the important homosexual element contributes to tenacious work problems in both sexes.

If, as suggested here, homosexual libido in women is normally absorbed in object relations of a sublimated kind, in the narcissistic self-image, and in sublimated activities, what then is the situation with regard to the overt homosexual? We might surmise that she on the contrary has met with severe impediments to the harmonious integration of her homosexual drives. . . .

The question of the limits to what is called "homosexuality" still remains to be defined. To begin with, even in all cases of *overt* homosexuality we are not necessarily dealing with the same clinical picture. That many homosexual women do not feel disturbed in such a way as to lead them to seek psychoanalytic help is in itself indicative. Although the capacity for heterosexual love is obviously impaired in the homosexual, there may be relatively unhampered capacity for social relations and for creativity, and such people are less likely to seek therapeutic aid. Others, however, find that all aspects of their lives are unfulfilling or arouse anxiety. For these women the self-image and feeling of identity are sometimes so damaged that they give rise to severe depression with suicidal ideas, or to outbursts of overwhelming anxiety, or again to episodic breakdowns in reality-testing with consequent difficulty in maintaining social relations.

Sometimes homosexual wishes themselves become the focus for conflict and anxiety and as such may motivate a decision to seek analytic help in order to understand and combat the homosexual fantasies. The question of "perverse" masturbation fantasy can be raised here. It seems to me that this is a typical expression of the *neurotic* structure, whereas in overtly perverse people sexual fantasy tends to be rigid and impoverished. One is tempted to posit in the latter an internal prohibition against fantasy which adds to the need to enact it in reality. When patients come to analysis because they are *troubled* by homosexual thoughts we are dealing more often than not with a neurotic structure in which these wishes, though warded off and repressed in the past, have surged back into consciousness, bringing guilt and panic in their wake. The woman who is overtly and exclusively homosexual on the contrary rarely feels strong guilt about her sex life. Although often sensitive to social censure of her proclivities, she usually believes that homosexual relations are an essential part of her life, which she tends to idealize rather than condemn. If she seeks the help of an analyst it is more often because of neurotic difficulties and suffering, which, indeed, are frequently mobilized by a breakdown in her homosexual relationship. Otherwise, she often defers seeking help for fear that her homosexual relations may be endangered.

This paper is not concerned with that large group of women who have created elaborate defenses against homosexual wishes as part of a neurotic picture, nor with that smaller group in which excessive guilt and anxiety over homosexual desires in a fragile structure leads to psychotic projection and paranoia. While the homosexual element is an essential pillar of these patients' psychic structure, it seems misleading to describe them as "latent homosexuals"; the term might in a greater or lesser degree apply to anybody.

There are, however, two broad clinical patterns which are related, though in different ways, to that of the overt homosexual. The first is that of the strikingly "mannish" woman who takes pains to display little femininity in manner and dress and shows a marked preference for the company of men. Such women are frequently referred to as homosexual in spite of the fact that they have no sexual desires toward women. Indeed, they distrust women, deprecate femininity, and often claim that in character they are more like men than women. Men are felt to possess superior intelligence, superior ethical values, superior courage, and so on. In being "masculine" they feel that they, too, share these interests and ideals. With few exceptions the patients of this type whom I have in mind were married and had children. Sexual relations, however, were invariably associated with disagreeable sensations ranging from suffocation to vaginismus, and with feelings of panic or disgust—such symptoms frequently being a leading motive for seeking therapeutic help. Their "virile" personality on the other hand was felt to be ego-syntonic and not regarded as a symptom. None of these patients had any conscious homosexual fantasy, and apart from banal childhood games, reported no history of homosexual experiences. When submitted to analytic scrutiny, the differences between the women of "masculine" character and the overtly homosexual women are more striking than their similarities. It does not seem justified to include them under one single clinical heading as some analytic writers have done, even though we might expect them to have certain features in common.

The second group to which I referred has more in common with the homosexual from the point of view of

psychic and economic structure. This is due to the fact
that the troubled identifications and inner turmoil which
seek expression through homosexuality might equally
well express themselves *in other forms of behavior*. I
have found certain cases of kleptomania and of alcohol-
ism to reveal a psychic structure and parental imagoes
almost identical with those of the homosexual women. . . .
Although kleptomania is not invariably a psychic equivalent to sexual deviation, in the cases I have in mind the
erotic element underlying the stealing was evident in
various ways. One young woman, for example, described
her "bouts" of shoplifting in terms more appropriate to
sexuality than to compulsion. She explained: "I try to
fight the urge to steal. Days go by and then little by little I
find I am thinking of nothing else. It's like an unbearable
tension. Finally, I give in and the feeling is just like deep
relief. It's so exciting and then it's over with, and I can
sleep calmly until the next time." Her pleasure was intensified if she could induce a girl friend to join her in the
shoplifting expeditions. The whole cycle of events carried
a scarcely disguised orgastic meaning for this patient. (It
is interesting to note that similar descriptions are often
applied to creative work also. Here sublimation rather
than perversion has been achieved as a solution to con-
flictual desire through the medium of fantasy elaboration.
The work has been successfully desexualized and the aggressive elements integrated in the creation itself and in
the implied competitiveness. In sexual deviation and
other symptomatic behavior, such as kleptomania, the
aggressive as well as the erotic elements are poorly integrated.) . . .

MASCULINITY AND HOMOSEXUALITY

As already indicated, a manifest desire *to be a man*
and an *overt sexual desire for women* do not necessarily
stem from a common unconscious structure. While both
desires clearly imply a disturbance in the feeling of sexual

identity, there is a considerable difference between the
"masculine" woman, who regards her *ego ideals and her
identity* as basically male (accompanied by a disparaging
attitude to women), and the homosexual one, who has
made *a masculine type of object-choice* in seeking love
relations with a woman (accompanied by a disparaging
attitude to men). What factors have hindered the harmonious integration of the ambivalent Oedipal attachments and the potential conflicts of the pre-Oedipal
phases to such an extent as to distort the feeling of sexual
identity? And what are the common features and the differences between the two groups?

To begin with it becomes clinically evident that both
groups repudiate any identification with the *genital*
mother, particularly in her role as sexual partner to the
man and to a lesser extent in her capacity to bear children. The homosexual woman does not seek to attract
men sexually and usually does not believe she could even
should she desire it. At the same time she is afraid of men
and constantly fears sexual attack. The masculine
woman, although not afraid of men, is usually distressed
and angry at the idea that she might be an object of
sexual desire for them, and she frequently acts as though
insulted if sexual approaches are made to her. Her sexual
relations with lover or husband are not infrequently accompanied by mental and physical pain—a fact which
she usually endeavors to hide.

Apart from the question of sexual relations, bitterness
toward men (conscious in one group and unconscious in
the other) affects work capacities in both and can affect
the maintenance of satisfactory social relations with men.
Homosexual women often seek to exclude men altogether
from their lives, thus imposing rigid limits on their activity. Masculine women, although socially at ease and consciously identified with men, are frequently frightened by
intense rivalry feelings which they attempt to stifle, and
they become inhibited to a pathological degree from creating or working at anything successfully.

Thus, women of both categories complain of feelings of inadequacy, of insecurity, and of confusion about what they want from life. All are liable to periods of depression or anxiety. Although their difficulties are determined in part by a common failure to identify with the genital mother, to understand their divergence it is necessary to discuss the sharp differences in the parental imagoes in the two groups of women. The virile woman has to some extent eliminated the mother image, and with her all other women, as objects of libidinal value. By contrast the homosexual constantly seeks other women for tender and eroticized relations, which have in addition the quality of a mother-child relationship.

With regard to the paternal image we find the situation reversed. The homosexual girl appears to have eliminated the father and all other men as possible objects of libidinal investment. The masculine girl constantly seeks relations with men, but on a nongenital basis. She accepts the sexual relationship with conflict and misgiving.

The following quotations, from a woman of each group, epitomize their respective positions when they seek to justify them consciously. One of my "masculine" patients, a physicist, married, with children, says: "It's just too bad being a woman. Women don't like other women and men can't stand them either! To be born a woman is to be condemned in advance." Her position closely resembles that of a Paris journalist well known for his misogynist views, who in a radio interview, to the question: "It appears, Monsieur, that you do not like women at all?" replied, "Who does?"

In contrast, a patient whose relationships were exclusively homosexual often proclaimed: "What could one possibly hope for from a man? Only women are capable of disinterested love or of understanding the pain of another human being."

Clearly, the two patients quoted here are both endeavoring to maintain a precarious sense of integrity and identity, but the complex series of identifications by

which they have attempted to solve their conflicts are
different. Each runs the risk of failure, with consequent
pain and disillusionment, in the field of sexual as well as
of sublimatory activities. A secure feeling of sexual and
personal identity can be achieved only through adequate
identification with *both* parents. This allows the integration of primitive omnipotence and primitive instinctual
drives toward both parents and is a necessary prerequisite
to the renunciation of incestuous wishes and to the establishment of secondary identification—in other words to
the resolution of the Oedipal conflict. Lacking such basic
identifications the possibility of maintaining ego identity
through adequate social and sexual relations is constantly
threatened and likely to lead to neurotic illness or to
perverse "solutions" of the Oedipal situation. It is within
the scope of psychoanalysis to provide conditions in
which such integration, blocked since early childhood,
may once again become possible.

*   *   *

5

Fathers, Mothers, and Sex Typing

EVELYN GOODENOUGH PITCHER

This study investigates the problem of whether boys of nursery school age differ from girls in their interest in persons, and whether there is anything in the attitudes of parents that might make a difference in boys' and girls' interests.

The problem emerged from a preliminary general study of sex differences of nursery school children. An interview structured around 16 open-end questions was administered to 80 parents (i.e., 40 married couples) of children aged two through four years. In this pilot study the investigator was interested in the general area of sex differences, but had not yet settled upon a single aspect of the problem for study.

As the interviews progressed, the more personal nature of the mothers' replies, the more ideational nature of the fathers' became increasingly apparent. A preliminary hypothesis began to emerge, namely, that the material from the interviews might show that females are more interested in persons than are males, and that parents might be promoters of this difference in their children.

A second trend suggested by the pilot study was that the mothers tended to treat their sons and daughters much more alike than did the fathers. The fathers seemed much more than the mothers to differentiate expectations for boys from those they had for girls. Fathers seemed to insist that boys must be boys and girls girls, to an extent

SOURCE: From "Interest in Persons as an Aspect of Sex Difference in the Early Years" by Evelyn Wiltshire Goodenough, in *Genetic Psychology Monographs*, 55 (1957), pp. 287–323. Reprinted by permission of The Journal Press and the author.

that mothers did not. This suggested a second hypothesis, that the fathers' influence might be stronger than the mothers' in the general area of sex-typing. These two hypotheses were tested by the analysis of material from six of the original 16 questions of the interview.

*   *   *

RELATIVE CONCERN OF FATHER AND MOTHER WITH SEX-TYPING

It was suggested as the second hypothesis of this study that the father tends more than the mother to differentiate sex-typed rôles. Material bearing on this hypothesis was brought out when the parents were asked, "For your first child did you prefer a girl or a boy, and why? Would you be disturbed if your child showed an excess of the characteristics of his opposite sex? If you knew all you know now, and could determine your sex, would you yourself prefer to be a male or a female?" . . .

In view of . . . material which has pointed to the greater personal orientation of the female, it seems relevant that the women's reasons for preferring a male child involve a concern for people. The reasons she gives refer to her personal experiences (because she had, or had not had, an elder brother), to her husband's wish, or to her mother's wish. Men show more interest in the abstract concepts of carrying on the family name, in sharing a sense of maleness with their sons.

One mother remarked: "Having a girl first seems to be easier for a father. Having a son seems to call for something particularly mature in a father. A son won't take him as he is. Relation to a child of the same sex brings up a parent's own childhood problems more strongly." If this statement contains some truth, it is apparently not reversible for the sexes. Mothers, perhaps more understanding and accepting of all children as children, make

no mention of a greater understanding for girls than for
boys. And although **four** men state that they worry lest
there be too many women in their lives, there is no corresponding report of fear of males on the part of females.
On the other hand, that 10 fathers say they "understand"
boys better suggests that they understand girls less well.
The father's presumed stronger identification with his son
than with his daughter perhaps calls for a stronger identification of the son with the father than is common in the
mother and daughter relationship.

These considerations support the thesis that, to the
male, masculinity is something special and apart from
femininity, but the female is not so apt thus to consider
that her sex-typing requires the exclusion of all masculinity. Insofar as it is true that the father may be more
concerned with the differentiation of sex-typed roles, the
father may also be more strongly the sex-typer than the
mother.

. . . When questioned directly as to whether they would
be disturbed at evidence of opposite-sex behavior in children, more fathers than mothers indicated disturbance,
though the difference is not statistically significant. Yet
the material from the interviews seems to indicate that
the father holds stronger views than the mother concerning sex differences in children.

Examples from the first two questions of the interview,
in which many parents comment on the affection of children, show the father appreciating and perhaps encouraging manifestations of feminine coquetry in his daughter
in a way that the mother does not. It has already been
noted that men alone commented on sexuality as a mark
of difference between the sexes: Sex appears to be a matter
of more direct and open concern to them. Perhaps, being
more sexually responsive, the father tends more than the
mother to differentiate the sexes.

The father's more direct tendency to differentiate the
sexes may be illustrated by the way *Affection* has been

reported as a trait. In the first question on personality, where affection is spontaneously mentioned in descriptions of both boys and girls, fathers exercised a restraint in mentioning a son's affection that mothers did not. Fathers seem to feel more diffidence than mothers in speaking of affection of a person of one's own sex, even the affection of a small boy.

A difference comes out more sharply, however, when the daughter's affection is discussed. The fathers' remarks are scarcely differentiated from those of the mothers in the first question, which simply asks for a description of general personality, but when the fathers consider the *femininity* of their daughters, their reactions suggest much more personal involvement. The mother is more the observer and reporter; the father an active participator. The remarks seem to illustrate one father's comment about femininity in adults: "Femininity can't be divorced in my mind from a certain amount of sexuality." Ten fathers think the girl's affection or coquetry is a mark of her femininity. They say the following:

1. Very coquettish. Gallantry and consideration work with her. 2. Seductive, persuasive, knows how to get me to do things she can't get her mother to let her do. 3. Inclined to be coy and a little seductive. 4. A bit of a flirt, arch and playful with people, a pretended coyness. Sometimes she seems like a Southern girl—maybe a little flirt when she gets older. 5. Soft and cuddly and loving. She cuddles and flatters in subtle ways. 6. Engages in outward display of affection. 7. Her coyness and flirting, "come up and see me sometime" approach. Loves to cuddle. She's going to be sexy—I get my wife annoyed when I say this. . . .

Five mothers also report the flirtatious character of the daughter as an aspect of her femininity, but what they say shows a noticeable lack of personal involvement. That is, the father says in effect, "She flirts with me"; the mother says, "She flirts with her father or other people." Mothers say the following:

1. A little flirt. 2. Flirtatious, at least with her father. 3. Tenderness, kissing new baby brought to our house. 4. Outgoing and demonstrative in affection. 5. Flirts with boys and men on occasion. 6. She tries to make up to men.

Material from the interviews in answer to the second question, in which parents described their children's interests as sex-typed traits, . . . suggests that boys define their own sex rôles much more sharply than do girls. For parents indicate that little boys are very early in conscious opposition against the female sex. Fathers tell of the opposition their sons have to girls as follows:

1. He's not interested in dolls. He's not interested in playing with girls. He stays away from them completely —they're no fun to play with. 2. He likes men more than women. 3. Drawn to men, not to women. 4. Hates dolls, loves cowboys, spacemen. No playing house.

Mothers comment that little boys' interest in dolls rises largely from the desire to tease the girls, and that the boys dislike girls. They comment:

1. He will take Ann's doll away, just to drag it away. 2. He has a passionate devotion to little boys. He liked Emmy Lou till he found out that she was a little girl. 3. He never cared for dolls or stuffed animals. 4. He doesn't care about dolls except to annoy his sister. Doesn't love doll or play with it. 5. He never plays with dolls, just looks at his sister's dolls. 6. If I give him an animal in bed, he asks for a truck or steam shovel. He asked me to change the doll's diapers, but he never played with the doll. No tea parties. 7. He's a typical cowboy, Indian, spaceman. He won't look at dolls. Loves boys' stories not girls' stories.

There is not the same tendency on the part of parents to say that girls' femininity implies opposition to masculinity. Only three girls are reported as being opposed in any obvious form to boys or boyish activities—a girl not interested in cars and trucks, one who wished Peter Pan was a girl, and one who wanted long hair rather than short, since boys have short hair. Neither the parents of girls, nor the girls themselves, seem to see the need to take so strong a stand against masculinity in girls as is true of the need to take a stand against femininity in boys.

Although mothers tend in general to agree with the fathers in reporting boys' opposition to feminine things, the father's own opposition to feminine behavior in his son may set the stage for what becomes a typical masculine attitude. "He gets mad if I tease him about his interest in anything girlish, and therefore babyish," says one father about his two-year-old son. "His father was furious when I painted his nails red," said a mother about her husband's reaction to fingernail polish on his son. And another remarks, "On Halloween a boy can't wear anything feminine. Idea of lipstick horrifies a father."

The kind of contrast that appears between father and mother reporting femininity in their son is illustrated by the following remarks. A father, asked if he would be disturbed by aspects of femininity in his son, said, "Yes, I would be, very, very much. Terrifically disturbed— couldn't tell you the extent of my disturbance. I can't *bear* female characteristics in a man. I abhor them." A mother says, "Jimmy is not as masculine. But he'll grow up to be considerate and kind. Gentlemanly, rather than masculine." Another father is distressed and scornful by signs of his son's femininity. "He's always interested in flexing his muscles. Perhaps he has to prove that he's masculine—that's why I call him feminine." The same boy's mother admits that at one time she was very much concerned about her son's femininity, but reasoned thus, "I am aware these people make splendid contributions to the world. I'd try to help. I would turn all my energies to producing a good environment for him."

And just as the father is more likely to inveigh against, or deny the existence of, femininity in his son, so he is the more likely to appreciate femininity in his daughter, as his remarks about *Affection* in his daughter have already suggested (p. 86). Remarks collected from various questions in the interview show the father's concern to promote his concept of femininity.

One mother reports her husband's pleasure when she put their six-month-old daughter into a dress for the first time. "That's much nicer than these old pajamas," said the father. But he was much concerned, since they were visiting, because the infant kept kicking up her dress, and he constantly rearranged her skirts in proper fashion. The mother thought this absurd, and made fun of the fact that her husband called his daughter's overalls her pajamas. One mother reports that her husband blanched when he found she had cut her daughter's long hair. "Promise me that you will never, never cut it again," he said. Another father says, "The little girl is a flirt, not at all interested in women. When she sees a man, she goes into a seductive act. She kisses women without any coaxing, but won't kiss men unless she's really interested." The same girl's mother reports her daughter as being "100 per cent Mother Eve."

Another father teaches his son how to react to femininity in his baby sister. "His attitude toward his sister is masculine, very big-brotherly. I've impressed him with this—to be careful, treat her nice, 'oogle-google' with her." This boy's mother says, "My husband talks in a high voice to the little girl, in a deep base voice to Jimmy." Other remarks show that there is a tendency for the father to grant his daughter a special, privileged place: "It is so inevitable to spoil a first child, I'm glad my first child was a girl," and "I'd be stricter with a boy than with a girl, perhaps because my own father was stricter with me. Mary (daughter) once asked me which of my 'girls' I liked best—her or her mother. One is always conscious that there is a little sex factor between a little female child and her father."

Only sparse examples can be gathered from these interviews to indicate that the mother is playing an active part in encouraging her son to a more masculine rôle insofar as interaction between the sexes, or the cultivation of "manly" custom is concerned. The interviews afford only two examples of the mother's being interested in encouraging a chivalric rôle as a token of masculinity. One mother describes her little boy as his sister's "protector" and another has strong feelings of satisfaction that her sons are polite and courteous to their sister, affording her a rightful "first" place.

Although mothers report their daughters' interests in domestic activities and in dressing up in feminine clothes, it would seem that mothers are as likely to give their little girls overalls as dresses, and to take their sons to a tea party as to visit a railroad yard. It almost seems as if sex-typing goes on in boys independent of maternal influence, and goes on in girls with very little effort from the mother to exclude masculine influence.

*   *   *

6

Psychosexual Differentiation

JOHN MONEY

Development and differentiation are inseparable concepts in the embryology of sex. In the psychology of sex, it is good to remember that the same applies: psychosexual development is also psychosexual differentiation as male or female.

In psychosexual theory, it has been more or less assumed that, when psychosexual development proceeds in an orderly fashion, masculinity or femininity will somehow differentiate out of an innate, instinctive bisexuality.

The origins and regulation of this psychosexual differentiation, too long neglected in research, still cannot be fully specified. In this chapter, I propose to review the present state of knowledge.

Anatomic sexual differentiation in the embryo takes place according to two plans, either of which may offer a model for psychosexual differentiation. One plan is exemplified by the gonads [ovaries or testes] and subsequently repeated by the internal accessory structures. In both cases, the anlagen [foundations] for both male and female are initially laid down side by side. Then one set regresses and atrophies while the other proliferates and differentiates.

The other plan of sexual differentiation is exemplified by the external genitalia. Here the homologous male and female structures differentiate from the same embryonic anlagen. Thus, the genital tubercle [swelling] becomes

SOURCE: From *Sex Research: New Developments*, edited by John Money. Copyright © 1965 by Holt, Rinehart and Winston, Inc. Reprinted by permission of Holt, Rinehart and Winston, Inc. The figures originally accompanying this essay have been omitted.

either a penis or a clitoris; the skin covering of the penis
has the same origin as the clitoral hood and labia minora;
and the labioscrotal swellings either remain divided as the
labia majora or fuse in the midline to become the scro-
tum.

Though complete reversal of genetic sex has been
achieved in amphibian experiments, little is known about
the fundamental principles of regulation of gonadal differentiation in mammals—that is, about what controls
proliferation of the "rind" of the primitive gonad to become an ovary, versus proliferation of the "core" to
become a testis.

Once formed, however, the gonads themselves become
the source of hormonal organizer substances that regulate
differentiation of the remainder of the genital system. If
the embryonic gonads are removed in mammals, before
the critical time of genital-duct differentiation has passed,
then differentiation proceeds as female. The critical period is marvelously short. In the experiments by Jost
(Chapter 2 in Jones and Scott, 1958) on the rabbit,
castration before embryonic day 21 was early enough to
ensure complete feminization of all the remaining reproductive system. On the twenty-fourth day, it was already
too late for castration to interfere with masculine differentiation already begun. But on day 23, castration of
genetic males arrested masculine differentiation in favor
of resumption of feminine differentiation, with resulting
hermaphroditic ambiguity of appearance.

Mammalian masculine anatomy, as these experiments
show, is brought about by something added, failing which
the more basic disposition of the embryo toward the feminine asserts itself. One wonders whether to look for a
parallel in human psychosexual differentiation. In view of
the alleged higher incidence of psychosexual pathologies
in males, it is conceivable that masculine psychosexual
differentiation is more difficult to achieve than feminine,
and is more vulnerable to error and failure.

Jost did not report on the effects of the changes set in

motion by embryonic castration on the subsequent differentiation of sexual behavior. More recently, however, Grady and Phoenix (1963) performed castration experiments on neonatal rats and found more feminine behavior, in response to mounting by intact males, in animals castrated before ten days of age than after.

There are also behavioral reports on a type of experimental hermaphroditism easier to accomplish than that of Jost, namely masculinization of a female fetus. Phoenix, Goy, Gerall, and Young (1959) bred hermaphroditic guinea pigs by administering testosterone to the pregnant mothers. Some of the daughters were born with male external genitalia, the internal reproductive organs being female. These animals (and to a lesser extent their morphologically normal female counterparts which had also been exposed in utero to testosterone, but in lesser amount) gained scores in various subsequent mating tests that were closer to the scores of untreated control males than to those of untreated control females. The authors ventured the hypothesis that prenatal androgen had affected neural organization and thus the organization of behavior. It is of significance to note, however, that the masculine scores of the experimental animals reflected a quantitative rather than a qualitative sex difference. The affected animals did that which normal females might do, but which normal males readily do more frequently. . . .

While admitting that there are inconsistencies which need further elucidation, Levine and Mullins (1964) suggest that the central nervous mechanism controlling gonadotropin-release in the rat will develop so as to function acyclically, that is in the male fashion, only under the influence of androgen, presumably secreted by the infantile testes. Testosterone would thus be implicated as the active hormone organizing the sexual control system, both in terms of reproductive cycles and sexual behavior. It is already known that, at a critical period earlier in embryonic life, androgen is an active organizer substance without which the internal anlagen of the female morphology do not regress and the external anlagen feminize. In other words, without androgen, nature's primary impulse is to make a female—morphologically speaking at least.

The change from cyclic to acyclic release of pituitary gonadotropin [substance that stimulates gonadal activity] in the female rat by neonatal injection of sex hormone is the product of sex-hormonal action not on the pituitary itself, but on the neural centers of the adjacent hypothalamus. Segal and Johnson (1959) took the pituitaries from female rats that had been treated neonatally with androgen and whose ovaries consequently were anovulatory and sterile. Transplanted into normal hypophysectomized [pituitary gland removed] hosts, these pituitaries were capable of inducing complete reproductive function, since the host animals bore young and suckled them. It was imperative, however, for the donor gland to be transplanted in contiguity with the hypothalamus of the host female, thus demonstrating that the control of cyclic pituitary function was in the hypothalamus itself.

It is theoretically important to underscore the significance of timing, and of the critical-period phenomenon, in all the above experiments. The mechanism of hypothalamic regulation of cyclic pituitary functioning, and of attendant sexual behavior, can be abolished by exogenous hormone, but only if it is injected during a critical developmental period. This period must be ascertained empirically for each species (Goy, Phoenix, and Young, 1962).

There is a somewhat suggestive human parallel to the animal experiments with androgen to be found in human female hermaphrodites with the adrenogenital syndrome, virilized in utero from an excess of adrenal androgens. There is anecdotal evidence from some of these patients, who, in adulthood, have reported experiences more typically reported by normal males than females, namely, erotic arousal from visual and narrative perceptual material. The experience might be accompanied by erection of the hypertrophied [enlarged] clitoris and masturbation. The erotic content of the perceptual images and fantasies was suitably female, in keeping with their sex of rearing and psychosexual identity. Only the threshold and frequency of arousal followed the masculine pattern. The reaction has occurred in both the untreated and treated cases of the syndrome, but is attenuated by treatment, which consisted of feminizing clitoral surgery and hormonal correction with cortisone. There is a possibility, therefore, that there was also a residual androgenic effect, even after androgen levels were controlled to normal. . . .

Whatever the ultimate experimental verdict on prenatal influences, in human psychosexual differentiation it is also true that what happens before birth can be overridden to an extraordinary degree by postnatal events. The demonstration par excellence is that of two hermaphrodites of identical diagnosis and anatomical defect, one assigned as a boy, the other as a girl. In such cases, the differentiation of gender role and psychosexual identity ordinarily proceeds in agreement with assigned sex, particularly if three conditions are met. The first condition is that the parents resolve their ambiguities and doubts, at the time of birth, and achieve a feeling of complete conviction that they have either a son or a daughter, whom they will raise accordingly. This first condition is linked to the second: that genital surgery, at least the first stage to achieve a good cosmetic appearance, be delayed as little as possible after birth. The visual appearance of the sex organs dictates not only the expectancies of other people, but also contributes to the development of the child's own body image. This second condition is, therefore, linked to the third: that pubertal secondary sexual development be timed and regulated hormonally, possibly with adjuvant surgery, in conformity with assigned sex and psychosexual identity.

This ideal is not always attained. There are patients for whom all three conditions have not been met. Even so, some of these patients manage to achieve a unitary

gender role and psychosexual identity, despite gross contradictions of bodily sex. Perhaps the most surprising of
these are women with the untreated adrenogenital syndrome. Despite a penis-sized clitoris, an exaggerated
masculine physique, excessive hirsutism, and a deep
voice, it is not impossible for these girls to develop and
maintain a feminine gender role and psychosexual identity.

The incongruities among the variables of sex in
hermaphroditism are such as to permit one to show that
psychosexual differentiation can take place in opposition
to:

1. genetic sex, as revealed by either the sex-chromatin
mass (Barr body) or a full chromosome count;
2. hormonal sex, in other words, a hormonal balance
that is predominantly androgenic or estrogenic;
3. gonadal sex: ovarian, testicular, or mixed;
4. morphology of the internal reproductive organs;
5. morphology of the external genitals.

Psychosexual differentiation in hermaphrodites may
also take place in contradiction of the sex of assignment
and rearing. The same happens in cases of sexual psychopathology in people who are genetically, hormonally,
and morphologically normal in all respects, according to
presently-known criteria.

One must make the inference that psychosexual differentiation takes place as an active process of editing and
assimilating experiences that are gender-specific and that
derive ultimately from the genital appearance of the
body. These experiences include direct apperception—
visual, tactile, and proprioceptive—of one's own sexual
organs. They also include the multitudinous and cumula-
tive experiences that derive from genital appearance as it
has determined the sex of assignment and rearing—experiences that are defined by the gender of personal
nouns and pronouns, clothing style, haircut, and a thousand other gender-specific expectancies and attitudes.

The evidence of hermaphroditism indicates that the condition existing at birth and for several months thereafter is one of psychosexual undifferentiation. Just as in the embryo, morphologic sexual differentiation passes from a plastic stage to one of fixed immutability, so also does psychosexual differentiation become fixed and immutable—so much so, that mankind has traditionally assumed that so strong and fixed a feeling as personal sexual identity must stem from something innate, instinctive, and not subject to postnatal experience and learning.

The error of this traditional assumption is that the power and permanence of something learned has been underestimated. The experiments of animal ethologists on imprinting have now corrected this misconception.

The basic paradigm of imprinting is that there is in a species a tendency to respond behaviorally to a certain type of perceptual stimulus, the limits of variability in both the behavior and the stimulus being phylogenetically set. Further, there is a critical period in the life history when this stimulation and responding must take place if an effective bond between the two is to occur. Finally, once the bond has been established, it has extraordinary durability for an epoch if not the entire lifetime.

The acquisition of a native language is a human counterpart to imprinting in animals. So also is the acquisition of a gender role and psychosexual identity. The critical period in establishing psychosexual identity appears to be approximately simultaneous with the establishment of native language. Planned experimental evidence is, of course, for ethical reasons impossible to come by. But there are occasional experiments of nature, namely, when infant and juvenile hermaphrodites are subjected to sex reassignment.

Psychosexual differentiation follows in agreement with a sex reassignment made in the neonatal period or up to a year or eighteen months of age, provided the parents negotiate the change successfully. Thereafter, adjustment difficulties and the likelihood of residual psychopathology increase with the child's memory of life-history experiences and appreciation of gender concepts. By school age, psychosexual differentiation is so complete that a sex reassignment is out of the question, save for the rare instances of ambiguous psychosexual differentiation.

Judging by the prevalence in psychopathology of errors or partial errors of psychosexual differentiation, the process of differentiation is vulnerable to many interferences. The great vexation, scientifically, is that one knows little about the extent and precise nature of these interferences. Harlow's (1962) now famous experiments on the macaque have shown that ability to mate is adversely and lastingly affected when the young are deprived of play contact with their age mates. In the case of human beings, it is possible that any impedance of normal development and maturation, however seemingly remote from psychosexual identity, may have a noxious side-effect on psychosexual differentiation. Such impedance would include defects in the parent-child relationship and attendant hindering of normal ego mechanisms of identification and impersonation.[1] . . .

With the advent of puberty, the stage is set for the completion of psychosexual differentiation in courtship, mating, and parenthood. Puberty is also the time at which prior errors and defects of psychosexual differentiation announce themselves in full and prevent continued normal and desired completion of psychosexual maturity. Whether or not psychosexual pathologies may be induced at puberty is arguable, but it is certainly true that a great many of them have a long "psychoembryonic" period before puberty.

It is commonplace of social anthropology that, whatever their prepubertal history, a multiplicity of details of adolescent and adult gender role are specific to a particular ethnic group at a particular historical time. One may go further and say that the hormones that bring about

[1] See Brown, 1957; Kagan, 1964; Katcher, 1955; Lynn, 1959; Maccoby, 1966; Mussen & Distler, 1960; Rabban, 1950.

sexual maturation do not, according to all the evidence available, have any differential determining influence on the psychosexual, male-female direction and content of perceptual, memory, or dream imagery that may trigger or be associated with erotic arousal. On the contrary, there is strong clinical and presumptive evidence (Money, 1961a, b) that the libido hormone is the same for men and women and is androgen. Psychosexually, the androgenic function is limited to partial regulation of the intensity and frequency of sexual desire and arousal, but not to the cognitional patterns of arousal. In women, androgen may be secreted by the adrenal cortex or metabolically derived from the ovary's progestins, to which it is akin in chemical structure.

Sex differences in the androgen-estrogen ratio may conceivably account for some of the differences between men and women in their thresholds for erotically related behavior and activity. In the male, for instance, there is typically a greater expenditure of energy in the service of sexual searching, pursuit, and consummation. This energy expenditure extends also to adventurous, exploratory roaming, to assertiveness and aggression, and to the defense of territorial rights. Of course, the male does not have exclusive prerogative in these respects, but there does indeed seem to be a sex difference in the frequency with which these patterns of activity are manifest.

This difference is not exclusive to the human species. Harlow (1962) found that male children of the macaque monkey make many more threats toward other monkeys, boys or girls, than do the female children. The girls' threats, moreover, are reserved primarily for other girls. The young females retreat more often than the males, specifically by adopting the female sexual posture. The male youngsters initiate more play contacts, with playmates of either sex, than do females, and the males are the ones that engage in rough and tumble play. With increasing age, the male infants show increasing frequency of the male mounting position in their copulatory play. They show little grooming behavior, which in adults is more predominant in female than male sexual behavior.

Hormone-derived sex differences in behavior after puberty may be independent of social interaction, or they may be interactional, so that the behavior of the male is influenced by the hormonal cycle of the female. Michael and Herbert (1963) found that the time spent by the female rhesus monkey in grooming the male fluctuates rhythmically with the menstrual cycle and reaches a minimum at mid-cycle, near the time of ovulation. Reciprocally, it is precisely at this time that the male's grooming activity reaches a maximum, and very shortly thereafter that his mounting activity reaches its peak. These rhythmic changes in the mounting behavior of males and in the grooming activity of both sexes did not appear in one case of a nervous and excitable male, and were in all cases abolished by ovariectomy. The route by which the ovarian cycle of the female influences not only her behavior but that of the mating partner as well may conceivably be via the sense of smell, though this possibility remains to be investigated. The relationship of the ovarian cycle to sexual behavior in human beings also requires investigation. It is of interest to note that the peak of sexual desire and initiative in women has by several investigators been reported as occurring at the menstrual or progestinic phase of the cycle (Money, 1965), so that one may see an analogy with the female monkey whose grooming approach to the male is intensified at this time.

In the behavior of human beings, there is evidence that the sense of smell is related to the sexual cycle in women and is hormone regulated. Women generally have greater acuity than men, and the consensus of reports (Money, 1963) is that acuity is at its peak when estrogen levels are highest, that is, between the periods of actual menstruation in the monthly cycles. Acuity is lost after ovariectomy, but regained with administration of estrogen.

Hypophysectomy, which suppresses ovarian function, also brings about loss of the sense of smell (Schon, 1958)....

Another sex difference that relates perhaps to hormonal differences pertains to perceptual distractibility. More than woman, man is in his erotic pursuits fairly promiscuously distracted from one love object to another, especially over a period of time, except perhaps when he is in the vortex of having just fallen desperately in love. The female is more steadfastly tied to a single romantic object or concept. In the act of copulation, by contrast, it is the male who has a singleness of purpose, perhaps oblivious even to noxious stimuli, and who is likely to be unable to continue if successfully distracted by a competing stimulus. This sex difference appears to hold widely in the animal kingdom (Beach, 1947, p. 264). "A marked difference between the male and female cat," wrote Horsley Gantt (1949, p. 37), "is that the female's interest in food is not inhibited by the sexual excitation of copulation, for she, as well as a bitch, will accept food not only after coitus but even during the act. . . . The female is, however, much more strongly oriented about the offspring than about the sexual act; she undergoes a great inhibition of conditional reflexes and of some unconditional reflexes postpartum, a fact which has been demonstrated several times in my laboratory with dogs."

On the relationship of sex hormones to sex-differentiated behavior, there is in animal experimentation a remarkable new development in demonstrating direct hormonal action on the brain (Michael, 1961; 1962). By implanting micro-amounts of estrogen directly into the hypothalamus of the cat, Michael was able to induce in the animal a state of sustained sexual receptivity, though without any of the other physiologic signs of estrus. Then by using C^{14}-labeled estrogen and an autoradiographic technique, he was able to demonstrate that the action of the hormone was localized and consistent with the hypothesis that certain neurons of the hypothalamus are selectively sensitive to the action of estrogen. . . .

The many difficulties inherent in unraveling the neurohormonal basis of sexual behavior, including species differences, are further exemplified in the findings of Fisher (1956) on the rat. Injecting minute amounts of testosterone directly into the preoptic area of the brains of male rats, Fisher obtained maternal and sexual behavior in a series of males. Maternal behavior included nest building and persistent retrieving and grooming of litters of young. All aspects of mating behavior were seen, sometimes accentuated. One male continuously retrieved his tail when stimulated, and then repeatedly retrieved a female in heat. When pups and paper were supplied, however, the animal built a nest and retrieved and groomed the young, neglecting the objects to which he had previously reacted. In another male, maternal and sexual behavior were activated simultaneously. When presented with a female (not in heat) and with newborn rat pups, the male attempted copulation twice while a pup he was retrieving to a nest was still in his mouth. Variations in response to injected androgen appeared to depend on small variations in placement of the canula in the brain. . . .

The human brain maintains its adult pattern of psychosexual differentiation relatively stable and constant, for the most part, though as some people gain in age and experience there may be a lifting of restraints against behavior they once tabooed. Major psychosexual changes in adulthood are not the norm, but a sign of abnormality and deterioration, well exemplified in the psychosexual regression and dedifferentiation of senility. Psychosexual deterioration may also be a symptom of other brain disease, of toxic neurological disease, and of other psychotic conditions of late onset. Otherwise, aging is a process in which the psychosexual fires simply burn low, quickly for some, but for others retaining some glow until the end.

SUMMARY

Psychosexual differentiation is an active process that takes place after birth and needs the stimulus of interaction with a behavioral environment, in much the same manner as does acquisition of a language. In certain indicative cases the behavioral environment, reinforcing the sex of assignment, can override the influence of the physical variables of sex.

Of possible significance to human psychosexual differentiation are new animal experiments on neurohormonal activity in the fetus or newborn, whereby sex hormones affect the neural organization of subsequent sexual behavior. The chief effect would appear to be that androgen is needed to induce masculine cycles and frequencies, but not types of behavior.

A second type of new experimental work is providing evidence of a direct action of sex hormone on neural centers and individual cells of the hypothalamus, which are related to phylogenetic stereotypes in sexual behavior. To date, the specificity of the relationship of estrogen and androgen to the release of feminine and masculine behavior, respectively, is none too clear; and other chemicals may prove able to simulate their neural-triggering action.

The neural component of human sexual behavior might well include a neuroperceptual sex difference. Men appear to be more responsive to visual and narrative erotic stimuli and images, women to be more dependent on touch. Males are perceptually more distractible than females in erotic pursuits. Their greater expenditure of energy in initiating erotic pursuit may bear some phylogenetic relationship to the defense of territorial rights, a type of behavior widely occurring in the mating patterns of mammals.

Women have more smell acuity than men; and it varies with the menstrual cycle. Secreted odors may be the responsible agent in controlling reciprocal mating behavior relative to the menstrual cycle, according to experiments on the macaque monkey. Odors secreted by the male have been found, in the mouse, to regulate whether copulation will succeed in successful pregnancy or not. Such excitatory odors have been named pheromones.

In human beings, psychosexual differentiation is manifested in full at adolescence and thenceforth remains relatively stable in adulthood, though changes and regression are possible, especially in senescence.

REFERENCES

Beach, F. A.   1947   A review of physiological and psychological studies of sexual behavior in mammals. *Physiol. Rev.* 27, 240–307.

Fisher, A. E.   1956   Maternal and sexual behavior induced by intracranial chemical stimulation. *Science* 124, 228–229.

Gantt, W. H.   1949   Psychosexuality in animals. In P. H. Hoch and J. Zubin (Eds.), *Psychosexual development in health and disease*. New York: Grune and Stratton.

Goy, R. W., Phoenix, C. H., and Young, W. C.   1962   A critical period for the suppression of behavioral receptivity in adult female rats by early treatment with androgen. *Anat. Rec.* 142, 307.

Grady, K. L., and Phoenix, C. H.   1963   Hormonal determinants of mating behavior; the display of feminine behavior by adult male rats castrated neonatally. *Amer. Zoologist* 3, 482–483.

Harlow, H. F.   1962   The heterosexual affectional system in monkeys. *Amer. Psychologist* 17, 1–9.

Levine, S., and Mullins, R., Jr.   1964   Estrogen administered neonatally affects adult sexual behavior in male and female rats. *Science* 144, 185–187.

Maccoby, E. (Ed.)   1966   *The development of sex differences*. Stanford: Stanford University Press.

Michael, R. P.   1961   An investigation of the sensitivity of circumscribed neurological areas to hormonal stimulation by means of the application of estrogens directly to the brain of the cat. In S. S. Kety and J. Elkes (Eds.), *Regional neurochemistry*. Oxford: Pergamon Press.

Michael, R. P. 1962 Oestrogen-sensitive systems in mammalian brains. *Excerpta Medica, International Congress Series No. 47* (containing papers read at the XXII International Congress of Physiological Sciences, Leiden, The Netherlands) pp. 650–652.

Michael, R. P., and Herbert, J. 1963 Menstrual cycle influences grooming behavior and sexual activity in the rhesus monkey. *Science* 140, 500–501.

Money, J. 1961a Components of eroticism in man: I. The hormones in relation to sexual morphology and sexual desire. *J. nerv. ment. Dis.* 132, 239–248.

Money, J. 1961b Sex hormones and other variables in human eroticism. In W. C. Young (Ed.), *Sex and internal secretions* (ed. 3). Baltimore: Williams and Wilkins.

Money, J. 1963 Developmental differentiation of femininity and masculinity compared. In *Man and civilization: The potential of woman.* New York: McGraw-Hill.

Money, J. 1965 Influence of hormones on sexual behavior. *Ann. Rev. Med.*, Vol. 16. Palo Alto: Annual Reviews, Inc.

Phoenix, C. H., Goy, R. W., Gerall, A. A., and Young, W. C. 1959 Organizing action of prenatally administered testosterone propionate on the tissues mediating mating behavior in the female guinea pig. *Endocrinology* 65, 369–382.

Schon, M. 1958 Psychological effects of hypophysectomy in women with metastatic breast cancer. *Cancer* 11, 95–98.

Segal, S. J., and Johnson, D. C. 1959 Inductive influence of steroid hormones on the neural system: Ovulation controlling mechanisms. *Arch. d'Anat. micros. Morphol. expér.* 48 bis, 261–273.

II

MASTURBATION, SEXUAL INTERCOURSE, AND ORGASM

Introduction

Masturbation, sexual intercourse, and orgasm are areas in which society and the female body have most noticeably collided in Western culture. In an excerpt from "Authority and Masturbation," René Spitz, the psychoanalyst, shows how female masturbation remained unmentioned in the medical literature until the nineteenth century, when it emerged as an object of condemnation and remained so until well into the twentieth century. Medical wisdom held that techniques such as clitorodectomy—amounting to a direct attack on female masturbation and, indeed, on female sexuality itself—were considered essential in the "treatment" of this "problem." What may surprise many readers is Spitz's evidence that the growth of psychoanalytic theory was an important influence in modifying the approach of the medical profession.

Although Kinsey began his work in the thirties, much of his material speaks to issues that remain controversial to this day. He found, for instance, that more small girls masturbate to orgasm than do small boys, and suggested that better muscular coordination in girls is at least partly responsible. He found also that women's response in masturbation is very nearly as rapid as men's, and places the responsibility for the legendary slowness of women to respond in heterosexual intercourse squarely on the ineffective techniques employed by men. Based on his evidence, he further asserts that the capacity for sexual responsiveness grows with sexual experience, and that masturbation is a useful technique in gaining sexual experience. Most radical of all for its day was his flat denial of the Freudian tenet that masturbation is immature.

Mary Jane Sherfey, writing after both Kinsey and Masters and Johnson had turned in their evidence, reminds us that the famous division between the vaginal and the clitoral orgasm simply does not exist physiologically. She confounds both the clitoris-oriented feminists and the traditional vaginal-orgasm proponents by citing medical facts. Physiologically, the orgasm occurs in deep-lying tissues—components of the clitoral structure—that become engorged with blood during sexual arousal. Orgasm occurs when muscles contract to expel the blood. Furthermore, this process is essentially identical in both men and women; one could say that not only is there no difference between the clitoral and vaginal orgasm, but that, with the exception of ejaculation, there is essentially little physiological difference between the orgasm in men and women. In addition, Sherfey shows how sexual stimulation can come from any source, and that the clitoris is stimulated as effectively in heterosexual intercourse as by any manual means. In fact, whatever the process leading to arousal and orgasm, the clitoris, labia minora, and lower third of the vagina play the same roles. This evidence can be used to support proponents of heterosexual sex, of lesbianism, and of masturbation; it is to be hoped that it merely shows that the physiological process of sexual arousal and orgasm is the same no matter what the circumstances or context, and that we might better look to social and psychological evidence than to any innate processes for the problems both men and women have with sexual activity. One point is clear, however: Contrary to the assertions of the "clitoralists," the human female is physiologically well adapted to reach orgasm through heterosexual intercourse.

At the same time, as Niles Newton demonstrates in "Trebly Sensuous Woman," women have the jump on men in sexual activity simply because they have so many more contexts available for sexual arousal and satisfaction. Female sexuality involves labor, birth, and lactation as well as intercourse. Newton shows how the processes of natural childbirth can be similar to those of sexual arousal, and that sexual excitement also occurs in breastfeeding. Breastfeeding mothers are more likely to be sexually responsive in intercourse and to want to return to normal sexual relations as soon as possible after giving birth. All three of these activities are related neurologically and hormonally, and all three are extremely sensitive to the environment, which can easily inhibit them. Our culture has traditionally inhibited sexual response in childbirth and breastfeeding, and only comparatively recently has valued sexual response in intercourse. Newton points out that all these activities involve another person, and that, under the right circumstances, all three can trigger caretaking behavior in the adult participants. She suggests that sexual pleasure "conditions" adults to each other and the mother to the child, providing a biological foundation for the universal family structure.

Many people have criticized Masters and Johnson for their "mechanical" approach to sex; it is interesting to read an excerpt from their book *Human Sexual Response* describing the subjective response during orgasm of the women involved in their laboratory work. The women report a sensation of "pelvic throbbing," which has been correlated by Masters and Johnson with the contractions that occur in the orgasmic platform, or swollen tissue in the lower third of the vagina. Pregnant women seem to be more sensitive to orgasm. Masters and Johnson note that a woman's orgasm has never attained the status of the man's ejaculation in our culture, but provide no answers to the question of why this is so. But they do make it clear that there is no longer any reason for a woman to simulate orgasm to please a man, and suggest that the capacity for orgasm in a woman relates more to the acceptance of sexuality than to any innate "drive" such as aggression. This suggestion, of course, belies the concept that the capacity for sexuality is linked to "natural" masculine aggressiveness, which women are not supposed to have. The links between sexuality and aggression are deeply ingrained in our culture; if it can be shown that woman's capacity for strong sexual response is in no way dependent on aggressiveness, we might begin to question the traditional ties between masculine aggressiveness and effective sexuality. Such a question implies the possibility of reversal of thousands of years of social conditioning, but there is no reason to suppose that we are as irretrievably bound to our evolutionary background as many of the current apologists for aggression like to assert. Human sexual behavior is never unrelated to the body, but neither does it ever occur outside a social context, because each of us carries a social context around in our heads. Masculine aggressiveness may be as much a mask for insecure sexuality as traditional feminine submissiveness has been a mask for insecure female sexuality. The physiological revelations of Masters and Johnson, Kinsey, Mary Jane Sherfey, and others can only have the profoundest impact on our expectations of behavior; such expectations are themselves the basic motivations in any social context. If the expectations change, so must, ultimately, the nature of the social context.

The subjective experience of female orgasm is pointed up by Ruth Moulton in her invaluable review of psychoanalytic theory, in which she points out a number of basic misconceptions in early theory and the ways in which subsequent analytical writing has dealt with social factors and has stressed a primary feminine sexual development. One of the prime sources of confusion has been an equation of masculinity with activity and femininity with passivity. Moulton debunks the old concept that masochism can be equated with the feminine character, pointing out that adapting to the realities of pain is not the same thing as clinical masochism. (It would seem that the emphasis on the active-passive dichotomy to distinguish men from women is another carry-over from infantile impressions, based on fantasies derived from early observation of the difference between the sexes.) Moulton stresses psychological and social factors in orgasm and the fear of it—what is called frigidity. A repressive childhood can obviously inhibit physical sensuality; if a woman is afraid of losing control of emotions, and possesses a weak body image, orgasm may represent a threat to identity. Moulton does not mention that this phenomenon is as true for men as it is for women—another instance in which the sexuality of men and women possesses more common ground than real differences.

Moulton is deeply concerned with the role of the mother in conditioning her daughter favorably or unfavorably; a mother who cannot accept her own sexuality is bound to pass along her problems to her daughter. This is a sensitive subject for women today, who are justly tired of being blamed for their daughters' problems; but it makes sense when considered in relation to the continuity of generations of social conditioning, in which the individual woman—herself victimized as a daughter—becomes, in turn, a victimizing mother. The struggle to free ourselves from this cycle has become one of the aims of feminism. Like Betty Kronsky, Moulton points up the difficulty women have in developing a strong identity as female persons when sex roles label activity as "masculine." A strong self-image can evolve only if a woman is free to develop her potential socially as well as sexually, and the two areas interact; "the sexually responsive woman does better in all areas, not just in bed." It is interesting in this context to recall that Freud made the same connection for men; he saw sexual repression leading to intellectual timidity and stagnation. Until recently, of course, both intellectual and sexual repression were considered to be essential components of femininity. These ideas seem to have been so thoroughly a part of Freud's outlook that they remained unexamined, and were ascribed to constitutional factors.

7

Authority and Masturbation: Some Remarks on a Bibliographical Investigation

RENÉ A. SPITZ

Every culture worthy of the name is based on a social organization and on the norms and values shared by its members. Therefore it must regulate sexual life. The regulation may be pragmatic, with utilitarian aspects, or it may be so highly idealistic as to negate completely utilitarian aspects and lead to self-extinction. But within this wide gamut of possibilities some form of regulation can always be disclosed. Primarily, this regulation involves the function of reproduction in its relation to the group. Inevitably, however, other social institutions sooner or later impinge on sexuality and it is then that regulation of deviant attitudes and deviant sexual practices begin to be imposed.

Such regulations stem from authority, religious or secular, ruling the life of each social system. According to the culture and according to its ideals, it addresses itself to the various aspects of sexuality, that is, to the manifestations of the partial instincts, and to the form in which sexual activity is practiced. . . .

Masturbation is a sexual activity observed from earliest infancy. It is the only infantile autoerotic activity which is recognizable as such even to the lay public. Masturbatory fantasies shape the œdipus complex; they are

SOURCE: From "Authority and Masturbation: Some Remarks on a Bibliographical Investigation" by René A. Spitz, M.D., in *The Psychoanalytic Quarterly*, 21 (1952), pp. 490–527. Reprinted by permission of *The Psychoanalytic Quarterly* and the author. The charts and bibliography have been omitted; the footnotes have been renumbered.

the enemy against which defenses are organized in the
course of the liquidation of the œdipus complex; they are
determinants of the structure of character, of the conflicts
of puberty, and of eventual sexual adjustment. The significance of masturbatory fantasies for the individual and the
reaction of society to it convince us that the phenomenon
deserves further study.

From an extensive survey of the literature on the subject, we have learned that the repression of masturbation
is a phenomenon which developed in the course of history and ultimately underwent more or less overt institutionalization. . . .

*   *   *

It is only in the second half of the nineteenth century
that sadism becomes the foremost characteristic of the
campaign against masturbation. This aspect is not limited
to any one country, though its form varies according to
the culture in which the anxiety about masturbation arose
and led to hostility against its practice. The English advocated surgical intervention far more frequently than
either the German or the French. . . .

Nevertheless, drastic measures (surgery, restraint, severe punishment, fright) constitute at least fifty percent
of the measures recommended in *all* countries until 1904.
. . . The sadistic trend in antimasturbatory retaliation
died down in German- and French-speaking countries
earlier than in the United States and England. The great
increase, both relative and absolute, in the application of
progressive methods in German-speaking countries clearly
shows the first impact of psychoanalytic publications
beginning with this century. . . .

It is no mere coincidence that the sadistic trend in
antimasturbationist therapy came at a period in history
when people became aware of infantile sexuality. Helpless children are suitable objects for retaliation. The same
can be said about women: it is to be noted that in the
eighteenth century Tissot spoke primarily of male masturbation; and where he talks, in a few pages, of female

masturbation, his description fits female homosexuals and not masturbators at all. It is only much later that women received the attention which Tissot gave, in a benevolent manner, to men. But the interest focused on female masturbation was a sadistic one.

Although the campaign against masturbation started with Bekker's *Onania* in 1700, it took more than a century until the extremes of repression were developed. In Germany attention was focused on disciplining children. In England surgery was added to discipline.

Around 1858, Dr. Isaac Baker Brown, a prominent London surgeon who later became the much respected President of the Medical Society of London, introduced the operation of clitoridectomy.[1] The indication for this operation was that in his opinion masturbation (a term which the Victorian Dr. Baker Brown replaces by such expressions as "peripheral irritation of the pudic nerve," or "peripheral excitement") leads to hysteria, epilepsy and convulsive diseases. He sought to cure masturbation by removal of the organ on which it is performed. He performed this operation in a very large number of cases, children and adults, establishing a special home for women, The London Surgical Home. Of these operations he published forty-eight in 1866.[2] It was this publication which got him into trouble with the Obstetrical Society, of which he was a Fellow. He was expelled from the Society in 1867 after numerous stormy debates,[3] and it is to be assumed that after 1867 clitoridectomy was discarded by the medical profession in England.

Whether this desirable result was achieved or not I have not been able to ascertain. However, clitoridectomy seems to have come back to haunt humanity in different

[1] Medical Times & Gazette, I, 1873, p. 155.

[2] Brown, Isaac Baker: *On the Curability of Certain Forms of Insanity, Epilepsy, Catalepsy and Hysteria in Females*. London: Robert Hardwicke, 1866.

[3] The Lancet, I, 1867, p. 366; Medical Times & Gazette, I, 1867, p. 427; British Medical Journal, I, 1867, p. 395.

countries. Gustav Braun[4] in Vienna recommended it—
actually he was considered the inventor of the idea; some
French physicians took up this idea around the nineties,
but very soon abandoned it. And traces of this sadistic
intervention are to be seen in the different recommenda-
tions for blistering the thighs, the genitals, the spinal region, which were transmitted to us up to quite recent
years in the most authoritative compendia and textbooks.

One of our most widely known psychiatrists, the late
Dr. Bernard Sachs, recommended cautery to the spine
and genitals in the different editions of his handbook up
to 1905.[5] Infibulation of the prepuce and of the labia
majora was equally recommended. Circumcision in boys
was a prevalent practice up to a very recent date. A
leading textbook of pediatrics advises the use of a double
side-splint, such as is used in fracture of the femur.[6] The
same book, as do most other pediatric textbooks, rec-
ommends circumcision in boys and is not averse to circumcision in girls or cauterization of the clitoris. Indeed,
after 1925, ten percent of the therapeutic measures advocated in the United States were surgical interventions,
while in the other countries such measures were no longer
recommended.

From 1890 to 1925 at least, there existed in the
United States a peculiar medical organization called the
Orificial Surgery Society which offered training in surgery of the prepuce, the clitoris, and the rectum. Space
does not permit enumerating the startling treatments administered by this group of physicians, some of whom
operated on thousands and had their licenses rescinded.

[4] Braun, Gustav August: *Compendium der Frauenkrankheiten.*
Vienna: Braumueller, 1863.

[5] Sachs, Bernard: *Treatise on Nervous Diseases of Children.*
New York: Wm. Wood & Co., 1905 (first edition 1895), pp. 539–
540.

[6] Holt, L. E.: *Diseases of Infancy and Childhood.* New York:
D. Appleton Century, 1897 (and all subsequent editions up to
1936).

They even had a journal of their own.[7] Originally they
admitted only doctors, later also osteopaths and chiroprac-
tors. I quote from their textbook: "Circumcision of the
girl or woman of any age is as necessary as for the boy or
man . . . I have been astonished at the multitude of sins
concealed within the rectum."[8] Of course, they were much
concerned with the fate of women: "The condition of the
foreskin of boys has received more or less attention, at
least since the days of Moses. But the girls have been
neglected . . . I do feel an irresistible impulse to cry out
against the shameful neglect of the clitoris and its hood
because of the vast amount of sickness and suffering
which could be saved the gentler sex, if this important
subject received proper attention and appreciation at the
hands of the medical profession."[9]

How this society disappeared from the scene, I do not
know. The first volume of its journal is dated 1892, and
it still existed in 1923. A textbook appeared in 1912 and
was reprinted in 1925 in a revised edition.[10] The founder
of this school, E. H. Pratt, a Chicago surgeon of the Cook
County Hospital, published his first book on the subject
in 1890.[11] They seem to be the last followers to spring
from the original Baker Brown invention of the excision
of the clitoris.

Friendly reference to Baker Brown's practice is also to
be found in respectable medical journals of the period.

[7] Journal of Orificial Surgery, edited by E. H. Pratt, Holbrook,
et al., Chicago, 1892–1902. American Journal of Orificial Surgery,
Chicago, 1913.

[8] Orificial Surgery, Its Philosophy, Application and Technique.
Compiled and edited by B. E. Dawson, M.D.; assisted by E. H.
Muncie, M.D., A. G. Grant, M.D., H. E. Beebe, M.D., Newark: The
Physicians Drug News Co., 1912.

[9] Ibid., p. 402.

[10] Orificial Surgery. Kansas City: Western Baptist Publication
Co., 1925.

[11] Pratt, E. H., M.D., L.L.D.: Orificial Surgery and its Application to the Treatment of Chronic Diseases. Chicago: Halsey Bros.,
1890.

The treatment meted out to a luckless seven-year-old girl
by the consulting surgeon of St. John's Hospital in Cleve-
land, Ohio, is one case among many.[12] The presenting
complaint was that she masturbated and was nervous and
reluctant to answer questions. After having unsuccessfully
subjected the patient to a number of medical treatments,
including blistering and cauterization, the surgeon decided to operate on her clitoris. His first approach was to
bury the clitoris beneath the labia with four silver sutures.
The result was that the sutures were broken by the child
and masturbation continued. Thereupon a consultant was
called and, with the assistance of three other doctors,
clitoridectomy performed. The entire organ including a
considerable portion of the crura was removed. The operation was called successful, since the child showed no
signs of returning to her former habits save once, when,
six weeks after the operation, she tried to masturbate and
then confessed: "You know there is nothing there now,
so of course I could do nothing."[13]

A medical practice as widespread as this and reaching
so close to our own period might well tempt one to specu-
late on its origins and its consequences on the minds of
people. Resisting the temptation for the time being, I
quote one sentence from the German physician Villinger.
He compared masturbation to a "snake that has to be
throttled."

It is unnecessary to discuss further the innumerable,

[12] Eyer, A.: *Clitoridectomy for the Cure of Certain Cases of
Masturbation in Young Girls.* Int. Med. Mag., Philadelphia, 1894–
1895, 3, pp. 259–262.

[13] Marie Bonaparte, in an article which has come to our attention after the conclusion of this study, investigated the significance
of clitoridectomy from the libidinal-economic point of view with
the help of the exploration of several cases of clitoridectomized
women. These cases are mainly African (i.e., from a continent in
large parts of which clitoridectomy is institutionalized). She concludes that clitoridectomy will neither suppress masturbation nor
render the woman frigid. (*Note sur l'excision.* Revue française de
Psychanalyse, XII, 1948, pp. 213–31.)

varied and subtle practices of a refined cruelty. I believe
it necessary to cite these few examples because even in
psychoanalytic circles one does not always realize how
extremely cruel the persecution of the masturbator has
been up to our day; nor is it generally known that these
sadistic practices found support among authoritative
physicians and that they were recommended up to almost
a decade ago in official textbooks.

*   *   *

8

Masturbation

ALFRED C. KINSEY,
WARDELL B. POMEROY,
CLYDE E. MARTIN,
and PAUL H. GEBHARD

Of the six possible types of sexual activity, heterosexual
petting is the one in which the largest number of females
engage before marriage, and marital coitus is the one in
which the largest number of females engage after marriage. Masturbation is the one in which the second largest
number of females engage both before and after marriage.

Among all types of sexual activity, masturbation is,
however, the one in which the female most frequently
reaches orgasm. Even in her marital coitus the average
female fails to achieve orgasm in a fair proportion of her
contacts, and this is true in most of the petting which she
does prior to marriage; but in 95 per cent or more of all
her masturbation, she does reach orgasm.

This is due to the fact that the techniques of masturbation are especially effective in producing orgasm. Socio-
sexual relationships usually demand some adjustment of
the interests, the desires, the physical capacities, and the
physiologic reactions of the partner in the activity. In
coitus, a female who is not strongly aroused by the psychologic aspects of the relationship may find that some of
the adjustments which she has to make interrupt the

SOURCE: From *Sexual Behavior in the Human Female* (Philadelphia, W. B. Saunders Company, 1953). Excerpts from pp. 132–
146, 163–173. Reprinted by permission of the Institute for Sex
Research. Tables, graphs, footnotes, and cross-references have
been omitted.

steady flow of her response, and she is, in consequence, delayed or completely prevented from reaching orgasm. She may prefer the socio-sexual relationship because of its psychologic and social significance, and the delay in reaching orgasm may in actuality increase her pleasure, but the fact remains that the techniques of masturbation usually offer the female the most specific and quickest means for achieving orgasm. For this reason masturbation has provided the most clearly interpretable data which we have on the anatomy and the physiology of the female's sexual responses and orgasm. . . .

DEFINITION

Masturbation may be defined as deliberate self-stimulation which effects sexual arousal. In the human animal, motivations for the activity lie in the conscious realization that erotic satisfactions and some release from erotic tensions may thus be obtained. Instances of orgasm induced by accidental self-stimulation are not, strictly speaking, masturbation. Masturbation may or may not be pursued to the point of orgasm, and it may or may not have orgasm as it objective. While the original forms of the word, *manusturbo* or *manustuprum*, associate the phenomenon with *manus*, the hand, the techniques, particularly in the female, may also include other means of stimulating the genitalia or some other part of the body, stimulation by way of some of the other sense organs, and psychologic stimulation.

* * *

MASTURBATION AMONG PRIMITIVE HUMAN GROUPS. The anthropologic record indicates that masturbation is widely known among the females of many human groups. It did not originate in our European culture. The published studies record masturbatory activity among the females of some thirty-five or forty primitive groups, including in particular those in the Pacific area and in Africa where the anthropologists have made the most extensive studies. Once again, however, the record is notably fragmentary and probably gives no idea of the true spread of the phenomenon. The anthropologist's inform- ant may neglect to refer to female masturbation, or only incidentally remark that it occurs, but a more system- atic survey might disclose that the activity was wide- spread in many of these groups. Human males through- out history and among all peoples have been most often concerned with the sexual activities of the female when those activities served the male's own purposes, and her solitary and even homosexual activities have often been ignored.

Typical of this lack of interest in the female's solitary activities is the fact that practically none of the anthro- pologic literature ever records the presence or absence of orgasm in the female's masturbation, and sometimes it uncertain whether she does anything more than touch her genitalia as she might touch any other part of her body. Certainly it would be unwarranted to conclude on the basis of the available information that the inci- dences or frequencies of masturbation among European and American females are any higher or any lower than they are in other cultures elsewhere in the world. . . .

LEARNING TO MASTURBATE

SELF-DISCOVERY. Most of the females in our sample had discovered how to masturbate as a result of their exploration of their own genitalia. Since the child's expe- rience from the day it is born has shown it that satisfac- tions may be secured from the tactile stimulation of vari- ous parts of its body, one might expect that all children would sooner or later discover, quite on their own, that the greatest satisfactions may be obtained from such geni- tal stimulation as masturbation might afford.

A considerable portion of the masturbation which we have found among infants and young pre-adolescent girls in our sample appears to have been self-discovered. Some

70 per cent of the older pre-adolescent girls who had begun to masturbate before adolescence also appear to have discovered the possibilities through their own exploration. . . .

Interestingly enough, many of the older individuals who did not begin to masturbate until they were well along in their twenties or thirties, and even in their forties and fifties, were still discovering the possibilities of such activity through their own exploration. This provides striking evidence of the ignorance which is frequent among females of sexual activities which are outside of their own experience, even though they may be common in the population as a whole. . . .

*   *   *

RELATION TO AGE AND MARITAL STATUS

In our sample, masturbation had occurred among females of every group, from infancy to old age.

AMONG CHILDREN. We have records of 67 infants and small girls three years of age or younger who were observed in masturbation, or who as adults recalled that they had masturbated at that age. We have one record of a seven-month-old infant and records of 5 infants under one year of age who were observed in masturbation. There were undoubtedly many more females who engaged in true masturbatory activities when they were young; but it has been impossible to calculate incidence figures from the available records.

Our records, however, include specific and repeated observations on several children whose responses were unmistakably erotic. We have records of 23 girls three years old or younger who reached orgasm in self-masturbation. There are more records of small girls than there are of small boys masturbating to orgasm at such an early age. It requires some experience and some development of muscular coordinations to effect the rhythmic manual

movements on which masturbation depends, and the
small boy does not so often manage to achieve that end.
Some 19 per cent of the girls had masturbated prior to
adolescence.

ACCUMULATIVE INCIDENCE. About 62 per cent of all
the females in the sample had masturbated at some time
in the course of their lives. About 58 per cent had masturbated at some time to the point of orgasm. The 4 to 6
per cent which had masturbated without reaching orgasm
was chiefly a group of females who had made only single
or desultory and infrequent trials of their capacities, for
nearly all of those who had seriously experimented soon
learned to reach orgasm. . . .

The active incidences of masturbation were lowest in
the younger groups, and highest in the older groups of
females. . . . There may have been several explanations of
these higher incidences of masturbation among the older
females: (1) There may have been an actual increase in
erotic responsiveness at the older ages. (2) The availability of socio-sexual outlets had been reduced at older ages,
and this may have forced an increasing number of females to masturbate. (3) There was often a reduction of
inhibitions among the older females. (4) The older females, having had more experience in petting and coitus,
had learned, thereby, that similar satisfactions are obtainable through self-masturbation. . . .

The active incidences of masturbation to orgasm
among the single females (ranging from 20 to 54 per
cent) were somewhat higher than they were (23 to 36
per cent) among the corresponding married groups.
Many of those who had depended on this outlet before
marriage had stopped masturbating when marital coitus
became available. On the other hand, there were some
females who had not begun masturbating until after they
had learned from their pre-coital petting experience in
marriage that self-stimulation could also bring sexual satisfaction. Some women who fail to reach orgasm in coitus
are then stimulated manually by their husbands, or they

masturbate themselves until they reach orgasm. Some of the married females, on the other hand, confine their masturbation to periods when their husbands are away from home. . . .

FREQUENCY TO ORGASM. . . . Between the ages of sixteen and fifty among the single females, and between the ages of twenty-one and fifty-five among the married and previously married females, there had been only slight changes in the . . . frequencies of masturbation. . . . This is more or less true of the frequencies of several other types of female activity and of the total sexual outlet of single females. This is one of the most remarkable aspects of female sexuality, and one which most sharply distinguishes it from the sexuality of the male. Hormonal factors may be involved.

Since the frequencies of masturbation depend primarily on the physiologic state and the volition of the female, they may provide a significant measure of the level of her interest in sexual activity. Heterosexual activities, on the other hand, are more often initiated by the male partner and, in consequence, they do not provide as good a measure of the female's innate capacities and sexual interests.

In some of the histories, there was a record of the female's masturbation being confined to the period just before the onset of her monthly menstruation. This is the period during which most human females are most responsive erotically.

INDIVIDUAL VARIATION IN FREQUENCY. Among those females who had masturbated, some had not had such experience more than once or twice in a year. Most of them, however, had masturbated to the point of orgasm with frequencies which ranged from once in a month to once in a week. There were, however, about 4 per cent who had masturbated with frequencies of 14 or more per week at some period in their lives, and a few who had experienced orgasm from this source as often as 30 or more times per week. In the sample there were females who had regularly masturbated to the point of orgasm several times in immediate succession, and there were some who had masturbated to orgasm as often as 10, 20, and even 100 times within a single hour. This is an example of the individual variation which may occur in any type of sexual activity. While considerable individual variation also occurs among males the range of variation in almost every type of sexual activity seems to be far greater among females.

*   *   *

SPEED OF RESPONSE TO ORGASM. Some 45 per cent of all those females in the sample who had ever masturbated reported that they usually reached orgasm in three minutes or less, and another 25 per cent in something between four and five minutes. The median for the whole group was a few seconds under four minutes. Many of those who took longer to reach orgasm did so deliberately in order to prolong the pleasure of the activity and not because they were incapable of responding more quickly.

These data on the female's speed in reaching orgasm provide important information on her basic sexual capacities. There is a widespread opinion that the female is slower than the male in her sexual responses, but the masturbatory data do not support that opinion. The average male may take something between two and three minutes to reach orgasm unless he deliberately prolongs his activity, and a calculation of the median time required would probably show that he responds not more than some seconds faster than the average female. It is true that the average female responds more slowly than the average male in coitus, but this seems to be due to the ineffectiveness of the usual coital techniques.

*   *   *

SIGNIFICANCE OF MASTURBATION

PHYSIOLOGIC SIGNIFICANCE. Most females masturbate for the sake of the immediate satisfactions which they may obtain, and as a means of resolving the physiologic disturbances which arise when they are aroused sexually and are restrained by the social custom from having socio-sexual contacts.

We have already noted that a variety of physiologic disturbances, including a considerable development of neuromuscular tensions, are involved whenever there is sexual arousal. When the sexual responses lead to orgasm, these tensions are suddenly released and the individual thereupon returns to a physiologically normal or subnormal state. Then she may function more efficiently in her everyday affairs. But without the release which orgasm can bring, most males and some females may continue to be disturbed for some period of time, and the prolongation of such a disturbance may distract or otherwise interfere with one's general efficiency. The individual may become nervous, irritable, incapable of concentrating on any sort of problem, and difficult to live with. Most persons live more happily with themselves and with other persons if their sexual arousal, whenever it is of any magnitude, may be carried through to the point of orgasm.

* * *

PSYCHOLOGIC SIGNIFICANCE. When no guilt, anxieties, or fears are involved, the physical satisfactions which may be found in any type of sexual activity, whether socio-sexual or solitary, should leave an individual well adjusted psychologically. But in view of the more than two thousand years of religious condemnation of masturbation, fortified by the ostensibly scientific opinions of physicians and other professionally trained groups, it is not surprising that many individuals, both female and male, are considerably disturbed when they masturbate. Among the females in the sample who had ever masturbated, approximately half had experienced some psychologic disturbance over their experience. Some of them were disturbed for only a single year or two, but the average (median) female had been disturbed for six and a half years. Some 30 per cent had been disturbed for more than ten years. This means that some millions of the females in the United States, and a larger number of the males, have had their self-assurance, their social efficiency, and sometimes their sexual adjustments in marriage needlessly damaged—not by their masturbation, but by the conflict between their practice and the moral codes. There is no other type of sexual activity which has worried so many women.

Freud and most of the psychoanalysts have recognized that masturbation does no physical harm, but they have introduced new sources of psychologic disturbance by rating the activity infantile, immature, and a personality defect which merits psychiatric attention when it occurs in an adult. But these objections merely perpetuate the Talmudic traditions which are now being fortified with a new set of terms which appear to have scientific significance. Many adults who are not immature in any realistic sense do masturbate, and there is no science in refusing to recognize this fact.

SOCIAL SIGNIFICANCE. Whatever may affect the efficiency of some millions of individuals may be considered of social concern. Whether masturbation provides a satisfactory source of sexual outlet or becomes a source of psychologic disturbance is, therefore, a question of some social import. Masturbation may be of still greater social importance if it affects an individual's sexual adjustments in marriage.

Some of the psychoanalysts have suggested that masturbation, because it depends primarily upon clitoral and labial stimulation, concentrates erotic response in the external genitalia and does not train the individual for the "vaginal responses" which they consider must be present before there is any "sexual maturity." But actually the vagina is, in most females, quite devoid of end organs of touch. It is incapable of responding to tactile stimulation, and the areas primarily involved in the female's sensory responses during coitus are exactly those which are primarily involved in masturbation, namely the clitoris and the labia. We have seen very few cases of females who had encountered any difficulty in transferring their masturbatory experience to coitus, although we have seen some hundreds of cases of females who were considerably disturbed because they were unable to accomplish the anatomic impossibility of "transferring their clitoral reactions to vaginal responses."

It is true that the girl who has nothing but masturbatory experience prior to marriage encounters a new type of situation when vaginal insertions are first encountered in coitus. She would, however, have the same problem to meet if she had never masturbated. . . .

Much more important is the evidence that pre-marital experience in masturbation may actually contribute to the female's capacity to respond in her coital relations in marriage. It has been pointed out repeatedly, and our own data confirm the opinion, that a considerable portion of the sexual maladjustment in marriage arises from the fact that the average female is aroused sexually less often than the average male, and that she frequently has difficulty in reaching orgasm in her marital coitus. There are a variety of factors involved in this failure, the most significant of which seems to be the female's inexperience in orgasm prior to her marriage. Some 36 per cent of the females in our sample had not experienced orgasm on even a single occasion, from any type of sexual activity, prior to marriage. Only half of them had had a regular outlet prior to marriage.

Calculations on the marital histories indicate that those females who had not responded to the point of orgasm prior to marriage, failed to respond after marriage three

times as often as the females who had had a fair amount
of orgasmic experience before marriage. It is true that
there were many individuals who did respond promptly
after marriage even though they had not experienced
orgasm before then; but the chances of working out such
adjustments seem to have been materially reduced for the
girl who had not previously learned what it means to let
herself go and respond uninhibitedly in sexual orgasm.
The girl who has spent her pre-marital years withdrawing
from physical contacts and tensing her muscles in order
to avoid response has acquired a set of nervous and muscular coordinations which she does not unlearn easily
after marriage.

The type of pre-marital activity in which the female
had acquired her experience did not appear to have been
as important as the fact that she had or had not experienced orgasm. This appears to have been true whether
her pre-marital experience was in coitus, in petting to the
point of orgasm, in homosexual relations, or in masturbation. Since masturbation was the activity in which the
largest number of females had reached orgasm, it was of
particular significance in these correlations.

Among those females in the sample who had never
masturbated before marriage, or whose masturbation had
never led to orgasm, about a third (31 to 37 per cent)
had failed to reach orgasm in their coitus during the first
year, and in most instances during that first five years of
their marriages. But among those who had masturbated
to the point of orgasm before marriage, only 13 to 16 per
cent had been totally unresponsive in the early years of
marriage. A selective factor may have been involved. The
more responsive females may have been the ones who
masturbated before marriage, and the ones who responded more often in their marital coitus. On the other
hand, a causal relationship seems also to have been involved. In many a specific history it appeared that the
quality of the marital response was furthered by the fe-

male's previous knowledge of the nature of a sexual orgasm. In any event, it was certain that the capacity to respond in orgasm in marital coitus had not been lessened by the pre-marital masturbatory experience of the females in the sample.

9

Clitoral Erotism and the Sexual Response Cycle in Human Females

MARY JANE SHERFEY

... [Helene] Deutsch suggested that the clitoris may be a primary organ of sexuality in women. Not that she was the first to propose that the clitoris may play an important, if not the only, role in the orgastic response. For example, C. S. Ford and F. Beach (2) tentatively put forth what amounts to the same idea in their classic cross-cultural, cross-species study, *Patterns of Sexual Behavior*, published in 1951....

The Kinsey study, *Sexual Behavior in the Human Female* (3), was probably the outstanding contribution in the 1950s to the theory that clitoral erotism is the only erotism in women. Backed by their considerable statistical data, the Kinsey authors state bluntly that their findings confirm the proposition that the vaginal orgasm is a biological impossibility. We cannot lightly dismiss the fact (although we have been doing so) that endocrinologists have maintained since the early 1940s that the clitoris is normally the primary source of sexual arousal, and androgen the primary sexual hormone in women although not the only one (7, p. 1390). The same is held by the gynecologists, I believe, although they tended to avoid the issue until the Masters and Johnson research began appearing in 1959....

*   *   *

SOURCE: From *The Nature and Evolution of Female Sexuality*, by Mary Jane Sherfey. Copyright © 1966, 1972 by Mary Jane Sherfey. Reprinted by permission of Random House, Inc. Diagrams and a chart have been omitted; references have been renumbered.

ANATOMY

... Judging from the biological, medical, and psychiatric literature (and patients' statements), there is still a widespread tendency to forget that the clitoris is not just the small protuberance at the anterior end of the vulva.* The deeper-lying components of the clitoral system are almost never taken into consideration, let alone the deposition and size of the veins and muscles surrounding the lower third of the vagina....

Since the cryptic clitoral structures will double or triple in size during sexual arousal (judging from the space provided them), it is apparent why so much functional importance can be attributed to them. On the other hand, the tiny clitoral shaft with its tinier glans comprises only the distal one fourth to three fourths inch of the total clitoris and less than one tenth its volume; this discrepancy is even greater during arousal when the cryptic structures may increase threefold in size, while the shaft and glans hardly do so at all.

EVOLUTIONARY PERSPECTIVES

... In human males, the length of the penile shaft is remarkably constant, varying less with body size than does any other body part. Conversely, the penile bulb varies considerably in size relative to body size and from one man to another (1, p. 763). Therefore, the size of the distended bulb must play a more important role in producing the intensity of the orgasm than does the length of the erect shaft. The same considerations would apply to the female's vestibular bulbs and clitoral shaft in producing the orgasm. ...

---

* *Vulva*: the external sexual organs of the female.

THE SEXUAL RESPONSE CYCLE
OF THE HUMAN FEMALE

. . . Masters and Johnson present their findings objectively with few interpretations and no theories. Hence, unless otherwise noted, all interpretations, deductions, and speculations derived from these findings are entirely mine. . . .

Similarity of Cycles

Of course, there are wide variations from the charted pattern among different women and in the same woman at different times. However, the variations are those of timing (duration of each phase), intensity of all reactions, differences due to whether or not the woman has borne children and the extent of obstetrical damage, and differences related to the time during the menstrual cycle when arousal occurs. The basic anatomical and physiological responses are always the same, with the responses appearing in their charted sequence uniformly in all women under all conditions of arousal. The authors state (5, p. 254): "From an anatomic point of view, there is absolutely no difference in the response of the pelvic viscera to effective sexual stimulation, regardless of whether stimulation occurs as the result of clitoral area manipulation, natural or artificial coition, or, for that matter from breast stimulation alone. . . . The female's physiologic responses to effective sexual stimulation . . . develop with consistency regardless of the source of the psychic or physical sexual stimulation."

Source of Pelvic Sexual Tension

Effective stimulation from any erotogenic source produces an immediate and intense vasocongestion (blood accumulation) of the entire pelvic area, primarily involving the pelvic venous plexi (capillary vasodilatation also occurs in the peripheral circulation, especially in the skin and the breasts). Venous dilation and congestion are quickly followed by the passage of fluid from the venous networks into the tissue spaces. So rapidly does this fluid pass through and edema occur that the *first* discernible sign of arousal is the appearance of droplets on the vaginal wall *within thirty seconds* from the moment stimulation begins. As the initially collapsed vaginal walls expand, the droplets coalesce, forming a well-lubricated vaginal barrel. In the upright position, the fluid begins flowing into the vestibule within a few minutes; in the supine position, its appearance will be slightly delayed. The rapid appearance of this fluid makes it similar (but not homologous) to the rapid appearance of the erection in men. This transudate, or fluid, is the chief, if not the only, source of vaginal lubrication (cervical secretions are absent, and greater vestibular glands secretions negligible). The vaginal transudate appears just as rapidly with effective psychological stimulation alone.

Masters states (4, p. 65): ". . . this transudatelike material is the result of a marked dilation of the venous plexus concentration which encircles the entire barrel of the vagina. . . ." . . .

During the plateau phase, the total pelvic venous congestion and edema create a broad "platform" of distended tissues; especially involved are the lower third of the vagina, the vestibular bulbs, the labia minora—and labia majora in women who have borne several offspring —anterior commissure, and the uterus. In short, pelvic sexual tension is purely a vascular phenomenon of venous congestion and edema induced by effective stimulation of any erotogenic zone, physical or psychological. . . .

Cause of the Orgasm

As in men, when the vasocongestive distension reaches a certain point, a reflex stretch mechanism in the responding muscles is set off, causing them to contract vigorously. These contractions expel the blood trapped in the tissue and venous plexi, creating the orgasmic sensations.

The muscles of primary response . . . are exactly the same muscles producing the orgasm and ejaculation in the male. Masters states (4, p. 71; 6, p. 90): ". . . the female responds to sexual stimulation . . . in a manner essentially akin to the localized congestive reaction which accomplishes erection in the male penis. . . . [And] actual orgasmic experiences are initiated in both sexes by similar muscle components."

*   *   *

Clitoral Retraction and the Preputial-Glandar Mechanism

One of the most significant findings of Masters and Johnson is that the clitoral glans is kept in a state of continuous stimulation throughout intravaginal coition even though it is apparently not being touched and appears to have vanished.

Clitoral erection causes the shaft to retract into the swollen prepuce or clitoral hood and occurs in every woman, regardless of the type of stimulation, coital position, degree of clitoral tumescence or the initial clitoral size. This phenomenon occurs much later than the homologous erection in the male, approximately one and a half to three minutes before the orgasm. Retraction occurs whether or not the clitoral area is stimulated during [earlier phases], although it generally takes place a minute or so sooner with prior clitoral-area manipulation than without it.

Masters and Johnson stress that retraction removes the clitoris from the vaginal orifice even further, making penile contact all the more impossible. . . .

. . . In both women and most primates, thrusting movements produce two actions on the glans: the prepuce is pulled over the glans and the shaft is pulled partially out of retraction. The former is the primary source of glandar friction, the latter is the secondary source. . . .

Masters and Johnson have shown that repeated relaxations and retractions of the shaft take place, equal in number to the number of thrusting movements. Consequently the more the thrusting, the more the erotic arousal in the woman. To this I would add: the greater the swelling of the prepuce, the closer it will envelop the glans as it moves back and forth or as the prepuce is pulled over the glans. The greater the retraction of the shaft, the greater will be the distance through which the glans moves during thrusting. The greater the labial swelling, the tighter the prepuce will be over the glans and the better the traction. Therefore, only if the clitoral shaft does *not* retract and seemingly disappear, due to inadequate stimulation, is it removed from participation in the erotogenic build-up.

It is now clear why so few women (or primates) employ digital stimulation of the lower vagina during masturbation or prefer it during foreplay as a primary source of arousal. The glans has a much higher erotogenic potential than does the mucous membrane of the lower third; moreover, considerable distension of the vaginal orifice must occur before traction on the labia can be effective. The fingers cannot substitute for the erect penis in this action.

Furthermore, it is also obvious why the thrusting movements of the penis will necessarily create simultaneous stimulation of the lower third of the vagina, labia minora, and clitoral shaft and glans as an integrated, inseparable functioning unit, with the glans being the most important and, in by far the majority of instances, the indispensable initiator of the orgasmic reaction. With these observations, the evidence seems overwhelming: *it is a physical impossibility to separate the clitoral from the vaginal orgasm as demanded by psychoanalytic theory.*

SOURCES

1. Brash, J. C., ed., *Cunningham's Textbook of Anatomy*. London: Oxford University Press, 9th ed., 1953.

2. Ford, C. S., and Beach, F. A. *Patterns of Sexual Behavior*. New York: Harper, 1951.

3. Kinsey, A. C., Pomeroy, W. B., Martin, C. E., and Gebhard, P. H. *Sexual Behavior in the Human Female*. Philadelphia: Saunders, 1953.

4. Masters, W. H. "The Sexual Response Cycle of the Human Female." *Western Journal of Surgery, Obstetrics, and Gynecology*, Vol. 68, 1960, pp. 57–72.

5. ———, and Johnson, V. "The Sexual Response Cycle of the Human Female. III. The Clitoris: Anatomic and Clinical Considerations." *Western Journal of Surgery, Obstetrics, and Gynecology*, Vol. 70, 1962, pp. 248–57.

6. ———, and ———. "The Sexual Response Cycle of the Human Male." *Western Journal of Surgery, Obstetrics, and Gynecology*, Vol. 71, 1963, pp. 85–95.

7. Money, J. "Sex Hormones and Other Variables in Human Eroticism," in *Sex and Internal Secretions*, edited by W. C. Young. 2 vols. Baltimore: Williams & Wilkins, 3rd ed., 1961, Vol. 2, pp. 1383–1400.

10

Trebly Sensuous Woman

NILES NEWTON

When males think about female sexuality they usually focus on the one aspect that is of most interest to them: intercourse. When they set out to study female sexuality, they usually investigate only the dimensions that have direct bearing on the pleasure and performance of adult males. After all, mature men can form *reproductive* relationships only with women, and only through one act: intercourse.

Female sexuality, however, includes at least three reproductive acts that involve two persons: coitus, parturition (labor and birth), and lactation. It is my thesis that these three functions are closely interrelated, physiologically as well as psychologically. What occurs on the delivery table, in other words, is very pertinent to what occurs later in the marital bed; and a mother-infant relationship without enjoyable breastfeeding is in some ways similar to marriage without enjoyable sex.

REACTIONS. I first noticed the physiological similarity between childbirth and coitus some years ago. I had read Alfred Kinsey's voluminous descriptions of female orgasm: data that had come from interviews, observations of intercourse by scientifically trained persons, and reports from physiological experiments. Then I read Grantly Dick-Read's accounts of natural childbirth, based on his observations of 516 consecutive labors. It struck me that many of the reactions he described were the same as those that Kinsey had noted. Indeed, much of his data has since been corroborated by films taken of

SOURCE: Reprinted from *Psychology Today* Magazine, July, 1971. Copyright © 1971 Ziff-Davis Publishing Company.

women undergoing natural childbirth or a similar process, psychoprophylaxis. (Dick-Read made every effort to keep his women free from fear or disturbance in labor and thus uninhibited. Since in the U.S.A. it is customary to move, strap down, and otherwise disturb women in labor, the reactions he noted are not so frequent here.)

My analysis of Kinsey's and Dick-Read's data showed these comparisons in the chart below:

Undisturbed, undrugged childbirth	Sexual excitement and orgasm
Breathing During early contractions, breathing becomes deeper. Second stage of labor brings deep breathing with breath holding.	During early stages of arousal, breathing becomes faster and deeper. As orgasm approaches, breathing may be interrupted.
Vocalization Tendency to make noises, grunts, especially in second stage of labor.	Tendency to make gasping, sucking noises as orgasm nears.
Facial expression As birth climax approaches, the face gets an intense, strained look; observers often assume the woman is suffering great pain.	As orgasm approaches, the face gets what Kinsey *et al.* call a "tortured expression": mouth open, eyes glassy, muscles tense.
The uterus The upper segment of the uterus contracts rhythmically.	The upper segment of the uterus contracts rhythmically.
The cervix Mucus plug from opening (os) of cervix loosens.	Cervical secretion may loosen mucus plug, thus opening cervix for sperm.

Undisturbed, undrugged childbirth	Sexual excitement and orgasm
Abdominal muscles Contract periodically in second stage of labor; a strong urge to bear down develops as delivery approaches.	Abdominal muscles contract periodically during sexual excitement.
Position Woman flat on her back, legs bent and wide apart.	Typically, the "missionary position" (woman on her back, legs wide apart).
Central nervous system Woman tends to become uninhibited, particularly as baby descends the birth canal. Veneers of conventional behavior disappear in later stages of labor.	Inhibitions and psychic blocks are relieved and often eliminated as orgasm nears.
Strength and flexibility Delivery of the baby through the narrow passage requires unusual strength and body expansion.	Unusual muscular strength often develops. Many persons become capable of bending and distorting their bodies in ways they could not otherwise do.
Sensory perception During labor the vulva becomes anesthetized with full dilation so that the woman often must be told of the emergence of the baby's head.	The whole body of the sexually aroused person becomes increasingly insensitive—even to sharp blows and severe injury.
There is a tendency to become oblivious to surroundings as delivery approaches.	As orgasm approaches, there is a tendency to become oblivious to surroundings; there

Undisturbed, undrugged childbirth	Sexual excitement and orgasm
Amnesia develops. Suddenly, delivery complete, the woman becomes wide awake.	is loss of sensory perceptions, sometimes leading to moments of unconsciousness. After orgasm there is a sudden return of sensory acuity.

Emotional response	
After birth, there is a flood of joyful emotion, which Dick-Read describes as "complete and careless ecstasy."	After coital orgasm there is a strong feeling of well-being in most persons.

There is maybe yet another, even more striking, physiological similarity. An obstetrician has recently reported noting clitoral engorgement in some of his patients, beginning about the time the cervix is well dilated and lasting until he sews up the episiotomy. This phenomenon, he notes, is especially likely to occur when husbands are present in the delivery room. (His patients, incidentally, were emotionally prepared for childbirth and were given minimal medication.)

Similarly, Masters and Johnson reported on 12 women who, far along in labor, described their feelings as intense sensations progressing through orgasm. Each of these women had delivered at least one child without anesthesia or pain killers. The clitoral reaction that the obstetrician noted in his patients and the feelings that Masters and Johnson described with their subjects is, of course, characteristic of sexual arousal.

JOY. The survival of the human race has long depended on the satisfaction gained from the two voluntary acts of reproduction—intercourse and breastfeeding. These had to be sufficiently pleasurable to ensure their frequent occurrence. And so they are; but this is not the only similarity between the two processes. In both:

1. the uterus contracts;
2. the nipples become erect, and the breasts receive extensive stimulation;
3. the skin changes: sexual excitement causes marked vascular changes, while breastfeeding raises body temperature in the submammary and mammary areas.

LEAK. There are other connections. Masters and Johnson report that milk may flow from both nipples during and immediately after orgasm. This involuntary loss of milk control occurs during intercourse or masturbation. Berry Campbell and W. E. Petersen, who first reported this phenomenon, found that the degree of milk ejection appeared to be related to the degree of coital responsiveness in some women, who leaked milk easily. Direct breast stimulation and breastfeeding both can trigger orgasm in some women, although less marked reactions are more usual.

Women who breastfeed are apparently more responsive and tolerant in other sexual areas. Masters and Johnson noted that for the first three months after delivery, nursing mothers as a group reported the highest level of sexual interest. As a group, they wanted as rapid a return as possible to active intercourse with their husbands. Robert R. Sears and his colleagues found that mothers who had nursed their babies were later significantly more tolerant in regard to matters such as masturbation and sex play.

The sensuous nature of breastfeeding is seldom recognized in our society for the same reason that orgasm during delivery occurs so rarely: our culture makes a strenuous effort to keep sexual pleasure out of the nursing experiences. If we permitted intercourse only at scheduled times, set up rules for the exact number of minutes intromission should last, and initiated it in a strange semipublic environment, sexual orgasm would be unlikely to occur. Our society manages breastfeeding in a similar way that tends to ensure that the mother-baby relation will be in some measure inhibited. Mother and infant are separated except for brief contacts during their hospital stay; both are usually clothed and the mother may even use a "nipple shield" for "protection." Rules about timing and amount of sucking permitted are invented and enforced by persons who usually have never successfully breastfed even one baby. Natural rhythms between mother and infant are often effectively inhibited by such initiation rituals.

While there are specific points of similarity between any two of the three processes I have been considering, there are also similarities across all of them. Coitus, childbirth and lactation have common biological roles and they share at least three characteristics:

1. they are based on closely related neurohormonal reflexes;
2. they are sensitive to environmental stimuli, being easily inhibited in their early stages;
3. they all, in certain circumstances, trigger caretaking.

SHEEP. M. Debackere, Georges Peeters and N. Tuyttens in Ghent, Belgium, did a classical experiment that illustrates the common neurohormonal reflexes in all three processes. The investigators joined the circulatory systems of pairs of sheep, using plastic tubes to connect their jugular veins. In some pairs, they joined the rams with lactating ewes, and massaged the seminal vesicles and penis shafts of the rams to the point of emission. Within 30 seconds there was a sharp rise of pressure in the ewes' udders. The milk-ejection mechanisms had been triggered by the blood of the sexually stimulated rams.

In other pairs, the researchers joined two ewes, repeatedly distending the vagina of one with a balloon (simulating the vaginal dilation that occurs normally in both coitus and parturition). The stimulation of the vagina in one ewe caused milk ejection to occur in the other.

These experiments indicate that sexual arousal, lactation and birth share a common neurohormonal level (oxytocin is one of the substances involved; in fact, oxytocin may be so much involved that I am prompted to call it "the hormone of love").

SAFETY. There may be a sound biological reason why these acts are easily inhibited in their initial phases by outside disturbances. All three processes leave the participants incapable of fight or flight, thus vulnerable to danger. During coitus sensory acuity lessens, making the couple less aware of the outside world. The female is maximally defenseless during birth as the offspring's movement down the birth canal interferes with ability to run. During breastfeeding, a mother with offspring attached is also less mobile.

Survival, therefore, would be most likely for individuals and species able to regulate intercourse, childbirth and suckling so that they could occur in safe surroundings. Among human beings, folkways and cultural patterns have long recognized this and have established customs and traditions designed to assure safety and shelter.

Coitus is almost everywhere a private affair. Even members of the most sexually permissive preliterate societies have intercourse in the semi-isolation of the palm grove, the garden patch, or the shelter of darkness.

MICE. Similarly, we have long known that fear and disturbance have a deleterious effect on labor in both animals and humans. My colleagues and I did a series of experiments on mice, showing delays in delivery and increased pup mortality for pregnant mice that had been disturbed in labor.

Finally, nursing mothers show definite sensitivity to their environments. Dairy farmers tell us that cows do not produce much milk when they are put in strange barns or when strangers milk them. Fordyce, Ely and Petersen supported the farmers' lore experimentally: when they placed cats on the cows' backs and banged paper bags in their ears, the cow produced less milk. Michael Newton and I did a similar experiment with a human mother and got the same results.

CARE. Intercourse, birth and breastfeeding, all may trigger "caretaking" behavior, an essential and important aspect of successful reproduction.

In most human societies males care for the women with whom they live. Each society channels this care differently, but usually the male defends and protects his vulnerable childbearing mate and gives her economic support.

Similarly the female accompanies her sexual relationship with an urge to care for the man in ways socially available to her: cooking for him, making a home and so on.

The intense emotions that orgasm arouses—and the pleasure that both male and female gain from intercourse —tend to condition each person to the other, binding them in a partnership and thereby increasing the chances that the children will have two adult caretakers.

Operant conditioning, reinforced by sexual pleasure, may be the biological foundation on which patterns of family life are built.

There is some statistical evidence for the speculation that sexual satisfaction and mutual cooperation are related. Lee Rainwater, using a lower-class sample, found that among white couples in which wives shared some activities with their husbands, 64 per cent greatly enjoyed sex. Only 18 per cent of those who did not share other activities with their mates reported such enjoyment of intercourse.

DIRECTION. The relationship between breastfeeding and caretaking has been studied extensively, and studies of human beings tend to show more maternal interest in breastfeeding mothers on the average. However, the personality and attitudes of the mother are themselves related to her decision to breastfeed in the first place, so human statistical studies do not show causal direction.

Animal studies, however, can get around this problem. Dudley Peeler and I worked on a colony of mice, performing sham operations on some and excising the nipples in others. We then bred these mice so that they would deliver at about the same time. We placed one nippleless mouse in a cage with a mouse that had undergone a sham operation, both of which had delivered the same day. We gave them a newborn litter belonging to neither of them and observed their maternal behavior over several following days.

We found no significant differences between the lactating and nonlactating mice in simple tests in which both adoptive mothers were given the opportunity to carry the mouse pups back to the nest. But when we placed barriers between the mice and their adoptive litters, the lactating mothers showed a significantly stronger drive to get to the young than the nonlactating mothers did. Lactation, apparently, influences maternal behavior, possibly because of the conditioning involved: the pleasure of nursing the young increases the female's desire for close contact with them.

Women, it appears, have a more varied heritage of sexual enjoyment than men. Kinsey's huge volume purporting to cover *Sexual Behavior in the Human Female* deals, in fact, with only one dimension of female sexuality: coitus and orgasm. I have no intention of underestimating the pleasure and importance of that dimension; but also to be noted are the pleasure and importance of the other reproductive partnerships that women experience as part of their female sexuality.

11

Psychologic and Sociologic Factors of Orgasm

WILLIAM H. MASTERS
and VIRGINIA E. JOHNSON

PSYCHOLOGIC FACTORS OF ORGASM

It is well to restate from time to time the necessity for maintaining a concept of total involvement when any facet of human sexuality is to be considered. . . .

Female orgasm, whether it is attained within the context of an interpersonal relationship (either heterosexual or homosexual) or by means of any combination of erotically stimulative activity and/or fantasy, remains a potpourri of psychophysiologic conditions and social influence. Many theoretical as well as individually graphic accounts of the female experience at orgasm have been offered in the professional literature of many disciplines and are even more widespread in general publications. This vast amount of published quasiauthority depicts both objective and subjective female reaction to orgasm with almost every possible degree of accuracy and inaccuracy.

Without referring to the prior literature, a description of subjective response to orgasmic incidence has been compiled from reports of 487 women, given in the laboratory in the immediacy of the postorgasmic period, obtained through interview only, or developed from a com-

SOURCE: From *Human Sexual Response* (Boston, Little, Brown and Company, 1966), pp. 134–139. Copyright © 1966 by William H. Masters and Virginia E. Johnson. Reprinted by permission of Little, Brown and Company. References have been renumbered; cross-references have been omitted.

bination of both sources. This composite is offered as a baseline for a concept of the psychologic aspects of the human female's orgasmic experience.

The consensus drawn from the multiple descriptions has established three distinct stages of woman's subjective progression through orgasm.

Stage I

Orgasm has its onset with a sensation of suspension or stoppage. Lasting only an instant, the sensation is accompanied or followed immediately by an isolated thrust of intense sensual awareness, clitorally oriented, but radiating upward into the pelvis. Intensity ranging in degree from mild to shock level has been reported by many women within the context of their personal experience. A simultaneous loss of overall sensory acuity has been described as paralleling in degree the intensity and duration of the particular orgasmic episode. . . .

During the first stage of subjective progression in orgasm, the sensation of intense clitoral-pelvic awareness has been described by a number of women as occurring concomitantly with a sense of bearing down or expelling. Often a feeling of receptive opening was expressed. This last sensation was reported only by parous study subjects, a small number of whom expressed some concept of having an actual fluid emission or of expending in some concrete fashion. Previous male interpretation of these subjective reports may have resulted in the erroneous but widespread concept that female ejaculation is an integral part of female orgasmic expression (8, 11, 30).

Twelve women, all of whom have delivered babies on at least one occasion without anesthesia or analgesia, reported that during the second stage of labor they experienced a grossly intensified version of the sensations identified with this first stage of subjective progression through orgasm. Reports of this concept also have appeared from time to time in the literature (6, 26).

Stage II

As the second stage of subjective progression through orgasm, a sensation of "suffusion of warmth," specifically pervading the pelvic area first and then spreading progressively throughout the body, was described by almost every woman with orgasmic experience.

Stage III

Finally, as the third stage of subjective progression, a feeling of involuntary contraction with a specific focus in the vagina or lower pelvis was mentioned consistently. Frequently, the sensation was described as that of "pelvic throbbing."

Women with the facility to express sensate awareness frequently separated this final stage of subjective progression into two phases. The initial phase was expressed as contractile, followed immediately by a throbbing phase, with both sensations experienced as separate entities. The initial contractile feeling was described as localized vaginally, subsequently merging with the throbbing sensation which, though initially concentrated in the pelvis, was felt throughout the body. The "pelvic throbbing" sensation often was depicted as continuing until it became one with a sense of the pulse or heartbeat.

Only the two phases of this third stage of subjective progression during orgasm afforded positive correlation between subjective response and objective reaction. This correlation has been developed from a composite return of direct interrogation of female study subjects during investigative sessions. The phase of contractile sensation has been identified as paralleling in time sequence the recorded initial spasm of the orgasmic platform.

Regularly recurring orgasmic-platform contractions were appreciated subjectively as pulsating or throbbing sensations of the vagina. Although second-phase sensations of pulsation coincided with observable vaginal-platform contractions, consciousness of a pulsating sensation frequently continued beyond observable platform contractions. Finally this pelvic-throbbing sensation became one with a subjective awareness of tachycardia [fast heartbeat] described frequently as feeling the heartbeat vaginally. Subjective awareness of orgasmic duration was somewhat dependent upon the degree of intensity of the specific orgasm.

Rectal-sphincter contraction also was described by some anatomically oriented or hypersensitive women as a specific entity during intense orgasmic response.

Observation supported by subjective report indicates that a relative norm of orgasmic intensity and duration is reflected by approximately five to eight vigorous contractions of the orgasmic platform. A level of eight to twelve contractions would be considered by observer and subject to be an intense physiologic experience. An orgasmic expression reflected by three to five contractions usually is reported by the responding female as being a "mild experience" unless the woman is postmenopausal. These physiologically recordable levels of orgasmic intensity never must be presumed arbitrarily to be a full or consistent measure of the subjective pleasure derived from individual orgasmic attainment (18, 20, 27).

Pregnancy (particularly during the second and, at times, the third trimester) has been noted to increase general sensitivity to the overall sensate effects of orgasm. To date, an increase in contractile intensity of the pregnant woman's orgasmic platform as compared to that in her nonpregnant state has not been corroborated by physiologic tracings. Orgasmic contractions of the uterus recorded during the second and third trimesters consistently have been reported as subjectively more intense sensations than those of nonpregnant response patterns. Of interest from an objective point of view is the fact that tonic spasm of the uterus develops in response to orgasmic stimulation and has been recorded during the third trimester of pregnancy.

SOCIOLOGIC FACTORS IN ORGASM

In our culture, the human female's orgasmic attainment never has achieved the undeniable status afforded the male's ejaculation. While male orgasm (ejaculation) has the reproductive role in support of its perpetual acceptance, a comparable regard for female orgasm is still in limbo. Why has female orgasmic expression not been considered to be a reinforcement of woman's role as sexual partner and reproductive necessity? Neither totem, taboo, nor religious assignment seems to account completely for the force with which female orgasmic experience often is negated as a naturally occurring psychophysiologic response.

With orgasmic physiology established, the human female now has an undeniable opportunity to develop realistically her own sexual response levels. Disseminating this information enables the male partner to contribute to this development in support of an effective sexual relationship within the marital unit (4, 25). The female's age-old foible of orgasmic pretense has been predicated upon the established concept that obvious female response increases the male's subjective pleasure during coital opportunity. With need for pretense removed, a sexually responding woman can stimulate effectively the interaction upon which both the man's and woman's psychosocial requirements are culturally so dependent for orgasmic facility.

Impression formed from eleven years of controlled observation suggests that psychosocially oriented patterns of sexual expression evolve specifically in response to developing social and life cycle demands. When continuity of study-subject cooperation permitted long-range observation and interrogation, it was noted that major changes in social baseline were accompanied by actual changes in sexual expression. For the female study subjects, changes involving social or life-cycle demands frequently resulted in a reorientation of sexual focus. This was manifest in alterations in desired areas of stimulation, preferred actions of partner, and reported fantasy (12, 14, 21). Often variations in coital and masturbatory techniques were observed.

These alterations usually appeared gradually, although, depending upon the impact of the social change involved, there were occasions of sudden onset. To date, physiologically measurable intensity in orgasmic response has shown no specific parallel to onset or presence of these psychosocial influences. This may indicate that physiologic capacity, as influenced by purely biologic variations, remains a dominant factor in orgasmic intensity and facility (5, 9, 24, 29). Reported levels of subjective pleasure in orgasm did, of course, parallel reports of desirable or undesirable social change.

It became evident that laboratory environment was not the determining factor in the success or failure of female study subjects' orgasmic attainment. Rather it was from previously established levels of sexual response that the individual female was able to cope with and adapt to a laboratory situation (9, 15–17, 23).

There were no particular personality trends toward high- or low-dominance individuals among the participating female research group. The women's personalities varied from the very shy through the agreeably independent, and histories reflected sexual-partner experience ranging from single to many. The ability to achieve orgasm in response to effective sexual stimulation was the only constant factor demonstrated by all active female participants. This observation might be considered to support the concept that sexual response to orgasm is the physiologic prerogative of most women, but its achievement in our culture may be more dependent upon psychosocial acceptance of sexuality than overtly aggressive behavior (1–3, 8, 11, 13, 19, 22, 28).

REFERENCES

1. Benedek, T. Panel report: Frigidity in women. *J. Amer. Psychoanal. Ass.* 9:571–584, 1961.

2. Davis, K. FACTORS IN THE SEX LIFE OF 2200 WOMEN. New York: Harper, 1929.

3. Dickinson, R. L., and Beam, L. A THOUSAND MARRIAGES. Baltimore: Williams & Wilkins, 1931.

4. Duvall, E. M. FAMILY DEVELOPMENT. Philadelphia: Lippincott, 1957.

5. Ellis, A. Is the Vaginal Orgasm a Myth? IN SEX, SOCIETY AND THE INDIVIDUAL (A. P. Pillay and E. Ellis, Eds.). Bombay, India: International Journal of Sexology, 1953.

6. Ellis, H. MAN AND WOMAN. Boston: Houghton Mifflin, 1929.

7. Ellis, H. STUDIES IN THE PSYCHOLOGY OF SEX. New York: Random House, 1936.

8. Ellis, H. PSYCHOLOGY OF SEX (2nd ed.). New York: Emerson Books, 1954.

9. Ford, C. S., and Beach, F. A. PATTERNS OF SEXUAL BEHAVIOR. New York: Paul B. Hoeber, Inc., 1951.

10. Grafenberg, E. The role of urethra in female orgasm. *Int. J. Sexol.* 3:145–148, 1950.

11. Hamilton, G. V. A RESEARCH IN MARRIAGE. New York: Albert and Charles Boni, 1929.

12. Hollender, M. H. Women's fantasies during sexual intercourse. *Arch. Gen. Psychiat.* 8:86–90, 1963.

13. Kinsey, A. C., *et al.* SEXUAL BEHAVIOR IN THE HUMAN MALE. Philadelphia: W. B. Saunders, 1948.

14. Kinsey, A. C., *et al.* SEXUAL BEHAVIOR IN THE HUMAN FEMALE. Philadelphia: W. B. Saunders, 1953.

15. Kubie, L. S. Influence of symbolic processes on the role of instincts in human behavior. *Psychosom. Med.* 18:189–208, 1956.

16. Levy, D. M. MATERNAL OVERPROTECTION. New York: Columbia University Press, 1943.

17. Lorand, S. Unsuccessful sex adjustment in marriage. *Amer. J. Psychiat.* 19:1413–1427, 1940.

18. McDougall, W. AN INTRODUCTION TO SOCIAL PSYCHOLOGY. London: Methuen, 1908.

19. Marmor, J. Some considerations concerning orgasm in the female. *Psychosom. Med.* 16:240–245, 1954.

20. Maslow, A. H. Self-Actualizing People: A Study of Psychological Health. In SELF: EXPLORATIONS IN PERSONAL GROWTH (C. E. Moustakas, Ed.). New York: Harper, 1956.

21. Maslow, A. H., et al. Some parallels between sexual and dominance behavior of infra-human primates and the fantasies of patients in psychotherapy. J. Nerv. Ment. Dis. 131:202–212, 1960.

22. Masserman, J. H., and Siever, P. Dominance, neurosis, and aggression. Psychosom. Med. 6:7–16, 1944.

23. Meninger, K. A. Impotence and frigidity. Bull. Menninger Clin. 1:251–260, 1937.

24. Money, J. Components of eroticism in man: II. The orgasm and genital somesthesia. J. Nerv. Ment. Dis. 132:289–297, 1961.

25. Mudd, E. H., et al. Paired reports of sexual behavior of husbands and wives in conflicted marriages. Compr. Psychiat. 2:149–156, 1961.

26. Newton, N. MATERNAL EMOTIONS. New York: Paul B. Hoeber, Inc., 1955.

27. Reik, T. PSYCHOLOGY OF SEX RELATIONS. New York: Rinehart, 1945.

28. Stekel, W. FRIGIDITY IN WOMAN IN RELATION TO HER LOVE LIFE, Vols. I and II. New York: Liveright, 1926.

29. Tinklepaugh, O. L. The nature of periods of sex desire in women and their relation to ovulation. Amer. J. Obstet. Gynec. 26:335–345, 1933.

30. Van de Velde, T. H. IDEAL MARRIAGE. New York: Covici-Friede, 1930.

12

Multiple Factors in Frigidity

RUTH MOULTON

Despite all that has been written on the psychology of women in the last 50 years, our therapeutic results with frigidity—a key problem—are often unsatisfactory. Victorian restrictions on women's sexual pleasure have been largely removed, at least in this subculture; yet relatively healthy women, who function well in other areas, still have more difficulty in achieving complete sexual satisfaction than do a comparable group of men. In fact, cultural permission to enjoy sex, although it has removed some of the more overt inhibitions, has not only failed to solve the problem, but has led to new ones. In the past, a woman who had little or no sexual response could take solace in the idea that such was the lot of a lady. But permission to have orgasm has imposed a new burden, namely the feeling of inadequacy if she fails to achieve it. Instead of freedom to experience fully the wide variety of sensations and emotions that can find expression in sexual contact, a new self-consciousness has developed about frequency and type of orgasm in comparison to man. Woman is far from secure in her sexual as well as her social role and continues to be, to some extent, an enigma to herself as well as to man. The purpose of this paper is to explore some of the possible reasons for this and to give examples of some of the typical dilemmas in which women find themselves.

To begin with, multiple factors play a role in determin-

SOURCE: From "Multiple Factors in Frigidity" by Ruth Moulton, M.D., in *Science and Psychoanalysis*, Vol. X, edited by Jules H. Masserman, M.D., pp. 75–93. Reprinted by permission of Grune & Stratton, Inc. and the editor.

ing woman's sexual responsiveness, so that it is futile to look for *the* cause. Sometimes there are specific sexual fears based on childhood traumata, but these only gather importance due to reinforcement from pervasive attitudes of significant people, operating insidiously and covertly over long periods of time. Widespread cultural attitudes need to be taken into account, but, in themselves, they rarely cause massive inhibition unless applied rigidly by parents who themselves lack warmth and humanity. Sometimes there are no specific sexual fears; rather the frigidity reflects an overall attitude of unresponsiveness, a need to be separate, to withhold, to keep obsessive control of all emotion, of which sex is *one* but not *the* source. There may be a deep seated distrust of other people, male and female, or an inability to trust one's body to react appropriately or to withstand any excitement. Thus, sexual behavior may merely reflect personality structure rather than being a basic issue. Women's reactions to frigidity also vary widely; some are very troubled, while others tolerate it well or may hardly be aware of it. Sexual responsiveness in some is so labile that it is readily influenced by any change in feeling about the partner or the self, such as increased resentment, or suspicion, decreased self-esteem or depression. In others sexual outlet is such a reliable source of pleasure that it is sought as a universal antidote for misery. Such a variety of patterns defies neat structuring and requires exploration into diverse aspects of living.

Misconceptions about Female Sexuality

Frigidity was originally explained in terms of presumably universal vicissitudes of female sexual development as seen from a predominantly male point of view. Forty years ago, Horney[1] began to point out the inaccuracies inherent in assuming that all women feel castrated and accept having children only as a substitute for the penis. She felt womanhood had deep primary satisfactions of its own, that the girl's sense of inferiority was

secondary to reality restrictions, and that women should
not agree so readily with a masculine interpretation of
their true nature. Other women analysts, as did Marie
Bonaparte,[2] felt that to emphasize positive feminine characteristics was to be like a suffragette, an apologist for
the vagina. She assumed that women simply had less
libido than men, and that woman's "belated, debilitated
orgasm" gave her no choice but to accept a passive
masochistic role. Mary Jane Sherfey[3] recently suggested
that the suppression of woman's sexual drives was necessary to the development of urban life, because of her
inordinate, insatiable sexual capacity, ability for multiple
orgasms, and continuous hypersexuality which interfered
with maternal responsibilities and man's territorial and
property rights in the original matriarchal cultures. With
such disagreement, even among women, no wonder it has
been hard to arrive at an unprejudiced, balanced concept
of femininity.

It is important, before turning to clinical material, to
comment briefly on some of the basic misconceptions
that have been sources of confusion in this field.

1. *Penis-envy* was taken literally as the universal cor-
nerstone of all further constructions about female development. One should distinguish primary penis envy,
which may be almost ubiquitous and begins with the
early discovery of sexual differences, from its secondary
reinforcements.[4] Early envy is based on the obvious advantages of a visible organ, whose performance can be
seen and shown off in the present, whereas the value of
having babies is far in the future.[5] The vagina is much
more difficult to conceptualize and reassurance about its
intactness hard to obtain. This early envy does not preclude a growing enjoyment of femininity, unless it is reinforced by derogatory attitudes toward women coming
from significant people in the environment. If the father
was resentful of, or contemptuous of, the mother, or if he
rejected and turned away from his daughter at puberty
during her oedipal love affair with him[6] he makes her

feel inferior or unattractive as a woman. She may feel he prefers a son and she tries to emulate one, or she may turn back to the mother; if thwarted here, she may feel a penis is necessary to get mother's love. If dependency needs are great, she may envy the father not so much his penis, as his access to mother. Ferenczi has pointed out that a man can always *get* a mother vicariously through his wife, while a woman must *be* the mother. If she craves having a mother she is apt to fear pregnancy and may envy the male role because it seems easier. Fromm[7] has suggested that a woman may wish to have a penis in order to be independent of a man, as she resents being dependent on pleasing him; her resentment of his apparent physical and social power may be expressed by ridicule and undermining, the weapons of the disadvantaged.

Clara Thompson[8] emphasized the fact that penis envy could grow into a major obstacle only when there was an underlying doubt on the woman's part about her ability to be an adequate woman. If her own mother was inadequate, ineffectual and resented her role, the growing girl has no positive model to identify with or learn from. She develops a deep fear about her ability to bear or raise children, or be sexually attractive. She may attain great professional competence, but be terrified at running a house, although on the surface she may belittle this. She may envy the man not his penis but his freedom from these anxiety provoking responsibilities and his having a wider choice of outside activities for his fulfillment. Thus, if penis envy is taken literally, the pre-Oedipal determinants and the residual problem with the mother may be overlooked.

Erikson[9] has emphasized that women can have a positive attitude toward their generative organs which is autonomous and not just compensatory. Bieber and Drellich[10] studied premenopausal women who underwent hysterectomy, and observed their tremendous feelings of loss and regret not only of the childbearing function, but also of menstruation, even though their families were complete. These functions were valued, not just for their immediate use, but as evidence of femininity. These authors suggest that the female castration complex not only has a phallic component, based on the lack of a penis, but also a feminine component based on the positive meaning of the uniquely female organs.

2. *The Role of the Vagina* is a second source of confusion. Freud assumed that it was not discovered until puberty, but there has been increasing conviction about early vaginal awareness and pleasure in girls aged 3–5. Josine Muller in 1932[11] felt that sensations from the vagina were stronger and more significant than those from any other erotogenic zone, but underwent secondary repression due to fear of internal injury or other consequences of becoming a woman. Such a denial of the vagina[12] makes the girl more vulnerable to penis envy, because of fears of being a woman. Clitoral sensation is felt to be safer, so continuation of clitoral masturbation is not a primary cause of frigidity but the secondary result of deep-seated inhibition. Muller felt that frigid women expended so much energy repressing strong vaginal sensations that they suffered from "troubled perception and uncertainty of will." She felt women with full vaginal capacity were more successful in their careers, that they were more fully women, rather than being like men.

Other writers, such as Lorand,[13] have emphasized the repression of vaginal sensation in the dependent woman with an infantile hunger for affection; the vagina becomes like a hungry mouth that craves continual nourishment and fears the repetition of oral frustration. These women may have a clinging, insatiable need for continued contact, more affectionate than passionate, but often fear orgasm either because it means giving up comfort or because they see themselves as helpless children, easily hurt. They may feel they are too small to give a man pleasure, or else they resent giving when they want so much to be given to. They may be enraged at the man for depriving them, for not mothering them. The basic wish then may not be for a penis, but for a nipple.

3. A third source of confusion about women is the tendency to equate *activity with masculinity and passivity with femininity*. This assumes that activity must be visible and movement producing,[14] a type of activity more typically masculine. The inner activity of the vagina, with its invisible smooth muscle contractions and less spectacular mucous secretions, is certainly less tangible, more subjective, but not passive. Receptive aims do not imply inertness; the truly receptive vagina is sucking, grasping, secreting, and giving pleasure through its own functions, not just through erotization of pain. Women may learn to bear certain types of internal pain more than do men, but this adaptation to reality should be distinguished from clinical masochism, which is a pattern of accepting pain as a prerequisite to being loved or taken care of. Here, pain is exploited neurotically for an ulterior goal.[9] This type of adjustment is not necessary to healthy femininity; in fact it precludes it, as it feeds a vicious circle of resentment, blame and guilt. Masochistic women may be always available sexually but get their satisfaction from having done a favor rather than from mutual exchange. Submission to get approval is not apt to lead to healthy, active participation on the woman's part;[15] this results only from her playing her own unique role in love-making, being free to express choices and preferences. This does not mean she has a right to be demanding, any more than does man.

4. Misconceptions about the nature of *female orgasm* are a fourth source of confusion. The almost totally subjective nature of this phenomenon, unfortunately, makes us too dependent on woman's verbal ability and willingness to describe accurately what she feels. The effort to arrive at some objectivity is made even more difficult by assumptions that clitoral sensation is masculine and infantile and must be relinquished for mature and truly

feminine vaginal sensation. If vaginal sensation can be
discovered as early as is clitoral, as described above, this
thesis can be doubted on theoretical grounds. Marmor[16]
and others have also thrown doubt on it from a physiological basis. Marmor points out that a denser concentration of sensitive nerve endings occur in the clitoris than in
the penis or any other organ of the body, male or female.
It seems to him untenable that sensations in this area
could ever stop. Rather he feels that, with mature acceptance of the role of the vagina, sensations from this area,
are added to the more acute sensations coming from the
clitoris. He feels that the clitoral sensation is mediated
through local spinal cord reflex mechanisms. Vaginal
sensations are much more subject to cortical control, either inhibitory or facilitating. Thus psychological attitudes such as fear or strong positive feelings play a much
greater role in an ability to have, or awareness of, vaginal
sensations. Female orgasm is more complex than that of
a male because it involves sensations from two areas that
must be fused and integrated. Clitoral sensation seems to
be more explosive, more parallel to that of the penis, but
not necessarily masculine. Vaginal sensation is more
diffuse, harder to describe, takes more maturity to absorb
and withstand and, at its best, may allow a more complete response of the whole body than is usually available
to men. Many women have arrived at a greater enjoyment of sexuality when they gave up comparing their
responses to that of the man and allowed themselves a
sensation more uniquely theirs. This development is only
hindered by using the typical male sexual response as a
standard.

A recent article by Mary Jane Sherfey,[3] using modern
embryology and other biological data, demonstrates that
the concept of initial anatomical bisexuality is erroneous,
and that sexual priority in development actually goes to
the human female, as the male differentiates from the
female during the second month of embryonic life by
the action of fetal androgen. She also points out how the

clitoral apparatus includes more widespread structures than just the glans clitoris, and that its arousal, whether by masturbation or heterosexual contact, cannot be separated at any time in the life cycle from that of the lower third of the vagina, which acts as a unit with it. She and Masters[17] make a clear physiological distinction between this and the upper two-thirds of the vagina, which balloons out during sexual excitement to facilitate impregnation, but is not involved in the process of arousal itself. They thus feel that there is no such thing as a vaginal orgasm distinct from a clitoral one. A woman's awareness of different qualities of orgasmic experience must therefore be seen as primarily a psychological, cerebral phenomena, rather than a local physiological one.

In addition to these sources of confusion about specific sexual issues, one must add that there are often *nonsexual forces* which prevent development or cause repression of all sensual pleasure. In these instances, sexual anesthesia is secondary to a major personality distortion, and there need be no sexual trauma. A girl brought up in a puritanical, ascetic, impersonal environment, with no maternal physical tenderness, fails to develop her potential for the most primitive type of pleasurable sensation through the skin. It is as though this capacity fails to develop or atrophies from disuse due to lack of appropriate stimulation. Two women I have treated, with the most deep-seated sexual anesthesia, did not enjoy being caressed and could not bear to have their breasts touched. This latter especially is a bad prognostic sign, indicating an extreme rejection of femininity. Both girls had rejecting, cold disinterested mothers, who gave them no physical care. One was raised by a series of rigid, obsessional nurses, who did not believe in fondling or stroking. During analysis, she learned to enjoy the physical affection she had missed in childhood, got much pleasure from mothering her children but never arrived at true genital feeling. The other patient was deserted by her father, left with her grandmother, and bitterly resented her mother when she was finally returned to her. She compensated by trying to become completely independent and was most competent professionally. At first her husband seemed dynamic, but actually was quite dependent. She resented feeding, nourishing, or in any way "wifing" him, feeling his demands as illegitimate as those of a little boy. He became ill and depressed, creating a vicious circle. She wanted children, feeling that she would enjoy mothering them but she avoided intercourse, was completely unresponsive and also infertile, so she actually mothered no one.

A second nonsexual factor can be the *need to control all emotion* due to a deep-seated fear that any strong feeling is dangerous. This may be a specific fear of revealing hostility toward one on whom one is dependent, or of opening up tender feelings that leave one vulnerable to attack or injury, or there may be an obsessive need for total control. Orgasm is then feared due to its momentary lack of control or loss of consciousness,[18] which may be seen as death, a convulsion, insanity, falling off into the unknown. The woman may feel she has to "hold on tight" to preserve her shaky sense of physical intactness, due to an unclear or fragile *body image*. Such a woman described her fear of "letting go" as a need to stay intact, in one piece, and imagined an orgasm as "falling in pieces like a broken plate, which would scatter all over."

In other instances, the *self-image* or sense of personal identity may be the weakest spot, and the woman feels she will literally lose her sense of herself so that her personality, rather than her body, will disintegrate. She may assume her psychic integrity rests on conscious control or she may feel her attractiveness completely depends on clothing, make-up and external appearance, and therefore she cannot afford to let down her facade and forget herself long enough to enjoy herself. This type of narcissistic self-preoccupation may allow a woman to look sexually feminine, but prevent her from following through. Finally, it can be said that anything decreasing self-

esteem or adding to depression dampens sexual responsiveness, as the latter requires not only a belief in oneself
but also an affirmation of life and, therefore, is an act of
both hope and faith.

Clinical Material

There is no agreement as to a definition of the term
frigidity. In the past, analysts have used it to refer to
either complete coldness during intercourse or more specifically to the lack of vaginal orgasm. Neither concept is
very functional, since complete anesthesia is rare and
the role of the vagina is too debatable. Some women
cannot distinguish between clitoral and vaginal sensation,
either due to the interlocking nature of the two or inhibition of perception. Other women alternate between acute,
explosive clitoral orgasm and a more diffuse voluptuous
vaginal sensation that may radiate throughout the whole
body. Again, for those who are perceptive and verbal,
there may be infinite permutations of the two, so that
neat distinctions seem to be untenable.

The biologically oriented conceive of orgasm as a reaction of the whole organism; neuromuscular tensions,
radiating from the genital area, culminate in a peak followed by more or less sudden discharge involving wide
areas of the body. Sexual response can then be seen on a
sliding scale, where differences in quantity are of more
importance than differences in quality, since a sense of
deep satisfaction and relaxation can come about by such
varied routes. In this paper, I use the term frigidity in a
pragmatic way to refer to those women whose sexual
response is so limited that there is evidence of repeated
frustration or lack of any real satisfaction even with the
use of flexible criteria. If the patient finds intercourse
exciting, not merely pleasant, and reaches some climax
with relaxation, I would not consider her frigid even
though I felt she could achieve greater sexual pleasure
were she freer from conflict and anxiety.

The frequency of frigidity has been reported as from

15–90 per cent according to different observers. I briefly
reviewed the sexual adjustment of all female patients
whom I had treated intensively in the last 10 years. Most
of them were married, with problems related to marriage
and/or child rearing; many of them were competent professional women with conflict about their role as women.
Out of the total of 35, only 8 presented sexual problems
as a reason for entering treatment, but it became clear in
treatment that two-thirds suffered from some degree of
frigidity. In other words, only 10 out of the 35 had no
apparent sexual problems as such; even these had marital
problems, since 5 were divorced, although the conflict
seemed largely to be nonsexual, causing only momentary
or situational frigidity. There were 4 girls, who were vir-
gins at the onset, who not only needed help in starting a
sexual life but had difficulty with it when they did.

I then studied the most recent 10 cases, all in treatment in the last 4 years and all with such limited sexual
response that they either had no orgasm or only occasional limited climax which seemed to lack any vaginal
component. All were married and involved in moderate
to severe marital discord, with frequent refusal to allow
intercourse. Eight of the 10 had active professional
careers, either artistic or scientific. Four had children but
serious problems in raising them. All were neurotic, not
schizophrenic or even borderline. A recurrent pattern in
this group of 10 was frustrated love for the father, who
severely disappointed his daughter in each instance by
being rejecting, disapproving, disinterested or unreach-
able. There was always evidence of strong, unrequited
oedipal attachment; the father either overtly spurned the
daughter at puberty or failed dramatically to help her feel
she could become an attractive woman. Under this lay an
even deeper problem with the mother, who had not only
been cold and ungiving, but in all instances had been
unhappy with her own role as a woman. Contempt for
the ineffectual, submissive mother was dominant, although in three cases the mother was seen as controlling

and rigid. Rage at the mother was conspicuous in all cases except one, who had no access to her rage. In 7 out of 10, the patient tried to get her husband to fulfill the mother's role. In most instances there was marked fear of submitting to the husband, sexually and otherwise, and the greater this fear, the greater was the need for obsessive control permeating many areas of living. Seven felt considerable sexual disgust; 3 had deep anal preoccupations and 2 had gotten conscious sexual excitement from the anal area. Competitiveness with men was frequent, half were aware of having wanted to be a boy, and tended to be castrating to men, one to the point of being disturbed by fantasies of cutting off her husband's genitals. All showed fear of admitting deep feeling. To show tenderness would expose them to new rejection and increase their vulnerability to pain. If their rage became visible, their relation to dependency objects would be threatened. Obviously none of these factors is specific to frigidity, but an average of 10 out of a check-list of the 15 items mentioned were noted in frigid women, whereas only 2 or 3 were observed in nonfrigid women. The role of the husbands is not referred to here, since the emphasis is on the intrapsychic problems of the woman. However, it may be said in passing that none of the husbands was impotent or had severe premature ejaculation; they seemed to play a contributing rather than a major role.

*   *   *

Therapeutic Considerations

Theoretical concepts can have an important influence on therapy. If penis envy is taken literally as *the* primary issue, one may miss underlying factors, such as the fear of being a woman, or the wish to possess the mother. If the marital battle is largely a reenactment of the infantile battle with the mother, these pre-Oedipal dependency needs must be handled before significant change can occur. Negative attitudes toward men, hostility and competition, certainly must be analyzed, but interpreting such hostility as being due to biological lack, which must be accepted as inevitable, perpetuates the vicious circle by enhancing woman's rage at man, whose superiority is thus confirmed. She is then encouraged to see herself as a victim, an amputee with an inescapable compensation neurosis. If activity is seen as masculine, she is given no access to appropriate self-assertion, but made to feel even more unfeminine which further decreases self-esteem. She may get caught in the trap of assuming that all men dislike competence and strength in women and fail to see that the real problem is her tendency to use her strength *against* men rather than for a constructive goal. She may set up a false dichotomy between her marriage and outside interests, feeling she must give *them* up for *him*. This not only increases her envy of him, encouraging a hostile, masochistic surrender, but allows her to overlook the dependency or self-doubt that limits her effectiveness in both roles simultaneously. There is often a common denominator, such as a compulsive effort to substitute will for imagination, relying on mechanical devices due to doubts as to the validity of inner feelings, which kills the life essential to a profession or an art as well as to sexual fulfillment. The sexually responsive woman does better in all areas, not just in bed.

Another negative result of overemphasizing the wish to be a man, is that there may be insufficient therapeutic work on the problems of being a competent woman. Part of each woman yearns to find pleasure in her own femininity and to fulfill her role with dignity, but she may need active help in overcoming the negative concept of womanhood that she brought from her past. The therapist must believe in woman's positive potential in order to help her work toward an ideal she can respect.

One girl with two overt penis envy dreams was sheepishly amused by the manifest content; she knew that she was in competition with her husband and wanted to "wear the pants" in the family. What was more repressed and more anxiety ridden was the sense of humiliation at feeling herself to be unattractive, disgusting, and totally inadequate as a woman. She much preferred to ventilate her rage at men or her hostility to her mother, than to face her begrudging admiration of her mother or the few women she did admire and focus on the deep dependency needs that prevented her from being able to strive toward positive goals. She unconsciously identified with the most negative aspects of the mother, partly to show up the mother in revenge and partly to be rescued by the husband. The marital battle was a reenactment of the battle with the mother. In acting this out, she took her rage at her husband too literally and ruined her marriage.

The woman with drive, intelligence and talent, who is led to see her active potential as merely masculine and aggressive may not only develop more militant resistance or hostile masochism, but often forfeits a great deal of what might become valuable and attractive feminine effectiveness. Activity has primary satisfactions apart from competition with men.

Acceptance of narrow concepts of normal sexual function unnecessarily limits expression of individual activity patterns.[19] Normal intercourse should be seen as having active and passive components for both men and women, with tremendous variety available according to mood and character structure. Multiple drives and all erotogenic zones can participate. Both sexes may seek the breast and enjoy it vicariously in lovemaking, unless there is too much anxiety about dependency gratification. Such anxiety may prevent acceptance and integration of partial drives, so that they grow under repression and do not receive appropriate discharge. The sexual act may be said to reflect all aspects of a person, so that a creative analysis of it may be useful as a wedge to explore widely divergent areas. This is quite different from the assumption that sexual drives are, by themselves, the basic causes.

In reaction to the overemphasis on sexual etiology, some present-day students fail to investigate thoroughly sexual fears and fantasies. Detailed descriptions of the woman's reactions during sexual activity are necessary to unraveling the various factors involved, and can indicate the next direction for exploration, which varies throughout changing phases of treatment. Specific sexual fears may predominate at one time; the vagina is seen as too small or nonexistent, the penis may unconsciously be conceived as having a bone in it and thus be very dangerous, pregnancy may be feared as equivalent to death, etc. At other times, or in other patients, nonsexual factors play a greater role, reinforcing the sexual.

Reintegrative aspects of treatment rest on affirmation of woman's productive potential, so that she can build up a positive concept of her womanhood differing from her mother's, not yielding to that of her father or a narrow part of the culture, but more truly suited to herself.

REFERENCES

1. Horney, Karen. On the genesis of the castration complex in women. *Int. J. Psychoanal.* 5:50–65, 1924.
2. Bonaparte, Marie. Female Sexuality. New York: International Universities Press, Inc., 1953.
3. Sherfey, Mary Jane. The evolution and nature of female sexuality in relation to psychoanalytic theory. *J. Amer. Psychoanal. Ass.* 14:28–127, 1966.
4. Horney, Karen. The flight from womanhood. *Int. J. Psychoanal.* 7:324–339, 1926.
5. Lampl-De Groot, Jeanne. Problems of femininity. *Psychoanal. Quart.* 2:489, 1933.
6. Searles, H. Oedipal love in the countertransference. *Int. J. Psychoanal.* 40:180, 1959.
7. Fromm, E. Sex and character. *Psychiatry* 6:21–31, 1943.
8. Thompson, Clara. Penis envy in women. *Psychiatry* 6:12–35, 1943.

 9. Erikson, E. Inner and outer space: reflections on woman-
    hood. *In:* Daedalus, Spring 1964, pp. 582–606.
10. Bieber and Drellich. The female castration complex.
    J. Nerv. Ment. Dis. 129:235, 1959.
11. Muller, Josine. A contribution to the problem of libidinal
    development of the genital phase in girls. *Int. J. Psycho-
    anal.* 13:362–368, 1932.
12. Horney, Karen. The denial of the vagina. *Int. J. Psycho-
    anal.* 14:57–70, 1933.
13. Lorand, S. Contribution to the problem of vaginal or-
    gasm. *Int. J. Psychoanal.* 20:432–438, 1939.
14. Kestering, Judith. Vicissitudes of female sexuality. *J.
    Amer. Psychoanal. Assn.* 4:453–476, 1956.
15. Thompson, Clara. Interpersonal Psychoanalysis. Chap.
    26. New York: Basic Books, 1964.
16. Marmor, J. Some considerations concerning orgasm in
    the female. *Psychosom. Med.* 16:240–245, 1954.
17. Masters, and Johnson. Human Sexual Response. New
    York: Little, Brown & Co., 1966.
18. Keiser, S. On the psychopathology of orgasm. *Psycho-
    anal. Quart.* 16:378–390, 1947.
19. Cohen, Mabel Blake. Personal identity and sexual iden-
    tity. *Psychiatry* 29:1–15, 1966.

III

MENSTRUATION AND MENOPAUSE

Introduction

The question of whether women's responses to menstruation and menopause stem primarily from biological or from social and psychological factors has not yet been resolved. The onset and regular recurrence of menstruation—and the fact that its cessation marks the end of a woman's childbearing capacity—have undoubtedly been the major factors in establishing the popular myth that women are entirely subject to hormonal factors that rule their emotional lives and incapacitate them intellectually. Often accompanied by anxiety, painful cramps (called dysmenhorrea), and so forth, menstruation has been held to be the "curse"—part of the biblical punishment of women for their very sexual existence. Cramps have been described as neurotic reactions, as the inevitable accompaniment of changes in body chemistry that lead to water retention and other symptoms, and as the result of pelvic congestion needing only orgasmic release. The recurrence of premenstrual emotional symptoms such as anger and anxiety has been ascribed to changes in hormone levels during the menstrual cycle, and is offered even today as evidence of women's incapacity for stable, productive work. Too little attention has been paid to the biological appropriateness of some of women's responses; the cessation of menstruation among some women in concentration camps during World War II, for instance, was clearly a biologically adaptive response rather than a neurotic symptom.

It has long been known that mind and body can affect

each other profoundly in the areas of neurohormonal
activity. Perhaps the problem lies in a general insistence
on finding the answer in mind or body alone rather than
attempting to understand their interrelationships. However, because so much material has dealt with hormones,
the essays in this section have been chosen to demonstrate social factors in a woman's response to her menstrual cycle, including its onset at puberty, its recurrence
through adulthood, and its cessation at menopause. It is
important to see a continuity in this activity, rather than
to define menopause or puberty as isolated phenomena.
Only when the menstrual cycle is integrated into a view
of a woman's whole life can it be adequately understood;
it then becomes an aspect of a woman's sexual and social
identity.

Clellan S. Ford and Frank A. Beach, in an excerpt
from their pioneering work, *Patterns of Sexual Behavior*,
outline the hormonal and physiological stages of the menstrual cycle, and compare and contrast them to the same
events in primates and lower mammals. One of their key
points is that social factors become increasingly more
important than hormones in the sexual behavior of
mammals as they are located higher on the evolutionary
scale. They cite evidence showing that the sexual responsiveness of primates is greatest at the time of ovulation,
while most women report a peak of sexual desire just
before menstruation. Restrictions on both the sexual and
social activity of menstruating women are common in
primitive societies, and inhibitions about sexual activity
during menstruation remain a factor for many women in
our own culture. Ford and Beach suggest that the anticipation of sexual deprivation may play a role in increasing
sexual desire just before menstruation.

In her book *The Nature and Evolution of Female Sexuality*, Mary Jane Sherfey takes the evidence of Masters
and Johnson and others to indicate that in fact the conscious mind, or cortex, plays no role in sexual arousal.
She shows how Ford and Beach's theory of species evolu-

tion has been linked to Freud's theory of the clitoral-vaginal transfer, and to the traditional assumption of biologists that subhuman mammals do not experience orgasm. The result has been the assumption that the vaginal orgasm is a product of superior cortical control or development, supposedly achieved by relatively few women. Sherfey states that the high incidence of frigidity among women has thus been interpreted as "proof" that women are biologically and intellectually less evolved than men, whose frequency of orgasm in intercourse is relatively much greater.

Sherfey presents a valid argument, but Ford and Beach do not reach the same kind of conclusion; they cite evidence of women's continued sexual desire after ovariectomy and natural menopause to support their conclusion that the sexual behavior of human beings is less dependent on hormonal cycles than is that of the lower mammals. The irony of the fact that their work has been used to support the contention that women are inferior should not be lost on readers. Ethologists—from Harlow to Jane Goodall—have shown the critical importance of social factors in the development of sexual behavior patterns among primates. Ford and Beach suggest that adverse social conditioning is a major factor in sexual inhibition among human females; the cortex is thus seen as functioning within a social environment to allow or inhibit sexual activity. Ford and Beach's theory can perhaps best be taken to refute proponents of the traditional idea, or myth, that women are ruled exclusively by hormonal cycles.

Karen E. Paige, a psychologist at the University of California at Davis, argues that there is insufficient evidence to support the assumption that mood changes associated with the menstrual cycle are caused entirely by hormonal and chemical changes in the body. She thinks that social factors are easily as important as physiological changes, and cites social attitudes toward menstruation as messy, unclean, a visible sign of sexuality and therefore of sinfulness, and as a sign of women's inferiority. She found that women using oral contraceptives of the combination variety experienced a reduction of anxiety associated with menstruation; she links this directly to a reduced menstrual flow rather than to any greater hormonal stability. Women whose oral contraceptives did not produce a decrease in menstrual flow experienced the same anxiety as women who were not taking any pill. Women with reduced menstrual flow were also more likely to ignore the taboo against intercourse during menstruation. Paige hypothesizes, then, that at least part of a woman's emotional vicissitudes during the menstrual cycle is a socially conditioned response to her body's functions rather than an emotional state triggered by hormonal cycles. Paige did find, however, that the element of hostility is correlated with an increase in certain chemical activity that occurs in the body when estrogen and progesterone levels go down just before the menstrual period; but she reminds us of the fact that chemical and hormonal activity can be triggered by the emotions as well as the other way around. The evidence, then, is not yet all in, and it would seem that major research in this area remains to be done.*

In an excerpt from her paper, "A Re-evaluation of Some Aspects of Femininity through a Study of Menstruation: A Preliminary Report," Natalie Shainess, a psychiatrist and psychoanalyst, narrows down the factor of social influence on menstruation to the emotional response of the mother to a girl's first period, or menarche. She found that out of 103 women studied, only 15 percent reported that their mothers responded with pleasure

* The use of the pill in research remains a loaded issue, and inclusion of Paige's article should not be taken as an endorsement of oral contraceptives either in research or for general use. It seems absurd, however, to ignore the results of work that has taken pill users into consideration. Valuable work on the general effects of the pill has been presented by Barbara Seaman and others; there isn't adequate space in this anthology to deal with these issues.

to their first period. These same women were also the only ones in the survey who reported little or no premenstrual tension. Shainess suggests that the emotional climate surrounding a girl's first period is reexperienced to some degree with each successive period, and that negative feelings about her body and herself are intensified during her periods. The catch is, of course, that mothers who react negatively to their daughter's first menstruation are themselves only reflecting the emotional climate in which they matured. Shainess links the reactions of the mother and of the larger culture in an effective example of a girl who received a negative view of herself from both. Menstruation is not simply a physiological event; it signals the start of sexual maturity, of the capacity to bear children, and is inextricably involved in a woman's attitude toward her body—in both its sexual and reproductive capacities. As in the evolution of identity, body and culture are linked together. Physiological events occur in a cultural context that defines their meaning for the individual. Culture can be embodied in a single person, in this case the mother. Individuals contain their culture, and pass it along to their children.

If one views menopause as another phase of the overall menstrual cycle, it becomes possible to see the correlations described by Isadore Rubin in "Sex after Forty—And after Seventy," between active sexuality and menopause. Rubin reports on research by Kinsey, Masters and Johnson, and others, who have shown that the continuation of an active sex life after menopause is more dependent on regular sexual activity before menopause than on any "correction" of hormonal imbalances. While physiological changes do occur in women during and after menopause—for instance, the walls of the vagina grow thinner and may not lubricate as well as before—the effects of these changes seem to be more pronounced in women who have not had regular, and pleasurable, sex before the physiological changes began. If the work of Shainess and Paige is taken into consideration, one could suggest that continued sexual activity after menopause reflects a woman's pleasure in and acceptance of her body that is at least partly dependent on the kind of response her culture made to her menstrual cycle from its beginning. If the culture responds negatively, it becomes that much more difficult for a woman to achieve a positive attitude toward her body and its functions. On the other hand, if menstruation is surrounded by a great deal of anxiety, its cessation with the menopause could possibly free a woman from much anxiety about her body, and give her a new ability to take pleasure in sex. In any event, it seems clear that the various activities of the body are interrelated, so that it is in a sense artificial to consider the menstrual cycle separately from other sexual activity, and it certainly makes little sense to consider any sexual activity apart from the cultural context in which it occurs.

In her essay, "Middle Age," a chapter from an unfinished book on women published posthumously, Clara Thompson relates the problems of middle age directly to the whole life-style of women who may fear losing their youth, or regret opportunities not taken. Thompson's examples show clearly that middle age can also be a time of productivity and growth. The implication here is that the physiological events of menopause take on overwhelming importance only when the larger context of a woman's life is unsatisfying. If a woman's whole identity is defined by her menstrual cycle, which gives her validity in the culture only as a potential childbearing person, the menopause can be a painful and difficult time. But if she is able to make connections with the culture as a person in her own right, the biological events recede into perspective and no longer signal a kind of death-in-life.

13

Feminine Fertility Cycles

CLELLAN S. FORD
and FRANK A. BEACH

... The various physiological changes associated with the attainment of physical and reproductive maturity produce alterations in sexual behavior. The appearance of completely adult sexual performance in lower animals and, to a certain degree, in our own species depends in part upon the gradual development of certain glands and other organs involved in reproduction. This chapter and the one that follows are devoted to an analysis of the physiological forces that continue to influence the desire and capacity for sexual activity after adulthood is reached. One of the most obvious and powerful types of physiological control over behavior is exerted by the female sex glands; the present chapter deals with this topic.

PHYSIOLOGY OF THE FEMALE SEX CYCLE

Periodic menstruation occurs in human beings, in all species of apes, and in some kinds of monkeys. It is governed by the rhythmic secretion of certain hormones. Prime movers in the menstrual rhythm are two hormones produced by the anterior pituitary gland. These are the gonadotrophins. . . . Stimulated by the pituitary hormones, the ovaries produce and release into the circulatory system a hormone known as estrogen or, more ac-

Source: From *Patterns of Sexual Behavior* (New York, Harper & Row, 1951), pp. 199–213, 221–225, 249. Copyright © 1951 by Clellan Stearns Ford and Frank Ambrose Beach. Reprinted by permission of Harper & Row, Publishers, Inc. A diagram, a graph, and cross-references have been omitted.

curately, estrone,[1] which produces a series of changes in
the walls of the uterus. Under the influence of estrogen
the inner lining of the uterus grows thicker and develops
a very rich blood supply. The ovary's secretion of hormones is a cyclic affair. A week or so after the cessation
of the menstrual flow the production of estrogen begins to
increase, and it reaches a high point approximately fourteen days after the beginning of the preceding period of
bleeding. This is about two weeks before the next flow
begins. In most women ovulation occurs at or near this
stage of the cycle, and one or occasionally several eggs
are released from the ovary to enter the Fallopian tubes.

Just before or shortly after ovulation the ovary begins
to secrete increasing amounts of a second hormone,
progesterone. Progesterone prepares the uterus for the
"implantation" of any egg which may be fertilized. When
conception occurs, the fertilized egg descends the Fallopian tubes, eventually comes to rest against the wall of
the uterus, and is embedded there. Later the placenta
develops and connects the maternal and fetal organisms.
If fertile copulation does not take place, the lining of the
uterus, which has been built up by estrogen and further
stimulated by progesterone, disintegrates and is shed into
the uterine cavity. Preceding this degenerative change
there occurs a temporary shutting off of the coiled arteries that supply the new tissue with blood. Circulation is re-
established within a few hours, but in the interim the
capillary blood vessels that were temporarily deprived of
their blood supply have suffered. They burst when the
blood flow is resumed. Little pools of blood collect and
drain off with the dying tissues which cannot survive
without the blood formerly carried by the capillaries.
This sequence of changes produces the external signs of
menstruation. Except when pregnancy intervenes, the
cycle is repeated every twenty-eight days, more or less,

[1] There are a number of closely related hormones that have the
same effects as estrone. They are called "estrogenic hormones" or,
generically, "estrogen," the term that is used in this book.

from the time of puberty until the onset of the menopause.

The menstruation of apes and Old World monkeys is
characterized by the same physiological events that occur
in women. New World monkeys do not bleed externally
but they do show a regular rhythm of slight internal
blood flow. The length of the cycle in infrahuman primates varies from approximately three weeks to thirty
days depending upon the species, but in all species, as in
human females, differences between individuals are pronounced. Ovulation occurs during the mid-menstrual interval and in some primates it is accompanied by conspicuous swelling of the sex skin which lies next to the
external sex organs.[2] . . .

Menstruation does not occur in mammals that are
below primates on the evolutionary scale, but the remaining features of the ovarian cycle are present in modified
form.[3] The ovaries of guinea pigs, rats, cows, dogs, and
other lower mammals secrete estrogen in gradually increasing amounts as the time for ovulation approaches,
and then progesterone is secreted for a while. In these
species as in the higher mammals, progesterone prepares
the uterus for implantation of the fertilized egg.

Females of our own and other primate species display
regular ovarian cycles throughout the year and may conceive during any season, although in some cases, at least
in rhesus monkeys, cycles without ovulation are more
common during warm summer weather. Absence of a
well-marked breeding season is also characteristic of
some domesticated animals. Female cattle come into
heat periodically throughout the year. . . . Some wild

[2] In some kinds of monkeys the sex skin does not swell appreciably but it may become brilliantly colored during estrus.

[3] Female mammals of subprimate species do not menstruate but
may nevertheless show some vaginal bleeding at a particular stage
in the reproductive cycle. This occurs, however, at the time of
estrus and ovulation rather than during the period of infertility.
The bleeding of ovulation and the menstrual bleeding are quite
different phenomena.

animals are also polyestrous. Female lions, for example, come into heat at irregular intervals throughout the year, although heat periods tend to be more frequent during the spring.

Unlike the animals discussed thus far, the vast majority of mammals and nearly all the lower vertebrates are fertile for only one or two relatively short periods in each year. The remainder of the time the reproductive glands in these species produce relatively little hormone and sexual behavior does not occur. It is in these "seasonally breeding species" that the relationships between the secretory activity of the ovaries and the appearance of sexual behavior are most obvious.

RHYTHMS OF SEXUAL BEHAVIOR

LOWER MAMMALS. Female cats and dogs usually come into heat, or estrus, twice a year. At these times the sex glands manufacture and pour into the blood stream relatively large amounts of their hormonal products. As the level of estrogen increases, the female becomes sexually attractive to males, and it is only at this time that she actively seeks a sex partner and readily engages in intercourse. As a matter of fact in some species, such as the guinea pig and chinchilla, the vaginal orifice is completely closed by an epithelial membrane except when the female is in estrus. At other times the penis cannot penetrate the vagina. Only while the appropriate ovarian hormones are present in adequate amounts does the female desire sexual stimulation. And, of course, it is precisely at this time that her ovaries contain ripe eggs and she is capable of conceiving as a result of copulation with a fertile male.

In lower mammals, therefore, the female's sexual urge is rigidly tied to reproductive functions by means of chemical control through the ovarian hormones. In most of these animals the duration of the female's receptive period is predetermined by hormonal rhythms and is not affected by the occurrence of fertile mating. Many coital acts usually take place during this period. In a few species, however, this is not the case. Instead, the female loses her desire for sexual stimulation within a few hours or days after copulating. And at the same time she ceases to attract and arouse the male. The cat stays in heat several days if she is not mated, but she becomes unreceptive within approximately twelve hours after intercourse. Coitus apparently shortens the period of heat in several other species including the shrew, porcupine, and Alaskan seal. . . .

SUBHUMAN PRIMATES. Like females of lower mammalian species, apes and monkeys show a clear-cut rhythm of sexual desire. The female is maximally attractive to the male and most eager for sexual contact at those times when ovulation is imminent and copulation can result in conception. But the relation between reproductive physiology and sexual behavior is less rigid in primates than in lower mammals, and the result is that under certain conditions female monkeys and apes may accept the male when they are infertile and physiologically not in estrus. . . .

All observers appear to agree that individual differences in responsiveness to different consorts are of great importance in sexual relations between male and female chimpanzees. . . .

The following . . . illustration of variable behavior by a female toward different consorts is taken from Yerkes and Elder's monograph on the subject:

Mona, a large and courageous, mature, experienced female, was many times given opportunity to mate with Bokar, Pan, and Jack. For each pair of consorts the pattern was distinctive. When receptive she accepted any one of them eagerly and copulation occurred typically with only slight differences in behavior. But when she was slightly or non-receptive, Mona exhibited the following differential behavior: Bokar's advances she met aggressively, and by intimidating him she completely controlled the mating situation. Pan she treated somewhat indifferently, if he chanced to exhibit sexual interest or desire. Her attitude and behavior toward him indicated familiarity and confidence in his self-control. But in the presence of Jack she was alert, cautious, conciliatory, and defensive, and if necessary she would permit copulation. [Yerkes and Elder, 1936, pp. 31–32.]

Male chimpanzees show clear-cut preferences for certain feminine sex partners and individuals vary in the degree of their selectiveness. Apparently all males prefer copulation with a female when she is in the stage of greatest genital swelling, but some apes are sufficiently motivated sexually to copulate at other times if the female will co-operate.

In the sexual behavior of monkeys there first appears some evidence of a low degree of social control over responses that are almost completely dependent upon hormonal secretions as far as lower mammals are concerned. The more highly evolved apes display an even greater degree of emancipation from endocrinological domination of their mating activities. . . . Immature female mammals of subprimate species display none of the sexual reactions characteristic of the adult individual during her estrous period, whereas, in contrast, immature female monkeys and apes do engage in sexual games that involve assumption of the mating posture, manipulation of the partner's genitalia, and on occasion even attempts at heterosexual coitus. The infrequent but recognizable sexual activities of the nonestrous adult female and the incomplete mating attempts of the immature animal both indicate that in primates the role of the ovarian hormones, although still very important, is less marked than it is in lower mammals.

HUMAN FEMALES. The growing evolutionary importance of nonphysiological factors which becomes obvious in monkeys and apes is tremendously increased in our own species. As a matter of fact, it is difficult to differentiate between the physiological and social influences that combine to govern erotic responsiveness in the human female.

Many women in American society experience regular cycles of sexual desire that appear to be correlated with the rhythms of ovarian hormone secretion. Various investigators who have questioned hundreds of married women report that for most of the wives who recognize such cycles, the peak of excitability occurs just before or just after the period of menstrual flow. In some individuals there are two times at which erotic responsiveness is greatest—one just before and one immediately after menstruation. A much smaller number of women experience the most intense satisfaction from intercourse during the mid-interval between two periods of flow, at the time when ovulation is most likely to occur and when the ovaries are secreting maximal amounts of estrogenic hormone. . . .

If the human female's sex drive were strongly conditioned by the same ovarian hormones that produce heat and mating behavior in other mammals, one would expect it to attain a maximal level during the mid-interval when ovulation is about to occur and the concentration of estrogen has recently increased. It has been stated that a few women do experience the greatest degree of responsiveness during this time. In a purely biological sense this kind of relationship is adaptive, since, other things being equal, it would lead to more frequent intercourse in the woman's fertile period and thus increase the probability of conception. In other words, it favors perpetuation of the species. Why, then, is it true of only a small minority of those women whose attitude has been studied?

Various explanations for the differential importance of estrogenic stimulation in human females and other primates might be suggested. The factors involved undoubtedly are numerous and complex, but one significant fact may be that women in nearly every society are prohibited from engaging in any form of sexual activity during the period of menstrual flow. This interval becomes, therefore, one of total deprivation as far as sexual stimulation is concerned.

RESTRICTIONS PLACED UPON THE MENSTRUATING WOMAN. The attitudes taken by members of different societies toward menstruation furnish an excellent example of one way in which social forces influence human sexual life. In very few societies is the menstruating woman regarded as a suitable sex partner. Among the Marquesans the head husband has intercourse with a wife whose menstrual flow is unduly prolonged. This is thought to stop the blood and is considered a prophylactic measure undertaken for the sake of the woman, although menstrual blood is considered unclean. It is reported that the Trukese of the Carolines commonly engage in sexual relations during the wife's menstruation, and such behavior is permissible among the Walapai, with the specific exception of the woman's first menstrual period after marriage. The Maori wife who is menstruating is permitted to receive her husband if she so desires. Much more commonly, however, the menstruating woman is considered "unclean" and is expected to modify her behavior in a variety of ways. In some cases she is only moderately controlled, but in others she is surrounded by a multiplicity of restrictions that bring major changes in her daily life.

The most lenient mores merely direct that women forego sexual intercourse; they need make no other changes in their routine activities during menstruation. In some other societies there are additional minor interruptions of the usual schedule. These may include the avoidance of certain dietary items such as meat and salt, or temporary discontinuation of bathing, or discontinuation of special activities such as dancing. In contrast, a number of societies enforce a great number of restrictive rules that severely circumscribe the female's activities during menstruation, and some compel her to remain in virtual isolation from other members of the community.

Attitudes taken by different societies toward menstruation are rationalized in various ways, but the reasons advanced almost always are based upon the attitude of the woman's masculine partner or other associates; rarely do they seem to arise from any recognized alteration in her own desires or tendencies. . . .

Occasionally, there appears the belief that the woman will be the one to suffer if she has relations with a male while she is menstruating. The Reindeer Chukchee, for instance, are certain that any woman who makes this mistake will shortly become sickly and sterile. It is much more common, however, to consider the woman a potential source of contamination—so powerful a source, in fact, that she may affect other people without the occurrence of any sexual relations. . . .

Because coitus during menstruation is an accepted practice in so few societies, and because there is no detailed evidence regarding the wife's responsiveness in such instances, it is impossible to draw any conclusions concerning the effects of menstruation upon feminine erotic capacity. We have noted, however, that for other primate species in which menstruation occurs, copulation during the period of bleeding is rare. And when it does take place it appears to reflect the male's insistence rather than any genuine receptivity on the part of the female.

The evolutionary evidence would lead to the expectation that during their menstrual periods women might be relatively undesirous of intercourse for purely physiological reasons. But this does not explain the apparent rise in receptivity directly after menstruation, or the heightened responsiveness that precedes the occurrence of bleeding. As indicated earlier, no completely satisfactory explanation is currently available. We wish to suggest, however, that one factor in the situation may be the effect of social conditioning and learning. Since in the vast majority of

societies the menstruating woman is deprived of any form
of sexual stimulation, it may well be that the premenstrual peak in her curve of desire reflects the effects of
anticipated sexual deprivation, and a second rise following the flow may be due to several days of enforced
sexual continence. We repeat that this tentative explanation certainly does not account in full for the phenomena
under consideration. Nevertheless, we are convinced that
the difference between human beings and other primates
in this respect is due primarily to the lessening of hormonal control and the pronounced increase in the extent
to which social influences govern human eroticism.

*   *   *

ADDITIONAL EVIDENCE CONCERNING OVARIAN HORMONES

. . . EFFECTS OF REMOVAL OR REGRESSION OF THE
OVARIES. In the light of previously described findings
concerning the importance of ovarian hormones to sexual
receptivity in lower mammals it is not surprising to learn
that ovariectomy (removal of the ovaries) promptly and
permanently abolishes all sexual behavior in females of
these species. Ovariectomized rats, rabbits, guinea pigs,
cats, dogs, horses, and cows possess no sexual attraction
for males of their species and never display sexually receptive behavior.

Ovariectomy in the adult chimpanzee eliminates the
usual cycles of sexual responsiveness and drastically re-
duces the frequency of coital contacts. After this operation females have a relatively low stimulative value for
the male and they show little or no desire for intercourse.
They behave, in fact, somewhat like a normal animal
during the periods when she is not physiologically in
estrus. Nevertheless, the ovariectomized chimpanzee may
occasionally permit the male to copulate; this occurs
most often under circumstances in which sexual acquies-
cence affords a means of avoiding physical injury. Evi-

dence of this sort reinforces our conclusion that subhuman primates are not completely dependent upon sex hormones for the ability to mate, although the degree of such dependence is much greater than it is in the human female.

Ovariectomy is not uncommonly performed upon human females, but before discussing the effects of this operation we shall review evidence pertaining to the natural regression of ovarian function which takes place during menopause. In most women menopause occurs during the fifth decade of life. Individual differences are marked, however, and this change may take place at any age from the middle thirties to later than the fiftieth year. Menopause marks the cessation of ovarian function. Discontinuation of the periods of monthly flow is merely the outward sign of a complex series of internal changes. In some individuals the onset of the climacteric is dramatic and sudden, but in many others the process is gradual rather than abrupt. The physiological changes involved are more or less the converse of those that take place during adolescence.

Menstrual cycles tend to become anovulatory (lacking ovulation), and intervals between them grow increasingly longer. Eventually the female reproductive glands cease entirely to produce eggs and to secrete hormones. The disappearance of ovarian secretions is accompanied by a pronounced increase in the pituitary substances that previously stimulated the sex glands. Either the decrease in the estrogenic hormone or the increase in pituitary gonadotrophins, or both, produces in most women in our society one or several of the following symptoms: hot flashes, nervousness, morning insomnia, palpitation, sweating, vertigo, headache, depression, crying spells, irritability, and fatigue.

Some women state that their sexual desire and capacity are as great after menopause as they were during the preceding years, but other individuals just as confidently say that the climacteric marked complete and permanent loss of all erotic responsiveness. We consider it extremely unlikely that these two groups represent physiologically distinct populations. It seems more probable that non-hormonal factors are responsible for the changed sexual status of women who become unresponsive following menopause.

Somewhat more conclusive evidence on this score is found in case histories of women who have passed through surgical menopause—the condition resulting from complete removal of both ovaries. . . .

The careful study by Filler and Drezner indicates that the removal of the ovaries need not depress erotic sensitivity. They examined the effects of ovariectomy in forty women, all under 40 years of age. The characteristic menopausal symptoms appeared in 85 per cent of the cases, but sexual urges were not reduced in a single one of these women. Pratt agrees that ovariectomized women are capable of experiencing normal sexual desire and of participating successfully in coital relations. Mansfeld even states that ovariectomy occasionally is followed by an increase in the desire for and enjoyment of intercourse. We suppose that such positive effects are in part referable to removal of the fear of unwanted pregnancy.

In the face of evidence suggesting retention of full sexual responsiveness after natural and surgical menopause, how is one to account for the frequent claims that removal or regression of the ovaries produces a profound decrease in erotic desire? It is our opinion that the explanation rests upon the effects of suggestion, and that physiological changes consequent to ovarian failure are not primarily involved. Daniels and Tauber describe a female patient who experienced a marked decline in erotic sensitivity following ovariectomy. Psychotherapy sufficed to restore this function, indicating that hormonal changes had not been the sole agent in precipitating the sexual depression. As a matter of fact, the patient stated that after psychiatric treatment intercourse became more

frequent and satisfactory than it had been during the
eight years of marriage preceding the operation.

The major role of nonhormonal factors in controlling
the sexual reactivity of human females is apparent in the
histories of many of Dickinson's patients. One example
will illustrate the point. A young woman, married at 21,
engaged in intercourse with her husband once or twice a
week for five years until the first child was born. During
the first year or two she felt sexual desire but never
reached climax. After five years of marriage her desire
and responsiveness had grown to be as strong as those of
her husband. At this time, however, she discovered that
he was unfaithful, and for two years she refused to have
intercourse. Following this lapse sexual relations were resumed; but although the wife was easily aroused, she was
usually unsatisfied and rarely attained climax. Several
years later, after removal of both of her ovaries, her
capacity for complete response returned. At that time the
habitual pattern of sexual relations included half an hour
of foreplay, and a total of an hour to an hour and a half
of coitus. She usually had five or six orgasms; less than
two left her unsatisfied.

This single case history illustrates several general
points, and although some of them have been mentioned
earlier they are sufficiently important to justify repeated
emphasis. The first is that full sexual responsiveness including regular orgasm may not appear in the physiologically normal woman until she has had a considerable
amount of sexual experience. The second point is that
normal reactivity to erotic stimulation may be lost under
circumstances which have no demonstrable effect upon
reproductive physiology. The emotional trauma resulting
from discovery of her husband's extramarital affairs created a block in this woman's sexual response, with the
result that climax became difficult or impossible to attain
even though her ovaries were secreting normal amounts
of sex hormones. In a very general way it is probably

correct to say that the vast majority of "frigid" or sexually unresponsive women are products of adverse emotional conditioning rather than of an abnormal physiological constitution. Comparable explanations probably apply to the occasional female chimpanzee who never becomes behaviorally receptive although her physiological rhythms are normal.

The third and final point illustrated by the example from Dickinson is that complete and satisfactory sexual relations are possible in the human female despite the total absence of ovarian hormones.

REFERENCES

Daniels, G. E. and Tauber, E. S. "A dynamic approach to the study of replacement therapy in cases of castration." *Am. J. Psychiat.*, Vol. XCVII, 905–918, 1941.

Dickinson, R. L. and Beam, L. *A Thousand Marriages*. Baltimore: The Williams & Wilkins Company, 1931.

Filler, W. and Drezner, N. "Results of surgical castration in women over forty." *Am. J. Obst. & Gynec.*, Vol. XLVII, 122–124, 1944.

Mansfeld, O. P. "Eirstock und Geschlechtrieb," *Arch. f. Gynak.*, Vol. CXVII, 294–310, 1922.

Pratt. J. P. "Sex functions in man." *Sex and Internal Secretions* (ed. Edgar Allen). Baltimore: The Williams & Wilkins Company, 1939.

Yerkes, R. M. and Elder, J. H. "Oestrus, receptivity and mating in the chimpanzee." *Comp. Psychol. Monogr.*, Vol. XIII, 1–39, 1936.

14

Effects of Oral Contraceptives on Affective Fluctuations Associated with the Menstrual Cycle

KAREN E. PAIGE

Periodic fluctuations in women's emotions during the menstrual cycle have been a topic of continuing discussion and research. Numerous clinical reports (1–10) and empirical studies (11–21) show that almost all women experience at least some increase in negative affect during the premenstrual and menstrual phases of the cycle, and a substantial proportion report these shifts as debilitating. Normal emotional behavior usually is resumed after menstrual bleeding stops, and continues until the next premenstrual phase.

The prevailing view among medical researchers is that these cyclic fluctuations in emotion are caused by fluctuations in the activity of female sex hormones (3, 12, 22–24). The emotional stability observed during intramenstrual phases is thought to be maintained by high hormone activity. The onset of depression, irritability and anxiety just before menstruation, and the days of emotional distress that follow are seen as a response to decreased estrogen and progesterone activity. During the cycle, a number of other biochemical changes occur that are frequently cited as intermediary links between fluctuations in female sex hormones and women's emotional

SOURCE: From "Effects of Oral Contraceptives on Affective Fluctuations Associated with the Menstrual Cycle" by Karen E. Paige, Ph.D., in *Psychosomatic Medicine*, 33, no. 6 (November–December, 1971), pp. 515–537. Reprinted by permission of *Psychosomatic Medicine* and the author.

shifts. For example, when estrogen and progesterone are decreasing premenstrually, a substantial increase in monoamine oxidase (MAO) activity is observed in various body tissues (25). Southgate et al (cited by Grant and Pryse-Davies [25]) have noted a tenfold increase in endometrial MAO activity which is believed to reflect similar increases in sensitive brain centers—eg, the hypothalamus. The cyclic pattern of MAO activity is of particular interest since changes in MAO activity are often cited as a direct cause of emotional disorders similar to those experienced by menstruating women (22, 24). Cyclic changes in adrenocorticoid levels (11, 12, 23, 26), nerve excitability (27), and water and electrolyte metabolism (28, 29) have also been observed in women. These changes are often believed to be influenced by fluctuations in estrogen and progesterone and, in turn, they determine cyclic emotional changes.

Although medical researchers acknowledge the importance of considering the effects of social and psychologic factors on women's mood cycles, it is commonly argued that the most fruitful direction of future research in this area is further specification of their biochemical origins (12, 23, 24). However, to date there is no empirical evidence to justify the assumption that the specific affective changes experienced during the menstrual cycle occur in direct response to specific biochemical changes. In fact, the whole question of physiologic distinctions among the various human emotional experiences must still be considered an open question. Correlational data, after all, do not demonstrate causality.

It must also be recognized that menstruation is a social, as well as physiologic, event. The menstrual process, and particularly menstrual bleeding, is surrounded by superstition and taboo, and plays a central role in women's psychosexual development. Menstrual blood is universally abhorred, and its monthly flow has a significant impact on women's social and personal life. In nearly all societies, taboos exist to restrict the activities of

menstruating women. These taboos range in severity
from the banishment of women to menstrual huts to informal prohibitions against sex relations (30–35). In our
own society, the menstrual sex taboo is commonly observed (36, 37), and women always take great care to
avoid any sign of menstrual blood. Menstruation is only
discussed in private, if at all, and is viewed as unsanitary,
inconvenient and embarrassing. The profound anxiety
which menstrual bleeding causes in both men and women
is well documented in folklore, literature and numerous
psychoanalytic protocols. Deutsch (6) and Benedek (3)
argue that menstrual blood may offer reassurance of
woman's reproductive capacity and femininity, but it also
symbolizes sin, baseness, uncleanliness and woman's inferior social status.

It is equally plausible to suggest, then, that the cyclic
shift in negative affect which coincides with the onset of
menstrual bleeding may be determined by external factors. Menstruation-related depression, anger, irritability
and anxiety could be socially mediated emotional responses to a woman's own bodily functions rather than a
direct consequence of physiologic changes. If this were
the case, then the biochemical events associated with
periodic emotional distress would represent a spurious
correlation between the time of menstruation and the
affective response to menstrual blood.

Currently, an excellent opportunity exists to study systematically the possible causes of affective fluctuations in
the menstrual cycle. Millions of women are using oral
contraceptives for the purpose of preventing ovulation.
One of the major consequences of using the drug is the
elimination of many of those biochemical fluctuations
usually cited as determinants of women's shifts in mood.
During the use of oral contraceptives, fixed quantities of
synthetic estrogen and progestin are administered daily
for 20 or 21 days thus inhibiting secretion of natural
estrogen and progesterone by the ovaries. The *combination* oral contraceptive brands artificially maintain high

circulating levels of both hormones by including both
progestin and estrogen in each tablet. During the use of
the *sequential* brands, estrogen is taken alone for the first
15 or 16 days of the tablet cycle. A progestin is combined with estrogen only during the last 5 tablet days.
There is some speculation that administration of these
oral contraceptives alters the cyclic pattern of adrenocorticoid secretion and normal brain wave patterns (38),
although the evidence is not yet conclusive.

There is good evidence, however, that the use of oral
contraceptives eliminates the normal premenstrual increase in endometrial MAO activity (25). Grant and
Pryse-Davies performed endometrial biopsies on women
who were using either the combination or sequential
brands and found that MAO activity remained relatively
stable during the cycle. These researchers believe that
this pattern reflects a similar pattern of MAO activity in
the brain, and is the result of administering large doses of
progestin. They also found significant differences in the
overall magnitude of endometrial MAO activity between
combination and sequential brand users. Throughout the
cycle, endometrial MAO activity was greater among
combination users than among sequential users. . . .
Women using combination brands reported a greater incidence of general negative affect during the cycle than
women using sequential brands.

Another important consequence of using oral contraceptives is a substantial reduction in menstrual flow. The
likelihood that menstrual flow will be reduced, however,
depends largely on the type of oral contraceptive used.
There is substantial evidence to suggest that only combination brands have a significant effect on menstrual flow.
Most women using sequential brands report no change in
the volume of flow, and some even report an increase
(39–43). In contrast, the majority of women using combination brands report a substantial reduction in flow
(40, 41, 44)....

Each of the physiologic changes described could influence the typical pattern of fluctuations in negative affect during the menstrual cycle, and each is related somewhat differently to social versus biochemical determinants of these affective shifts. The differential effects of oral contraceptives on cyclic variability in the levels of female sex hormones, cyclic pattern of endometrial MAO activity, and volume of menstrual flow lead to a number of testable hypotheses about the origins of menstruation-related negative affect.

In the present study, the pattern of negative affect during the menstrual cycle was measured among women with natural cycles and among those using various oral contraceptives. Negative affect patterns were then compared between (a) combination brand users and women with natural cycles, (b) women experiencing different intensities of menstrual flow, and (c) women using different brands of oral contraceptives which are expected to have different effects on MAO activity. . . .

*   *   *

DISCUSSION

The results of this study indicate that fluctuations in negative affect commonly experienced during the menstrual cycle do not occur among women using combination oral contraceptives. Self-selection factors, the effects of oral contraceptives on menstrual discomfort, and women's expectations about the effects of the drug on menstrual distress did not account for this finding.

Further analysis demonstrated, however, that the absence of anxiety (but not hostility) fluctuations among those in the Combination group can be attributed largely to the effects of the drug on menstrual flow. When women most likely to experience reduced flow were compared to those most likely to experience normally heavy flow, *only* those with reduced flow show no increase in menstrual phase anxiety. Women using oral contraceptives who most likely experience normally heavy flow show the same increase in menstrual anxiety observed in women with natural menstrual cycles.

One might argue that physiologic changes coinciding with menstrual bleeding explain the results, rather than flow intensity. First, the low dosage of progestin used by women most likely to have reduced flow may have caused the lower anxiety levels. Second, women with reduced flow may experience less physical discomfort while bleeding, and consequently express less anxiety.

With respect to the dosage argument, although reduced flow is associated with the use of low progestin brands, there is no reason whatsoever to believe that progestin activity should affect anxiety level at only one phase of the cycle. Progestin activity, after all, is continuously active throughout the tablet cycle. If the use of progestin has some yet unspecified direct influence on the magnitude of anxiety, then one should reasonably expect the effect to be observed throughout the cycle rather than just at menstruation. The differences in anxiety patterns by dosage level clearly indicate that this is not the case. Only at menstruation is there a significant difference in anxiety means by dosage group. At each of the remaining 3 cycle days, there are no differences in mean anxiety scores between the 2 dosage groups. When flow intensity was estimated on the basis of self-report data, women with reduced flow showed lower anxiety not only at menstruation but throughout the cycle. However, a large proportion of these women were using the higher dosage brands as well as the 1-mg brands. Dosage level alone, then, cannot account for this result.

The second argument that may be raised suggests that women with reduced flow may experience less physical discomfort during the menses, and consequently experience less anxiety. Analysis of the relationship between complaints of physical symptoms and flow intensity, however, show that symptom complaints were not significantly less frequent among women with reduced flow than among women with normal flow.

The empirical relationship between the intensity of menstrual flow and the magnitude of menstrual anxiety thus raises the possibility that emotional disturbances most often associated with menstruation are a socially mediated response to a woman's own bodily functions. The woman perceives the bleeding, must take sanitary precautions, and becomes anxious in social situations because of possible embarrassment. This is, of course, a hypothesis which is contrary to most medical opinion on the causes of menstrual distress. Nevertheless, the results of this study suggest that it may in fact be true, particularly for menstrual anxiety.

Further analysis provided a number of reasons to suggest that menstrual distress is related to the intensity of menstrual flow. First, sexual abstinence during menstruation was shown to be significantly related to flow intensity. Women experiencing normally heavy flow, whether or not they used oral contraceptives, were almost twice as likely to abstain than women experiencing a reduced flow. Further examination also showed that sexual abstinence could not be accounted for by the degree of physical discomfort at menstruation: Women who did *not* abstain were just as likely to report menstrual physical discomfort as did those who abstained. Reduced menstrual flow, then, is associated with lower anxiety *and* ignoring the menstrual sex taboo. As noted earlier, menstruating women are specifically forbidden to engage in sexual relations in nearly all societies. Stephens (33) and Young and Bacdayan (35) have shown that cultural variation in the severity of menstrual restriction is related to specific aspects of the social structure and socialization process, such as indices of male sexual anxiety and castration fears, social rigidity and male solidarity. In our own society, the menstrual sex taboo is still commonly observed, despite the fact that medical evidence shows that it is neither physically harmful nor unsanitary.

It should also be mentioned that the data showed an association between women's emotional reaction to menarche and adherence to the menstrual sex taboo. In this sample, 70% of the women with negative reactions to menarche adhere to the sex taboo as compared with only 40% of the women with positive reactions, and 54% of those with no emotional reaction. Since reactions to menarche were based on recall data, these findings cannot be taken as evidence of actual menarche experience. Instead, they may be another index of women's subjective feelings about how one should react to the menstrual process.

While the social explanation seems reasonable for menstrual anxiety, replication of the Grant and Pryse-Davies results regarding group differences in hostility (depression, anger and irritability) suggests that one aspect of the menstrual cycle mood fluctuations may be biochemically determined. As discussed earlier, Grant and Pryse-Davies found that the magnitude of depression, anger and irritability during the cycle was directly related to the magnitude of MAO activity in endometrial tissue. These researchers believe that endometrial MAO activity reflects similar changes in MAO in sensitive brain centers, and that such biochemical changes determine emotional behavior. At present, of course, one can only state that the activity of MAO as well as that of other biochemical agents (eg, adrenocorticoids) is *correlated* with observed emotional changes. The direction of causality is still unclear. Indeed, there is abundant evidence to suggest that biochemical changes occur in *response* to socially mediated emotional changes as shown by the work on biochemical reactions to stress and other psychologic states (24, 45). Nevertheless, the kinds of affects measured by the Hostility scale are those which Grant and Pryse-Davies found to be associated with changes in endometrial MAO activity. In this study, premenstrual increase in Hostility produced by the Normal group was not observed for either the Combination or Sequential group. Also, the general level of Hostility was significantly lower for the Sequential than for the Combination group, as predicted.

SUMMARY

This study attempted to determine possible causes of menstruation-related affective fluctuations by comparing the patterns of negative affect in women with natural cycles and in those who use oral contraceptives. Negative affect was measured at four different phases of the menstrual cycle by an instrument that is not distorted by self-report or social expectations about menstruation. All hypotheses tested in the study made predictions about the relationship between the magnitude of negative affect (anxiety and hostility) among oral contraceptive users and menstrual cycle phase. Women with natural cycles were used as a control group, since cyclic mood patterns during the natural cycle have already been established.

The first hypothesis, which predicted that cyclic affective changes should be eliminated for combination oral contraceptive users, was supported. One hundred percent of the variability in Total Negative Affect scores accounted for by the cycle day was eliminated for the Combination group. . . .

The question of spuriousness was considered by examining factors that may determine the results other than oral contraceptive use. It was shown that group differences in negative affect patterns could not be determined by self-selection, prior expectations or differences in physical discomfort.

Two additional hypotheses were tested in order to examine possible mechanisms by which oral contraceptives eliminate mood fluctuations. One hypothesis proposed that oral contraceptives reduced menstruation-related negative affect by reducing the intensity of menstrual flow. This hypothesis was supported for Anxiety, which suggests that menstrual anxiety is a socially mediated response to menstrual bleeding.

A third hypothesis proposed that oral contraceptive use eliminated mood fluctuations by eliminating cyclic shifts in endometrial MAO activity, as argued by previous researchers. Examination of group differences in Hostility patterns replicated the findings of Grant and Pryse-Davies about the relationship between endometrial MAO activity and negative affect in women.

REFERENCES

1. Abraham, K. Manifestations of the female castration complex, Selected Papers on Psychoanalysis. Edited by K. Abraham. London: Hogarth, 1948, pp. 338–369.
2. Balint, M. A contribution to the psychology of menstruation. *Psychoanal. Quart.* 6:346–352, 1937.
3. Benedek, T. Sexual function in women and their disturbance, American Handbook of Psychiatry. Vol. I. Edited by S. Arieti. New York: Basic Books, 1959.
4. Benedek, T., and Rubenstein, B. The sexual cycle in women: the relation between ovarian function and psychodynamic processes. *Psychosom. Med.* 1:246–270, 1939.
5. Chadwick, M. The psychological effects of menstruation. Nervous and Mental Diseases Monograph Series 56: 1952.
6. Deutsch, H. Psychology of Women. Vol. I. New York: Grune & Stratton, 1944.
7. McCance, R. A., Luff, M., and Widdowson, E. Physical and emotional periodicity in women. *J. Hyg.* 37:571–611, 1957.
8. Rose, R. A. Menstrual pain and personal adjustment. *J. Personality* 17:287–307, 1949.
9. Shainess, N. A re-evaluation of some aspects of femininity through a study of menstruation: a preliminary report. *Comp. Pychiat.* 2:20–26, 1961.
10. Silbermann, I. A contribution to the psychology of menstruation. *Int. J. Psychoanal.* 6:346–352, 1937.

11. Coppen, A., and Kessal, N. Menstruation and personality. *Brit. J. Psychiat.* 109:711–721, 1963.
12. Dalton, K. The Premenstrual Syndrome. Springfield, Ill.: Charles C Thomas, 1964.
13. Fluhmann, C. F. Management of Menstrual Disorders. Philadelphia: W. B. Saunders, 1956.
14. Garron, D., and Shekelle, R. Mood, personality, and the menstrual cycle. Unpublished data, 1969.
15. Gottschalk, L., Kaplan, S., Gleser, G., et al. Variations in magnitude of emotion: a method applied to anxiety and hostility during phases of the menstrual cycle. *Psychosom. Med.* 24:300–311, 1962.
16. Ivey, M., and Bardwick, J. Patterns of affective fluctuations in the menstrual cycle. *Psychosom. Med.* 30:336–345, 1968.
17. Levitt, E., and Lubin, B. Some personality factors associated with menstrual complaints and menstrual attitudes. *J. Psychosom. Res.* 11:267–270, 1967.
18. Moos, R. The development of a menstrual distress questionnaire. *Psychosom. Med.* 30:853–867, 1968.
19. Moos, R., Kopell, B., Melges, F., et al. Fluctuations on symptoms and moods during the menstrual cycle. *J. Psychosom. Med.* 13:37–44, 1969.
20. Paulson, M. J. Psychological Concomitants of Premenstrual Tension. Unpublished dissertation, University of Kansas, 1956.
21. Sutherland, H., and Stewart, I. A critical analysis of the premenstrual syndrome. *Lancet* 1:1180–1183, 1965.
22. Coppen, A. The biochemistry of affective disorders. *Brit. J. Psychiat.* 113:1237–1264, 1967.
23. Janowsky, D., Gorney, R., and Kelly, B. 'The curse': vicissitudes and variation of the female fertility cycle; Part I: psychiatric aspects. *Psychosomatics* 7:242–246, 1966.
24. U.S. Department of Health, Education, and Welfare, National Institute of Mental Health, Mental Health Reports-3. Public Health Service Publication No. 1876, Washington, D.C., Government Printing Office, 1969.
25. Grant, C., and Pryse-Davies, J. Effects of oral contraceptives on depressive mood changes and on endometrial monoamine oxidase and phosphates. *Brit. Med. J.* 28:777–780, 1968.

26. Rees, L. The premenstrual tension syndrome and its treatment. *Brit. Med. J.* 1:1014–1016, 1953.
27. DeCara, E. EEG studies of the bioelectrical activity of the brain during the menstrual cycle. *Acta Neurol.* 13:617–637, 1958.
28. Eichner, E., and Watner, C. Pre-menstrual tension. *Med. Times* 83:771–778, 1955.
29. Ferguson, J., and Vermillion, M. Premenstrual tension. *Amer. J. Obstet. Gynec.* 9:615–619, 1957.
30. Bettelheim, B. Symbolic Wounds. Glencoe: Free Press, 1954.
31. Ford, C., and Beach, F. Patterns of Sexual Behavior. New York: Harper & Row, Ace Books, 1951.
32. Hays, H. The Dangerous Sex. New York: G. P. Putnam's Sons, 1964.
33. Stephens, W. A cross-cultural study of menstrual taboos. *Genetic Psychology Monographs* 64:385–416, 1961.
34. Webster, H. Taboo—A Sociological Study. Stanford: Stanford University Press, 1942.
35. Young, F., and Bacdayan, A. Menstrual taboos and social rigidity. *Ethnography* 4:225–240, 1965.
36. Paige, K. Unpublished data.
37. Tietze, C. Forward. *Int. J. Fertil. Steril.* 12:65, 1967.
38. Scott, J. Personal communication.
39. Balin, H., and Wan, L. Chlormadinone, a potent synthetic oral progestin: evaluation of 1002 cycles. *Int. J. Fertil.* 10:127–131, 1965.
40. Drill, V. A. Oral Contraceptives. New York: McGraw-Hill, 1966.
41. Goldzieher, J., and Rice-Wray, E. Oral Contraceptives. Springfield, Ill.: Charles C Thomas, 1966.
42. Mears, E. Clinical experience in the use of oral contraceptives. *Proc. Roy. Soc. Med.* 57:204–207, 1964.
43. Palma, E., and Onetto, E. Our experience with a combination of estrogen-progestin in birth control. *Dec. Congr. Chileno. Obstet. Gynocol.* 2:615–617, 1963.
44. Pincus, G., et al. Effectiveness of an oral contraceptive. *Science* 130:81–85, 1959.
45. Mason, J. Organization of Psychoendocrine Mechanisms. Psychosomatic Medicine. Vol. 30. No. 5, Part II, 1968.

15

A Re-evaluation of Some Aspects of Femininity through a Study of Menstruation: A Preliminary Report

NATALIE SHAINESS

* * *

The onset of menstruation focuses on attitudes relating to
feminine sexuality. It is the start of the reproductive function, but also contains a summation of all the feminine
feelings and attitudes to that point. It is something experienced by every girl at approximately the same age, and
memories relating to this experience frequently contain a
few drops of the distillate of the mother-daughter relationship. I will give a brief example from the analysis of
a 40-year-old woman: As an 11-year-old girl who had had
no preparation for her menses, she awoke early one
morning feeling wet. She threw off her bed clothes and on
observing blood ran in panic to her mother's room. Her
mother seemed annoyed at being awakened, slapped her
face, then explained that the blood was her "period,"
which had really started too soon, and added, as an after-
thought, that it was a natural occurrence. She was told
what to do for herself hygienically, advised to take to her
bed for the day, but given no other information. At 14
she had the following experience: She had been the favorite grandchild of her maternal grandfather, an orthodox
Jew. Upon his death, she was denied admission to the

SOURCE: From "A Re-evaluation of Some Aspects of Femininity
through a Study of Menstruation" by Natalie Shainess, M.D., in
Science and Psychoanalysis, Vol. V, edited by Jules H. Masserman, M.D., pp. 278–285. Reprinted by permission of Grune &
Stratton, Inc. and the editor.

cemetery to participate in the burial ceremony. She was told that a menstruating woman is unclean and cannot set foot on holy ground. Thus, not only was she cut off from her grandfather by death, but from the last meaningful experience in relation to him and a structured occasion to work out her grief. She developed a deep feeling of resentment about being a girl. It seemed to her that people viewed a girl as a sickly, inferior creature, and her function of menstruation as something undesirable and abasing. Here we can see directly the cultural aspect of her self-devaluation as a woman, and the role of her mother and social group in contributing, in these instances, to its development.

It was with a view to focusing directly on this area of a girl's developing sexuality and the mother-daughter relationship, that the following study relating to menstruation was undertaken. There have been previous studies of menstruation, notable among which is Therese Benedek's *Psychosexual Functions in Women*.[1] However, her study, which correlated dreams and free associations with the cytologic state of the vaginal mucosa, was undertaken with a classic frame of reference and made the basic assumption that the mental products observed are a direct function of the endocrinological state at any given time during the monthly cycle. This provides a bio-instinctual base to all feminine ideation. It does not take into account the total ego structure, how it evolved or the effect of current experience and interaction.

In my study of 103 women, most of them married and of relatively high economic and educational level, a questionnaire was devised and submitted to five different groups, my patients constituting one group. The questionnaire elicited brief background data, and a detailed menstrual history, including anticipation of menstruation, circumstances of its discovery, responses to this discovery by both mother and daughter, and finally a detailed current menstrual history with emphasis on premenstrual tension, dysmenorrhea and amenorrhea. Although details of the study and interpretation of responses will be presented elsewhere, the results are relevant to a review of psychoanalytic thinking about the female castration complex. They also show an interesting correlation between the experience of menarche and subsequent menstrual events and attitudes.

Twenty-one per cent of the women had no advance preparation whatever for the onset of menstruation. It was from this group that several reported a fantasy of being damaged or cut. One might ask whether this is classic evidence of biologic defect, or, as Freud also suggested, anxiety over infantile masturbation; or rather, could it be a rational fear in which the lack of special knowledge permits resort only to the usual context in which blood is seen—that is, the result of some injury. Symbolically, one could formulate it as a castration by the mother—the result of her omission of information. At the opposite pole was the experience of 10 per cent of the girls of an active castrating gesture by the mother, in being slapped on the cheek without explanation—a traditional response among certain groups for which many rationalizations are offered. Three fourths of the group that had some advance knowledge, anticipated menstruation with anxiety, fear and dread. The first impulse of most girls was to find and tell their mothers, but 11 were careful to keep this occurrence a secret. A striking fact became apparent in evaluating the maternal responses to this event. *Only 15 per cent of all the mothers reacted with pleasure to this sign of maturation in their daughters.* Sixty per cent showed responses that were negative and damaging, and 10 were extremely destructive.

Of the total group, only 13 percent of the women were consistently free of symptoms of premenstrual tension. These were the same whose mothers had adequately prepared them for menstruation, and received the news of its occurrence with pleasure. This freedom from symptoms

suggests acceptance of their femininity. The remaining 87
per cent experienced symptoms of premenstrual tension,
and 15 of these suffered severe, disabling tension.

Goldfarb, a gynecologist, reported in 1958 that premenstrual tension is not well understood.[2] Medical
treatment involved the use of estrogen and diuretics, anti-
spasmodics and analgesics. Notable in his paper was the
implication, though not so categorized by him, that while
the symptoms referable to the emotional state *did* at
times improve under treatment, the physical signs of
water retention and endocrine change did not improve,
even though treatment for these conditions was presumably specific. In my study, breast engorgement, though
reported, was rarely troublesome. Other premenstrual
symptoms could be placed in two categories: (1) Hunger
and desire for sweets, wish to call mother, anxiety, depression, insomnia—all represent a yearning for love and
state of helpless defenselessness. (2) Irritability, quarrel-
someness, headache, nausea and vomiting and related
symptoms suggest an angry defensive reaction to anticipation of attack and feelings of vulnerability. Although
the second group may involve a higher order of adaptive
potential, both can be considered signs of impoverishment
of the ego, particularly relating to feminine self-acceptance
and, in the patient control group, were specifically related
to the concept of self as sexually undesirable. This
suggests that at a time when the body physiologically
recapitulates the experience of menarche, there is a compulsive repetition of the emotional climate of the experience, especially in relation to the mother—and there exist
intensified feelings relating to the self, particularly regarding femininity.

Dysmenorrhea—a symptom occurring only once in the
total group at onset of menstruation—is a more difficult
symptom to evaluate because of the large physical component. But where certain criteria suggested it was predominantly psychogenic, it seemed to be a somatization
of anxiety in women with hypochondriacal tendencies.

Patients suffering dysmenorrhea had had frightening introductions to the menarche, and had been led to expect it to be painful. Their attitudes in regard to femininity were characteristic of those traditionally considered masochistic and passive. Thirty per cent of the total experienced amenorrhea of varying lengths, at one time or another. Many recalled a precipitating event with intensive affective response; many related extreme changes in weight to this occurrence, difficulties with their mothers, or sense of guilt about some sexual experience.

The onset of menstruation heralds the possibility of motherhood, which, like all creative experiences, is inextricably linked with vulnerability. It is not surprising, therefore, if a certain amount of anxiety inevitably accompanies the menarche. Yet the degree of anxiety, the extent of its perpetuation, and the quality of the new awareness of self as a woman, depends in large part on the nature of the mother-daughter relationship.

SUMMARY

. . . 2. Some results of a pilot study of 103 women were presented, indicating that: (a) premenstrual symtoms fall into two main reactions—of helplessness and need for love, or defensiveness against anticipated attack; and are a constant compulsive recapitulation of devaluation of the self in relation to femininity and that (b) symptoms of premenstrual tension, and to some extent dysmenorrhea and amenorrhea, are directly related to unpleasant, humiliating, or unloving experiences in relation to the mother.

3. As part of a sequence of experiences influencing the development and awareness of the self, the onset of menstruation is a nodal area of high potential for enhancement or impairment of the self, especially in relation to femininity.

REFERENCES

1. Benedek, T. Psychosexual Functions in Women. New York: Ronald Press, 1952.
2. Goldfarb, A. Multiphasic management of premenstrual tension. *N.Y. St. J. Med.* 58:3647, 1958.

16

Sex after Forty—And after Seventy

ISADORE RUBIN

SMASHING A DANGEROUS
STEREOTYPE

One of the major contributions of Dr. William H. Masters and Mrs. Virginia E. Johnson has been their detailed laboratory study of the sexual responses of older persons. Their work helps fill the gaps in medical knowledge and clinical experience. It helps break the conspiracy of silence about sexuality in the later years. And it helps destroy the stereotype of "sexless old age," which has done such serious harm to the health and happiness of the aging. Masters and Johnson, it is true, did find important physiological changes in sex response occurring as the years go by. But their major conclusions are unequivocal: "There is no time limit drawn by the advancing years to female sexuality"; and for the male, too, there is, under favorable physical and emotional conditions, "a capacity for sexual performance that frequently may extend beyond the eighty-year age level."

These conclusions are supported by the findings of a growing body of research by other investigators.

In the past, the failure of society to recognize the sexual needs of older people was serious, but not critical. Today, when more than twenty-five million of our population have reached the age of sixty—a figure that is expected to mount to over thirty-one million by 1975—

SOURCE: From *An Analysis of Human Sexual Response*, edited by Ruth and Edward Brecher. Copyright © 1966 by Ruth and Edward Brecher. Reprinted by arrangement with The New American Library, Inc., New York, New York.

society can hardly afford to maintain the false myths about sexlessness in these years. In the early 1960's, over thirty-five thousand marriages a year took place in which at least one of the partners was sixty-five or older.

These myths are not limited to the years after sixty, although they take much greater hold in these years. For women who are not emotionally prepared for it, the end of menstruation may be a traumatic event. For many of them menstruation has been a badge of femininity and a symbol of youth. As long as it continues they may feel they are still young and attractive in spite of the changes that have taken place over the years. When menstruation ends, writes gynecologist Howard A. Novell, "a woman suddenly has the mirror of life thrust at her and she takes a long, agonizing look and begins a period of marked introspection and usually faulty reappraisal of herself." It is at this vulnerable time in her life that all the folklore related to the menopause comes to bear on some women with great force. One idea is that after the change of life a woman loses her sexual desire and is less capable of functioning sexually than before. This myth, of course, has no anatomical or physiological basis.

Every counselor who deals in any way with sex problems can report many cases of marriages that were brought to the point of disaster because one partner had suddenly decided that the couple was "too old for sex." "I am fifty-eight years old and my wife is fifty-five," wrote one husband to the physician conducting the question and answer column of *Sexology* magazine. "Until about three years ago our sexual life was quite normal, but since that time (contrary to my desires) my wife has not permitted intercourse. Her apathy is even greater since her change of life a year and a half ago. She says I am too old to be so 'foolish' concerning sexual relations and that nobody at this age has sexual desires." "My wife and I are over sixty-five years old but we still like to have sexual intercourse very much," another husband wrote. "Please give us advice in this case. What should we do?"

These examples indicate how older people—unsure about their roles in a new stage of life for which they have been little prepared—reflect the popular ignorance about sexuality. Such attitudes require the authority of the physician to correct them and to dispel the guilt that older couples may have about sexual needs and desires. All too often in the past, however, the physician has had the same ignorance about sex in the later years and has reflected the same guilt feelings about sex. In too many cases an older patient who has sought advice from a physician about waning sex ability and responsiveness is greeted merely with evasive laughter—or with the question, "What do you expect at your age?"

If these attitudes affected only the sex life of older persons, they would still be serious enough. However, they go far beyond this to strike at the whole self-image of the older man and woman, complicating and distorting all their interpersonal reactions in marriage. They have serious effects on the diagnosis of many medical and psychological problems and upon the administration of justice to older persons accused of sex offenses. Not least of all, they have unfortunate effects on the relationships of children and parents thinking of remarriage; the reaction of too many children is, "They ought to know better."

Today, with the benefit of the Masters-Johnson research—added to the surveys of behavior in the later years by the Kinsey investigators, by Drs. Gustave Newman and Claude R. Nichols at Duke University, by urologists at the University of California School of Medicine at San Francisco, by Dr. Joseph T. Freeman in Philadelphia, by *Sexology* magazine, and others—there is no longer any reason for anyone to continue to believe that sex, love, and marriage are the exclusive privileges of youth. The research has clearly established that—under the proper physical and emotional conditions—the capacity to enjoy sex is not lost in the later years but simply slows down gradually, along with other physical capacities.

THE RESEARCH EVIDENCE

A number of other investigators have surveyed the
sexual behavior of older persons. Masters and Johnson
were the first actually to observe the anatomy and physiology of their sexual response under laboratory conditions. Included in this part of the study were sixty-one
menopausal and postmenopausal women (ages forty to
seventy-eight) and thirty-nine men (ages fifty-one to
eighty-nine). Obviously, these numbers were not large
enough to provide biological data of statistical significance and further studies will be required, but they furnished important preliminary information.

When the orgasmic cycles of the women of this group
were studied, Masters and Johnson found that generally
the intensity of physiologic reaction, and the rapidity and
duration of anatomic response to sexual stimulation were
reduced with advancing years through all phases of the
sexual cycle. That is, the sex flush was more limited and
restricted in the older women, there was less lubrication,
there was delay in reaction of the clitoris to direct stimulation, reduction of duration in orgasm time, etc. However, they emphasized, they did find "significant sexual
capacity and effective sexual performance" in these older
women. "The aging human female," they concluded, "is
fully capable of sexual performance at orgasmic response
levels, particularly if she is exposed to regularity of effective sexual stimulation." They added that there seems to
be no physiologic reason why the frequency of sexual
expression found satisfactory for the younger woman
should not be carried over into the years after the menopause, with no time limit drawn by the advancing years.

As in the female, Masters and Johnson found that in
men after fifty the intensity and duration of physical responses during the orgasmic cycle are lessened; particularly after sixty, erection takes much longer, ejaculation
lacks the same force and duration, the sex flush is markedly reduced, etc. "There is no question," they state,

"that the human male's sexual responsiveness wanes as he ages." However, they add, when regularity of sexual expression is maintained in a sexually stimulative climate within the marriage, a healthy male's capacity for sexual expression could extend beyond the seventies and the eighty-year age level.

Masters and Johnson's findings that sexual activity continues—though on a reduced scale—into advanced old age in many persons is well substantiated by other research, as is their finding that there is no basis for any physiological effect of menopause on frequency of intercourse for women.

In the Kinsey studies the investigators also found little evidence of any aging in the sexual capacities of women. "Over the years," they reported, "most females become less inhibited and develop an interest in sexual relations which they may then maintain until they are in their fifties or even sixties." In their later years, sexual activity of course depends to a large extent on the desires and capacities of their husbands, who would generally average three or four years older. The responses of the average husband, in contrast to the average wife, drop with age. Thus, many of the younger women reported that they did not wish to have intercourse as often as their husbands, but in the later years of marriage, many of the women expressed the desire to have intercourse more often than their husbands.

As far as males were concerned, the Kinsey investigators did find evidence of a weakening of sexual response with age. Morning erections, for example, which had averaged 4.9 per week in the early years, had dropped to an average of 1.8 at sixty-five and to 0.9 per week at age seventy-five. However, for most males they found that there was no point at which old age suddenly enters the picture. One white male was still averaging seven ejaculations each week at the age of seventy, and an eighty-eight-year-old man and his ninety-year-old wife still continued their sexual life.

In 1959 a group of urologists at the University of California Medical Center at San Francisco reported on their study of 101 men who had come as patients to their outpatient clinics. There was a general decline with age, but sixty-five percent of the men under seventy were still capable of sexual relations. Of the males over seventy, one third of the number were still potent.

In 1960 a report was made by Drs. Gustave Newman and Claude R. Nichols of an investigation into the sexual activity of 250 persons living in the Piedmont area of North Carolina, ranging in age from sixty to ninety-three years of age. They found, out of the 149 persons still married and living with their husbands or wives, that more than half were still sexually active (54 percent). They concluded that "given the conditions of reasonably good health and partners who are physically healthy, elderly persons continue to be sexually active into their seventh, eighth and ninth decades."

This same general finding was reported by Dr. Joseph T. Freeman, who among other things found that by the age of eighty a number of men studied still reported no cessation of desire and some were still potent. Drs. L. M. Bowers, R. R. Cross, Jr. and F. A. Lloyd, who studied veterans applying for a pension, reached the same conclusion.

One of the largest surveys was conducted by *Sexology* magazine, which mailed questionnaires to men over sixty-five who had attained enough eminence in various fields to be listed in *Who's Who in America*. More than eight hundred men answered the series of questions. Of the married men who still had partners, over 70 percent indicated that they still engaged with some regularity in sexual intercourse, most with general satisfaction. Even in the group of 104 men aged seventy-five to ninety-two, almost one-half reported that intercourse was still satisfactory, and six engaged in coitus on the average of about eight times a month.

One interesting survey on the attitudes of women toward the menopause was conducted by Dr. Bernice L. Neugarten and her colleagues of the Committee on Human Development at the University of Chicago. They found that among the women who had not yet gone through the menopause there was a great deal of uncertainty about how the menopause would affect their sex lives, with the youngest group disagreeing most with the view that menopausal women may experience an upsurge of sexual impulse. "I was afraid we couldn't have sexual relations after the menopause," said one woman, "and my husband thought so, too." However, in the group of women who were between the ages of fifty-five and sixty-five, 21 percent of them felt that "after the menopause, a woman is more interested in sex than before."

It should be noted that none of these studies involved a sufficiently large or sufficiently representative group of men or women for the figures to be typical of the average older man or woman. However, all of them do confirm the Masters and Johnson findings that there is no particular stage of life or age that represents a cut-off point for sexual desire, response or ability, even though age does reduce the strength of sexual response.

THE IMPORTANCE OF REGULARITY

One of the points that Masters and Johnson keep emphasizing in their discussion of the factors necessary for maintaining sexual capacity and effective sexual performance is regularity of sexual performance. This, they say, is essential for both males and females.

As a result of lowered hormone production in the female in the later years, thinning of the vaginal walls and reduced lubrication make intercourse uncomfortable and even painful. However, three women past sixty years of age were repeatedly observed to expand and lubricate the vagina effectively despite obvious senile thinning of the vaginal walls and shrinking of the major labia. These

women had maintained regular intercourse once or twice
a week for their entire adult lives. On the other hand,
women, five to ten years after the end of menstruation,
who had intercourse infrequently (once a month or less)
and who did not masturbate with regularity had difficulty
in accommodating the penis during their rare exposures
to intercourse.

Regularity of sexual expression is also the key to sexual responsiveness for the aging male, say Masters and
Johnson. With loss of sexual outlet, many aging males
report rapid loss of sexual tension and potency. Regularity is important, apparently, not only in the later years
but in the earlier years as well.

"The most important factor in the maintenance of
effective sexuality for the aging male is consistency of
active sexual expression," Masters and Johnson assert.
"When the male is stimulated to high sexual output during his formative years and a similar tenor of activity is
established for the 31–40-year range, his middle-aged
and involutional years usually are marked by constantly
recurring physiologic evidence of maintained sexuality.
Certainly it is true for the male geriatric sample that
those men currently interested in relatively high levels of
sexual expression report similar activity levels from their
formative years. It does not appear to matter what manner of sexual expression has been employed, as long as
high levels of activity were maintained."

This finding, which indicates that there is a close correlation between activity levels in the earlier years and
those in the later years, is supported by the findings of the
Kinsey research. It does not, of course, prove a cause-and-
effect relationship, since it may merely indicate that those
with the strongest sex drives had greater sex activity both
in the early and later years. But it does effectively de-
molish one of the great myths about sexual activity that
has persisted from ancient days down to the very present
—the idea that one can use oneself up sexually and that
it is necessary to save oneself for the later years. This

myth is connected with the belief that the emission of semen through any kind of sexual activity weakens and debilitates. Many people still believe that each drop of semen emitted in ejaculation is equivalent to the loss of forty drops of blood. Such beliefs are hard to overcome since they go back thousands of years to ancient Chinese, Greek, and Hindu views.

"My husband," writes a woman to a doctor, "has reached the age of sixty-five. He had decided that, in order to ensure a longer life and health, he will no longer engage in sex activity. He is convinced that intercourse and the emission of semen are quite debilitating, particularly in his years." The feeling of this man is not unusual. Dr. Morton M. Golden reported that many of his patients had the distorted notion that males have a limited number of sperm and were convinced that masturbation had used up their supply of sperm cells and energy. "I have seen patients," he wrote, "who deliberately began a program of abstinence in the fourth decade to postpone the inevitable 'catastrophe of old age.' "

Actually, it is well recognized today that the emission of semen is no more of a loss than the expectoration of saliva. Both are quickly replaced by the body.

The notion that one can prolong sex life by being inactive in the earlier years and less active in the older years is particularly contradicted by the findings of the Kinsey group. They found that at age fifty all of the males who had been sexually active in their early adolescence were still sexually capable, with a frequency about 20 percent higher than the males who had begun activity later. "Nearly forty years of maximum activity," they say, "have not yet worn them out physically, physiologically, or psychologically. On the other hand, some of the males (not many), who were late adolescent and who have had five years less of sexual activity, are beginning to drop completely out of the picture; and the rates of this group are definitely lower in these older age periods."

There is no question that other leading sexologists

agree with Masters and Johnson on the importance of
regularity and consistency in maintaining effective sexual
functioning. Professor Tadeusz Bilikiewicz of the Medical Academy of Gdansk, Poland, points out that "the
most effective way to secure the longest possible functioning of organs is by letting them work continuously and
systematically." Hence, far from advising abstinence for
those who wish to preserve sexual life, he concludes that
the best advice that specialists in aging can give is: "Try
to maintain your intellectual and sexual activities as long
as possible."

Dr. John F. Oliven, an authority on sexual functioning,
has also emphasized regularity of intercourse. Very often
in the older years, the sexual life of a couple is disrupted
by a more or less prolonged period of abstinence because
of surgery or some health reason. Prolonging the period of
abstinence longer than is necessary invites certain dangers to the marriage, Dr. Oliven notes. He suggests to
doctors that as a general rule, the greatest possible sexual
freedom at the earliest possible time compatible with the
remedial program should be allowed, or even encouraged.

Thus, authorities are in agreement with Masters and
Johnson's emphasis on the importance of regular sexual
performance in helping maintain effective sexual capacity
for both men and women.

THE POSTMENOPAUSAL YEARS

One of the problems faced by women in their postmenopausal years is the loss of estrogen brought about as
the ovaries reduce their production of hormones. This
loss generally begins to manifest itself about five years
after the end of menstruation and is quite evident in most
of the women who have reached sixty years of age, although there are many individual exceptions. Masters
and Johnson note that, as the woman moves through her
postmenopausal years, the lining of the vagina becomes

very thin and atrophic. Instead of having the thick, ridged pattern characteristic of the vagina when it is receiving considerable estrogen stimulation, the walls of the vagina become tissue-paper-thin and, therefore, cannot protect the structures lying next to the vagina—the urethra and bladder—by absorbing the mechanical irritation of active intercourse. There is also a shortening of both vaginal length and width and a shrinking of the major labia, leading to constriction of the opening of the vagina.

In addition, once the woman is about five years past the menopause, the rate and amount of lubrication production diminish to an obvious degree. This is not true for all women, since Masters and Johnson observed three women over sixty, one as old as seventy-three, who consistently responded to sexual stimulation with rapid production of lubrication typical of women under thirty. All three of these women had very active sex lives throughout their mature years.

Another result of steroid imbalance is that contractions of the uterus, which take place during orgasm at all age levels, now become painful. For some women these contractions are so painful that they seek to avoid orgasm and even intercourse itself.

As a result of these changes, intercourse during the postmenopausal years may be painful in many ways. Some women find penetration and the friction of intercourse painful. Some complain of a burning on urination, which develops from mechanical irritation of the urethra and bladder because of the thrusting movement of the penis. It is not unusual for many to have an urgent need to urinate immediately after intercourse.

Fortunately, today, it is easily possible to make up for any lack of hormone production in the body with adequate hormone-replacement therapy. In some cases, local application of a simple lubricant between the lips of the vulva will relieve the discomfort entirely. If the tissues are very thin and tender, estrogen creams or suppositories applied locally to the vulva and vagina may restore the tissues to normal layers and cure the discomfort within a week or two. In addition, more and more women are being given general replacement therapy to make up for the loss of hormone production by the ovaries.

However, as Masters and Johnson point out, the effect of hormone imbalance on sexual adjustment after the menopause is not the major factor. Sexual performance in many cases depends far more on opportunity for regular intercourse and on numerous emotional factors than it does on hormone balance. Many women develop renewed interest in their husbands and have described a "second honeymoon" during the early fifties as a result of the ending of any fear of pregnancy. In addition, women beyond the years of fifty have resolved most of the problems connected with raising a family, and frequently there is a significant increase in their sexual activity. On the other hand, one must not overlook the fact that many women who have never been too happy about sex during most of their lives find in the menopause or in their advancing years a respectable reason for ending a duty that has always been onerous or distasteful to them.

*   *   *

17

Middle Age

CLARA THOMPSON

In important ways, the meaning of each stage of life is dependent on what happened in the preceding stages. During the years before middle age the average person is not quite so aware of this. He has the feeling, for instance, "Even if my childhood wasn't happy this is all going to be changed now by a happy marriage—or I'll have the satisfaction of making a better life for my children." Or, he doesn't like this job—he can look for another one. It may be that none of these things happens, but at least he hopes. He feels himself still young, strong, and capable of conquering. But the term middle age has a frightening sound for most people. Somehow it means you are passing the peak—your powers are beginning to wane—you are not as robust—you cannot start new things now. Especially for women there also lurks some vague nightmare called the change of life which in popular thinking is accompanied by terrible somatic difficulties and even the specter of insanity. You will argue that these superstitions cannot be wholly false. A fear that is so widespread must have some basis in observable fact.

Let us investigate these negative aspects and attempt to place them in their true perspective and then consider the too-little publicized positive satisfactions of middle age.

When we think of middle life, we think roughly of a period somewhere between the ages of forty and sixty

SOURCE: Chapter 35 of *Interpersonal Psychoanalysis*, by Clara Thompson, edited by Maurice R. Green. Copyright © 1964 by Maurice R. Green. Reprinted by permission of Basic Books, Inc., Publishers, New York.

years. But this was not always so, nor is it necessarily true of many people today. In the early 1900's, Freud was of the opinion that in the case of women not many changes could be made in their lives after thirty. He believed that somehow the difficult process of becoming a woman had so exhausted her adaptive powers that by the time she was thirty she was already fixed and rigid in her personality—one could say already past middle age in adaptability. Freud has usually been an accurate observer of facts but often he saw things as more unalterable, more biologically determined than they really are. Subsequent development of our way of life has certainly greatly altered this pessimistic appraisal of women. In 1900, a woman of thirty in middle-class European society usually found her life course rigidly determined. If she had not married by then she was doomed to spinsterhood—and that was a very limiting and bleak outlook. If she had married, she was inescapably committed. If her marriage was unhappy, there was no way of changing this, short of the death of her husband. Few women had been educated to the point of having other sources of interest or satisfaction. And, of course, as a psychotherapist, Freud was not consulted by the happily married woman. (I assume there were some in 1900.) Hence, the possibility of a woman's enlarging or enriching her life much after the age of thirty seemed indeed small at that time. However, today we have the increasing possibility of careers, greater freedom in general, especially greater educational opportunities and a relative ease of divorce, if one has made a bad start.

Anything which tends to limit a person's free development tends to make them rigid and prematurely old. A man caught in an uninteresting, routine job without the opportunity for advancement will also become rigid and old before his time, unless he has other compensations, such as a happy marriage or a lively interest in something other than his work. In other words, a person tends to remain young if he has a future, that is, if he can con-

tinue to grow and develop. One of the forces which tends
to prevent this is lack of opportunity. This lack of opportunity may be the result of inadequate educational advantages due to poverty, racial discrimination, or other restrictions of the particular social order under which one
lives. Another force leading to early old age is a limita-
tion within the personality itself, such as low intelligence
or crippling neurosis.

If we take these factors into consideration, it is apparent that the time of middle age is partly dependent on
social and personality forces and is not a definite chrono-
logic period. Thus one may be fixed and rigid at the age
of twenty, or one finds people such as Titian, Einstein, or
Goethe still creative and productive at the age of seventy
and even eighty. Although exceptions in both directions
exist, for practical purposes in this discussion, we will
stick to the average, i.e., what happens to most people
between forty and sixty.

What are the hazards of middle age? We begin to die
from the moment of birth. That is, throughout life, from
time to time, certain organs reach the height of their
function and begin to deteriorate. For example, the
thymus gland is one of the organs which begins to diminish at birth and in normal people has become rudi-
mentary by the age of five. In the meantime, other organs
are developing and for many years, physically, there is
more growth in the body than deterioration. Then comes
a period of relative equilibrium—this is middle age, a
kind of pause in life before our physical strength starts
downhill, that is, when the rate of deterioration is faster
than the rate of growth. However, not even in this physical sphere do all people arrive at this middle stage at the
same time. We encounter people with snow-white hair in
the twenties, and we find people in the seventies with
hardly a gray hair. I do not wish to give the impression
that white hair is necessarily a sign of general aging of the
body, but simply to illustrate the wide range of aging of
various parts. Much more important than hair in affecting

the whole personality are the variations in aging of the arteries and other vital organs.

In the physical sphere, middle age is best known to people in general as the time of the change of life in women. Sometime during middle age women come to the end of their capacity for reproduction. This is marked by the cessation of menstruation and is accompanied by a general readjusting of the endocrine balance in the body. The endocrines are organs secreting various hormones which when in balance cooperate with each other in aiding the functioning of the body. When one is changed, as, for example, when the thyroid gland becomes underactive, this affects the functioning of other endocrine glands. The ovaries, for instance, are then disturbed in their functioning and a woman with deficient thyroid may be unable to become pregnant, although there is nothing basically wrong with her ovaries.

In the same way, at the menopause, the ovaries gradually cease to function. With the diminishing of ovarian function the other endocrines are temporarily thrown out of balance, and this produces some of the physical discomforts of this period. The most well known of these are the so-called hot flashes that overtake a woman unexpectedly from time to time. Today, however, these physical discomforts can be markedly diminished, and in some cases entirely overcome, by supplying the missing hormones and withdrawing them more gradually than nature does. Women no longer need anticipate with dread the physical discomforts of the change of life. Many women experience almost no unpleasant symptoms and can mark the time of the menopause only by the cessation of menstruation.

But the question which concerns us here is why do women tend more easily to get upset at this time. Various factors play a part. One cannot deny that the physical instability just described contributes somewhat. When you never know when you are going to be too hot or too cold, when menstruation arrives at unpredictable moments or just as annoyingly fails to appear so that you never know whether you are pregnant or not, there is likely to be an increased feeling of uncertainty and this makes for increased irritability. One gets angry more easily, one weeps more easily. But if life in general is happy these disturbances are usually of a minor nature.

The serious emotional upsets of the middle years are due, not primarily to physical conditions per se, but to the awareness more or less consciously of the unlived life. The physical change brings a woman sharply up against the fact that she is beginning to age. She may have been drifting along from year to year in a frustrated, discontented, unproductive life, somehow continuing to hope that the future will be better. Suddenly, with the menopause, she realizes with dismay that it is too late now. The spinster, who has waited through the years for the right man to come along, is now faced with the fact that he has not come and probably will not. This type of woman is not so frequent today as she was formerly, but one still occasionally sees her in the psychiatrist's office.

For example, there is the case of an unmarried schoolteacher living in a private girls' school. For many years, she was happy in this adolescent atmosphere, living emotionally herself at the adolescent level. The beginning of the menopause suddenly threw her into a panic. She had always expected some day to get around to marrying—now she must hurry up to find the man; but this meant getting out of this girls' school. But, when she got out, she found, of course, that she was not prepared to find a man. She sank into a paranoid psychosis, in which she believed that all young men who came near her were trying to seduce her. The butcher was putting powder in her food designed to rouse her sexually. The mail carrier had his tricks. She moved from grocer to grocer, and job to job, trying to escape these persecutors. She even took a trip to Europe, but the persecutors were there. Although this woman was in torment, nevertheless in a distorted way she was denying that it was too late to find love.

Witness—all the men in the world are after her. Of
course, not every disappointed spinster becomes as disturbed as this.

Another who suddenly thinks it is too late is the un-
happily married woman who has remained with her husband for the sake of her children, or because she is afraid
to venture on her own. If she has remained in an unhappy
situation because of her children she usually thinks:
"When my children are old enough I will leave him," but
when the time comes she is unable to conceive of an
independent life, for now she doubts her sexual charm, or
she fears no men are available.

There is another type of woman for whom middle age
is a hazard, and that is the woman who has depended a
great deal for self-esteem on her ability to attract male
admirers. She may have been very beautiful or she may
have had unusual charm, but she lacks a firm foundation
within herself. At heart she does not believe in herself.
For her middle age brings panic as she begins to realize
that her way of adjustment is coming to an end. These
women in their forties often start a hectic pursuit of men.
They engage in frantic efforts to appear young. They indeed are in the roaring forties.

Even the happily married woman may have a few
qualms about her fears of loss of sexual attractiveness.
And one frequently gets inquiries such as "Will I still be
capable of sexual desire!" About the latter there is an
unequivocal yes. If you have enjoyed your sexual life up
until the menopause, you will continue to enjoy it in
many instances even into old age. In my practice I have
been consulted by women over seventy because they were
still "bothered by" (to use the expression of one) sexual
feelings. They feared that they were somehow depraved.
For these few who consult psychiatrists, there must be
thousands who continue to enjoy their sexual life after
seventy without conflict. At any rate, one does not have
to fear the loss of sexual interest after the menopause.

In short, emotionally the menopause poses the greatest

threat to two types of women: those who have postponed living until too late and those who have managed to maintain a feeling of importance and value only through the adulation of men. These are the people who have breakdowns and are consumed with self-reproaches about their misspent lives.

Many of these women live through this experience and come out successfully to find new interests. This is especially true if they have had psychiatric help, but some find their way back to an interest in life by themselves. Not infrequently they find an outlet in some form of cause which they adopt as a kind of religion or a genuine interest. But women are not the only ones who find middle life a frightening hazard. To be sure, men do not have an actual organic change of life. As you know, men keep the power of procreation until well into old age. Healthy men as well as healthy women also keep the power of sexual enjoyment until old age. But for men the fulfillment of this latter satisfaction is easier to obtain in middle age, and even in the sixties, than it is for women.

Furthermore, especially with women, but also to some extent with men, another situation usually occurring at middle age adds a hazard to the time. With the average marriage, children have reached adolescence by the time their parents are forty-five. They are beginning to leave home, to manage their lives more and more on their own. A hundred years ago, this was not so true. In the large families of the early pioneering days, a woman continued to bear children throughout her reproductive life. Therefore, she might still be concerned with raising a two- or three-year-old at forty-five. But today, in families of two or three children, most of them are breaking away when their parents are in the forties. This throws the parents back on their own inner resources. The woman sees her job which had required so much of her energies up until now disappearing. Presently two people married for many years and engaged in a joint enterprise find themselves alone together, the woman practically without em-

ployment and feeling insecure because of her diminishing
sexual charm. The way this situation works out depends
again on the nature of the intimacy of these two people
up to this point. Have there been many interests in common, mutual respect? Does the woman have a sympathetic interest in her husband's business, or has she the
initiative to seek new work for herself? Can he understand her problem without being threatened? If there was
no deep feeling of mutual liking and respect earlier in the
marriage, the marriage may break up by the husband
going elsewhere. The woman is likely to cling frantically
to her husband, to become more possessive and jealous,
or try to keep his attention and control him by obscure
physical complaints. These signs of panic on her part
often only increase the gulf between the two, although
sometimes it looks as if they had become more devoted
because she has managed to make her husband feel guilty
for his impulses toward freedom. But in spite of all these
hazards of middle age, a surprising number of people go
through it very well.

Although the onset of middle age is a period of crisis,
in that a new way of life is beginning, it does not have to
be a tragic period characterized by a frantic effort to hold
on to youth. Middle age definitely has its rewards, and
the door is not closed to growth and development for
those who have not been so successful earlier, if they will
turn toward the satisfactions available in middle life and
not try to become adolescents again.

First let us consider the happiest experience possible in
middle life. That is the experience of having arrived. The
early struggles in making a place for oneself in the business or professional world are ended. Uncertainties are
past. Years of devotion and experience have gone into
building a secure foundation in business or home, and at
last the results are apparent. You can see with satisfaction your own worth! A man of my acquaintance started
in a business as office boy at the age of fourteen. At sixty,
he became president of the company. Many years of

struggle and hard work lay between these two points. Unfortunately, such a success story seldom occurs today. He belonged to the generation before mine, but advancement in business still occurs and such men find themselves at fifty or sixty securely placed and recognized as experts in their fields.

The professional man or woman has the greatest opportunity to have the experience of recognized success. The successful medical man or lawyer, for instance, usually has more demands on this time than he can give by the time he is forty-five. Freed from anxieties about making a living he is able to devote himself to the more interesting aspects of his work. He can leave the drudgery to younger people. But you will say these are special cases; these are the ones who in the beginning either had special endowment or unusual opportunity, and that is true. Outstanding success comes to relatively few of the millions of Americans, but the satisfaction of having lived well and productively can be experienced for many other less spectacular achievements. For example, the man and woman who brought up a healthy family can look on with joy at their starting out in life. The man who has worked hard and finally is able to buy the home he always wanted can also have the feeling of having arrived. The woman who sees her first grandchild, the offspring of the happy marriage of her son or daughter, can also enjoy the feeling of achievement. Thus middle age can bring the fulfillment of earlier promise.

For the emotionally healthy person the feeling of having arrived is not a signal to stop growing. Many go right on growing in the same direction, e.g., the medical man continues to keep up with the advances in his field and is in a better position to contribute to them because of his long experience. The man who buys a house may become interested in beautifying it or developing his garden. But for many, continued growth in middle life may mean finding new interests, and this is especially true of most women. The gradmother cannot indefinitely find her chief joy in her grandchildren. Their actual lives in this generation usually touch her life infrequently. The woman of middle life who has been chiefly a mother and homemaker must find new interests that are personally satisfying if she is to continue to grow. Many women have a kind of rebirth after the menopause. Their general health is better. Freed from concern about possible pregnancy their sex lives often become more spontaneous and satisfying. Although there is no longer the fiery passion of youth, sex becomes expressive of a tried and trusted companionship and intimacy often more satisfactory in its total meaning than earlier experiences. Especially fortunate is the woman who earlier prepared herself for the years when she would have more time. For example, there is a woman who was a musician of modest talent before her marriage. The responsibilities of marriage, children and finally two years of nursing a dying husband led to neglect of her musical interests; but at fifty-five she turned back to it again. She became a professional accompanist in a small way and thus brought herself again into contact with a whole world of new interests which actually made her grow younger. Another woman had some experience in administrative work before marriage. She gave this up because of her husband's objection and there followed a childless marriage in which she was restless and increasingly hypochondriacal. She went from doctor to doctor and, as the menopause approached, it looked as if she could not escape a breakdown. But with some psychoanalytic help, she got the happy idea of using her earlier administrative experience in her husband's business. He was still rather old-fashioned about a wife's working, but he came to see that it was important for her psychic health and gave her the chance. From then on until his death and the sale of the business, this woman enjoyed better mental health than she had known since her marriage. She grew to love her husband more fully. Her middle age and old age proved to be productive periods of growth. I might say (although this is outside of middle age) that since her husband's death, she has found another job in which she is greatly interested, although she is now over seventy.

This last case brings us to our third consideration. We have seen that the fulfilled early life generally leads to a productive middle age, that serious frustration and discontent in the early years can lead to mental illness and despair in the middle years. Our last consideration is: do difficulty and unhappiness earlier have to lead to more unhappiness later? The case I have just mentioned is an example of triumphing over the unhappy past. Another example is a woman who consulted me many years ago. She was about fifty at the time, and she was married to a mean, parsimonious, hypocritically religious man whose temper had always terrified her. She had four children, the youngest of whom was then thirteen. All of the children had serious emotional difficulties—in fact, from her description the youngest seemed well on the way to schizophrenia. Needless to say, the woman was an excellent example of the menopausal type of panic one sees when the awareness of an unlived life dawns on a person. However, there was a quality of vitality about this woman that made me feel something could be done for her. She went far beyond what I had dreamed of for her. She had a native knack of being able to help people feel out their difficulties, but she had no education beyond high school and no type of training. Soon after her few talks with me—this was not an analysis—she left her husband, although he made it as difficult as possible for her, proceeded to put herself through college, taking a few courses a year while she supported herself doing this and that. Today she is a teacher and counselor in a sanitarium for crippled children, and has a regular column in her local newspaper on parent–child problems. I think she will get her degree in another year. It is true that her past life has left her with personality difficulties, but she has had a rebirth and she has more possibilities for growth and development than ever before. Also her two

younger children have shown improvement with her
change.

There is also the woman of fifty, who hopes, by dyeing
her hair, having her face lifted, and wearing youthful
clothes, to have the sexual charm and allure of a woman
of thirty. She is doomed to failure in her attempts at
salvaging her misspent life. People sometimes come to
analysis for miracles. One must first face and come to
terms with the fact that one can never make up for the
lost years. One can only hope to live from now on. And
for that, middle age is not too late to begin—to begin
with the pleasures and satisfactions possible in middle
life.

IV

PREGNANCY, BIRTH, AND CHILD CARE

Introduction

Perhaps in no other area of their lives do women today feel as much conflict between body and culture as in childbirth and child care. Both have been the primary factors in defining women's identity since history began. Now that, for the first time, women have the option of whether to bear children or not, the questions surrounding these two processes have come to rest increasingly on what is good for a particular woman. Women who bear children are interested in giving birth rather than in merely being delivered, and they are pressing for alternatives to the exclusive maternal care demanded by our society since the nineteenth century. It is well known that exclusive care of a child by the mother has not actually been the pattern in most cultures or even in our own until relatively recently. Sufficient publicity has been given to studies of the extended family and to the role of nannies, nurses, servants, and governesses to show that our cultural ideal has been more an anomaly than the norm.

The social pressure to bear children as a sign of "maturity" or "normalcy" still exists, and the guilt faced by many women who choose to work while their children are still young is testimony to the strength of traditional attitudes. Abortion, while legalized, remains an issue—whether for religious, psychological, or political reasons. It may not be too much to say that objections to abortion frequently boil down to a problem of men rather than of women; abortion is opposed as a violation of religious law or order, one which threatens traditional male control over procreation or even men's ideas about their virility. For women, the issue has come to be control over their own bodies, and this idea in itself remains threatening to many men, who predict collapse of the family and even of the entire society if women possess such control. These issues extend, naturally, to child care as well, where the male backlash has been particularly strong.

The essays in this section deal with the psychological processes of pregnancy and birth, with the social context in which birth takes place, and with child care.

Malkah T. Notman, of the Department of Psychiatry at Harvard Medical School, discusses the issues that confront the pregnant woman who is seriously involved in a career. Her focus is pragmatic; the real demands of professional work conflict with the demands of child care, and the solutions so far available are not very satisfactory. Further, the strength and independence that contribute to a woman's professional success can be threatened by the need for new psychological adjustments in pregnancy and child care. Conflicting role expectations concerning womanhood, femininity, and styles of mothering emerge and must be dealt with. Notman sees the availability of safe, legal abortion as extremely important for the self-image of women as people who have value outside the traditional childbearing role. Even if a woman never chooses to have an abortion, the fact that she has a choice supports the validity of non-family-oriented activity.

Grete L. Bibring, professor of psychiatry emerita at Harvard Medical School, regards pregnancy as a period of crisis in which a woman must adapt to profound psychological as well as biological changes. Pregnancy, like puberty and menopause, is a "point of no return"—a step in the evolution of the individual involving major psychological reorientation. Bibring views the crisis of pregnancy as "normal"; the problems of women confronting motherhood are developmental ones rather than indications of some neurotic condition. The pregnant woman must reorient herself in terms of the infant, her male partner, and her own mother. She must deal with the infant as a new element that is part of herself and yet separate. Her relationship to the child's father can become problematic if a woman regards herself as competing with the child for his love, or finds herself so absorbed in motherhood that she loses all interest in him. In relation to her mother, pregnancy can be for a young woman a period of growing independence, a time when early childhood conflicts are resolved.

Helene Deutsch, in an excerpt from her 1945 book, *The Psychology of Women*, may surprise many people with her attitude toward natural childbirth as important in allowing the woman to participate actively in the process of delivery. This was a radical idea at that time; Grantly Dick-Read's work had not yet been introduced in the United States, and in most cases it was routine for babies to be delivered with forceps and anesthesia, as it has continued to be. Deutsch offers an interesting description of some of the psychological processes a woman goes through at the time of delivery, including the withdrawal from identification with the fetus as part of the self, and the fear of death evoked by the coming separation of birth. Her work reflects an emphasis on the painful aspects of childbirth, seen as contributing to an innate masochism that was unfortunately taken to be typical of women by many psychoanalytic writers until quite recently. (Andrea Ostrum offers a lucid analysis of Deutsch's theoretical formulations at the beginning of her selection, which follows Deutsch's.) However, like Bibring, Deutsch sees the process of pregnancy and birth in terms of the need to reintegrate the psyche in a new way.

Deutsch describes delivery as a period of regression. This should not be taken to mean that the woman in labor is seen as a helpless child. Rather, Deutsch sees birth as a creative act in which, as in other forms of creativity, one becomes open to the unconscious and whatever may lie unresolved within it. Many women may say that they were not aware of any such fears of death or of other conflicts at the time of birth, but Deutsch as a psychoanalyst is concerned with the unconscious as it manifests itself in the conscious mind and in present activity. All the major phases of female sexuality—puberty, pregnancy and birth, and menopause—involve an opening up of the self to regressive or unconscious states; "regressive" refers simply to the fact that the unconscious mind is largely formed in infancy and early childhood. Crises in development involve an incorporation and reorganization of the unconscious into a new mode of conscious being—an adolescent girl has the same task of integrating her childhood relationships and identifications into a new, independent self.

In an excerpt from her thesis, Andrea Ostrum, a feminist and psychologist, discusses the psychoanalytic, anthropological, and neuropsychological theories of childbirth. She cites Margaret Mead's evidence that the climate of childbirth is culturally determined, and that cultural attitudes profoundly affect both a woman's expectations and the actual process of delivery. If the cultural attitude is relaxed, labor tends to be short and relatively painless. Ostrum offers an invaluable historical summary of the various methods of "natural" childbirth, and cites statistics of the American Society for Psychoprophylaxis in Obstetrics (ASPO), an organization dedicated to the psychoprophylactic methods first developed in the Soviet Union and introduced in the United States by Marjorie Karmel in her book, *Thank You, Dr. Lamaze.* The psychoprophylactic method is what most of us think of when we speak of natural childbirth—with training involving physical exercise, breathing, relaxation, and psychological suggestion. ASPO has a small membership indeed, relative to the number of hospitals and obstetricians in this country. Ostrum argues persuasively that childbirth patterns relate closely to the general cultural patterns of any country, and shows that the isolation of women in childbirth, the prone position (which has rarely been used in other cultures), and the automatic administration of anesthesia have all been inventions of men. Childbirth in our culture is treated, in fact, as if it were a disease rather than a normal process, and the woman is prevented from actively participating in and enjoying it. Ostrum feels that this state of affairs is likely to continue until women are in control of the childbirth policies of hospitals and clinics.

Child care has been recognized as a crucial process since Freud's work came upon the scene, but hardly anybody agrees on the optimal conditions under which children should be raised. A number of years ago reports by such people as René Spitz and John Bowlby disclosed that infants and small children placed in institutions such as orphanages and residence hospitals often died, and the cause was laid to the effects of maternal deprivation. If children did not die, they suffered emotional and intellectual impairment. It was seen that these infants and children received inadequate attention and stimulation, often remaining immobilized in cribs. Children separated from their mothers after about six months of age, by which time a strong mother-child bond had been formed, were particularly hard hit by maternal deprivation. It was doubtless not the intent of these authors that their work be picked up by a post–World War II society intent on glorifying a return to Mom and apple pie, and be used as justification for enforcement of an exclusive mother-child bond in suburban households—cut off even from the servants and relatives that in other times brought some relief from the intensity of this relationship. Several generations of mothers have been subjected to strong pressure to remain at home, with one result being a series of vociferous masculine protests against Momism, from Philip Wylie to Philip Roth. Another result, of course, was the feminist reaction, beginning with publication of *The Feminine Mystique*; and feminists, many of them professionals, have made important contributions to the growing protests against this cultural injunction. Some have gone too far, denying the value of almost all interpersonal relationships. But the best have not denied the core of Bowlby's and Spitz's concern—that infants do need loving care, stable relationships, and an environment sufficiently stimulating to promote growth. Bowlby stated that severe discontinuity in the mother-child relationship in the first three years of life has severe effects on a child's personality, impairing its ability to grow and relate to other people. Bowlby has said that, although a primary mothering figure is essential, it need not be the biological mother, nor is supplementary care by other people, including the father, precluded. Despite this disclaimer, most of Bowlby's work on attachment has been written in terms of the mother-child relationship, and those differing with his views have tended to focus on the exclusive mother-child bond as it has been structured in our culture. Two papers in this section provide interesting reviews of work that has been done: Rochelle Paul Wortis reviews psychological and ethologic studies and describes the feelings and attitudes of mothers themselves; Margaret Mead offers impressive cross-cultural evidence to show that the exclusive mother-child bond is peculiar to modern Western culture and indeed dependent on modern urban conditions for its very existence.

Rochelle Paul Wortis demonstrates that many studies do not explore positive alternatives to extreme, traumatic separation, such as day care or other forms of supplementary care. Although studies of the children of working mothers have found no detrimental effects as compared to the children of full-time mothers, Wortis points out that the culture continues to resist the establishment of adequate day care facilities for working mothers. Ethologic studies, utilizing instinct theory, tend to stress the advantages of the "natural" mother-child tie; in general, social scientists have been biased in favor of the status quo, or the ideal of the exclusive mother-infant relationship. Wortis looks at accounts by mothers themselves, as well as the professional literature, to point up some of the negative effects of an overintensive mother-child bond and of the home as an environment isolated from the culture at large, restrictive to both the mother and the child. She emphasizes the need for men to be actively involved in child care and domestic tasks, and for work schedules to be adjusted so that both parents can share these activities. Parent-controlled day care, communal living experiments, and other social models being explored by feminists and others are important in developing new, less alienating social relationships that will benefit fathers, mothers, and children.

Margaret Mead brings the full arsenal of her vast anthropological knowledge to bear on the question of forms of child care, and makes some devastating points. She compares standard Western institutional care to the primitive method of exposing unwanted babies or of simply "allowing" them to die through subtle forms of emotional neglect. Where breastfeeding is universal and not supplemented by bottle feeding, she points out, many infants die because they do not "fit" well with that particular mother or because, for whatever reason, they simply cannot nurse. In such cases, the failure of a mother's milk is biologically appropriate behavior—only sound infants will survive. We, however, believe in keeping all infants alive, and so utilize alternative methods.

Furthermore, Mead shows that no form of childbirth or child care can be considered "natural"; all human behavior is organized within a cultural context, and ties between women, men, and children are no exception. In primitive cultures the exigencies of maternal work at food-gathering, agriculture, and so on, are most likely to dictate some form of multiple mothering, even multiple breastfeeding. Finally, Mead makes the interesting point that the form of child care has profound effects on the character structure of the child: kibbutz children have been found to be excessively dependent on their peers, and studies of Hutterite children, raised in isolated groups, have found them "unfitted for venturing forth as individuals." By contrast, multiple mothering seems to provide security for the child and—not such a plus in today's world—tends to result in a high birth rate.

Neither Wortis nor Mead, it should be pointed out, advocates drastic or extensive separation from the mother; both recognize the need for stable relationships, love, and security. It is important to realize that most feminists do not advocate the abolition of all forms of maternal care; rather, they see the need for viewing child care as a social responsibility, so that the choice of motherhood does not automatically preclude participation in other activities. Neither mother nor child, it seems, benefits from total isolation from the world at large, and it is to be hoped that the alarmists who somehow extrapolate from day care to the breakdown of the entire social fabric can see that, in fact, alternative methods of child care may provide one answer to the problem of structuring human relationships in a society that can no longer enforce the old ideal of *materfamilias*.

18

Pregnancy and Abortion: Implications for Career Development of Professional Women

MALKAH T. NOTMAN

PREGNANCY

For the professionally active woman, her pregnancy often provides the first challenge to a life-style that may have functioned well and adaptively until that time. When she discovers she is pregnant, she has to make a choice whether to have the child or whether to have an abortion. Marriage may be included in this decision. Most professional women who do have children are married. Although increasing numbers of unmarried mothers elect to keep their babies rather than offer them for adoption, their educational and class background is generally different from that of career women. This, therefore, is not a widely accepted alternative for the women with a career.

Having a baby then brings a whole range of consequences. Some are related to the experience of the pregnancy and some to the impact of the child on family roles and responsibilities.

Many of the discussions about femininity and feminism these days waver between assertions that women are no different from men in any respect that really matters on the one hand, and to pleas for appreciation of those qualities which are specifically feminine on the other.

SOURCE: Reprinted from *Women & Success: The Anatomy of Achievement*, edited by Ruth B. Kundsin, Sc.D., published by William Morrow & Company, Inc., 105 Madison Avenue, New York, New York 10016. Copyright © 1973 by The New York Academy of Sciences under the title *Successful Women in the Sciences: An Analysis of Determinants*.

Certainly in most professional occupations there are few ways in which women must inherently function any differently than men in regard to the actual character of their work. There are, however, many ways in which they may choose to arrange their lives differently from the prevailing patterns for men. The most marked of these concern their family relationships and the most compelling have to do with the care of children.

Numerous obstacles complicate a woman's gaining access to a career and then achieving recognition and the standard rewards or professional advancement within it. The problems posed by the external barriers of overt discrimination, subtle prejudices, and the inner conflicts such as those concerning the competitiveness and aggressiveness necessary for successful achievement may be solved in a number of ways, varying with the individual backgrounds and personalities of the woman involved. One possible option a woman has is to minimize the distinction between the sexes; that is, to work "like a man." She can insist on equal hours and on undertaking work of equal challenge, and can try to participate fully in all the informal exchanges of information, banter, and social communication. We have heard a good deal about the dubiousness of accepting these masculine role models, but it does remain difficult to modify or abandon them if one is after success. Whatever possibilities exist for managing this solution for the woman graduate student or young professional become smaller or vanish in some fields once a woman plans to have children.

She has the theoretical option of insisting that there be no differences in her work conditions except for maternity leave and the immediate postdelivery period for a short while afterward, or she can ask for "special" consideration that takes some account of the integration of work with the human needs of her family and herself. The latter is actually not always feasible. Flexible work arrangements may not exist in certain work settings, particularly in the sciences, and the woman may be reluctant to "buck the system" and thus make herself more conspicuous and vulnerable. She often feels guilty at needing something "special" in the way of arrangements, because this is regarded as a disruptive rather than as a legitimate aspect of one's life. She is then forced into an either-or decision: either she adopts a discontinuous work pattern and stops for a few years after the baby is born or she makes a commitment to a full work schedule where she may inhibit her own full response to her pregnancy and its meaningfulness for her. This, in effect, devalues both the particular rewards of her life that childbearing can represent, and the child as well. In addition to its unavailability, men's and some women's depreciation of part-time work contribute to the dilemma.

The particular alternative ways of working out one's family roles are very difficult for the woman to conceptualize in the abstract before a baby is born. Partially this is true because plans theoretically conceived do not always take into account the real strains, pleasures, and tasks of parenthood. Most women bring to this role complex and sometimes confused expectations and fantasies of what it means to be a mother and care for a child. These derive in part from her own experiences and memories of being mothered, which are not always conscious. Another reason for the difficulty in anticipatory planning has to do with the growth that takes place during pregnancy—not only in girth, but also psychologically. A first pregnancy holds considerable developmental potential in the transition a woman makes to being a mother and caretaking person.

It is interesting that woman students who are contemplating careers have difficulty thinking through how the family-career integration is to be managed. They suggest innovative and interesting ideas, but often these are unrealistic, sometimes almost mathematical in their concepts of the division of time. If the woman students become interested in how other professional women have managed, this can often help lend some reality to their

plans. The value of a variety of role models provided by
women in the professions with a range of different life-
styles has been properly stressed in many discussions of
this problem.

The birth of a child puts a strain on what may, up until
then, have been a successful arrangement with the husband, because prior to this point it is more possible to
function in essentially parallel ways, with sharing and
rearrangement of responsibilities. When a child is involved, however, and the issues of who is to provide care
and how this is to be done become an insistent reality,
many deep-seated expectations of each other's roles come
into play. These deeper feelings may conflict with newer
ideas, derived from ideological considerations or rational
plans. For a woman to work seriously, some resolutions
of these conflicts must be achieved in at least a relatively
harmonious fashion.

Past identifications with parents and other important
figures play a crucial role in determining the concept each
person has of how one behaves as a woman—or a man—
and how these should interrelate. Pregnancy stirs up
these old identifications; particularly important for the
woman is her relationship with her mother, which is
revived emotionally. On the verge of being a mother
herself, her mother's life-style assumes particular importance. She may feel conflicted at choosing a solution different from her mother's, or disturbed at what might seem
to be outdoing her in status or achievement. She may feel
uncertainty about her career plans, arising from the new
appeal of her mother's pattern.

Pregnancy does obviously differentiate men from
women. The experience is something potentially shared
with all women. Although the care of a child can be
divided with her husband and others, the bearing of a
child is a woman's experience alone. There is evidence
from the life histories of women who have chosen the
socially deviant path of intellectual interests and serious
commitment to careers that as girls they felt outside the

more generally accepted group, which stressed prettiness and popularity. Residual doubts or uneasiness about her femininity may even seem to be confirmed by success in scientific pursuits. Faced with these feelings, even if they are not very prominent, pregnancy can bring a sense of being like other women. Surprising pleasure may accompany sharing this experience and having a common bond with "those other" women. If womanhood, femaleness, or femininity brings conflicts, and if it is disturbing to be linked with "those other" women, the pregnancy will be a trying time and may be avoided.

Pregnancy may threaten some well-established patterns. Psychologically and realistically, a woman is often more vulnerable during pregnancy; she may find herself more volatile, more fatigued, and be less in control of her body. This experience may be very threatening to someone whose self-image is based on being strong, competent, and in control. In the process of developing a career, many women develop defenses that make unacceptable anything appearing to be weakness in themselves, even the temporary symptoms of a pregnancy. These feelings may lead a woman to resist modifying her life patterns while she is pregnant and force herself to carry on just as before. Of course, many women feel no need to modify anything, since they feel well and prefer to work. But flexibility in making this choice is important.

For many women the pregnancy provides their first experience with being a patient—and a participant in the nonmutual relationship that some obstetricians seem to encourage. The passivity and dependence connected with being a patient runs counter to their other modes of functioning, which have been adaptive in their work development. It is frustrating for someone oriented to solving problems and valuing knowledge to be treated as someone who does not need to know what is going on in her pregnancy.

The pregnancy may also be the first encounter with such an intimate responsibility for another human being.

The impact of the first child and the consequent expansion of the family unit is considerable. New responsibilities are added, often precipitating a realignment of roles and priorities. The range of plans that seemed theoretically possible in earlier thinking narrows down to those necessary to meet the real needs of a real child—but heavily affected by deeply held expectations of how to raise it. These may be difficult to modify by good intentions alone. Experience is important. The complexity, juggling, and ingenuity needed are considerable. Certain personality traits become particularly valuable for both parents. Among these are tolerance of conflict, ability to forego perfectionism, and the capacity to concentrate in the face of distraction. It would be valuable to know more about those personality traits which facilitate the integration of family and work.

Even where a husband and wife adopt a pattern of real sharing it is usually the woman who assumes the responsibility of the overall planning and availability to the child. Men tend to perform specific caretaking functions —feeding a baby, bathing, story-telling, and so on. Our clinical impressions suggest that the woman's role is conceptualized as providing the primary care for very young children. It is usually the woman who feels she has to find coverage for herself if she works seriously, and usually the woman who feels the conflict and guilt at working. This conflict is present especially when children are young and separation is traumatic, but also persists when they are older.

ABORTION

When the pregnancy is unwanted, the implications of the availability of abortions for facilitating a woman's choices of the timing of the phases of her career and freeing her for professional activities are clear. Several colleagues and I are now completing an intensive study of the outcome of therapeutic abortion in 100 women in

Boston. Thirty-eight percent of these randomly selected women sought abortions for reasons related to work or educational conflict, although these may not have been the only reasons in each case. After the abortion they did return to work or school.

There are many reasons for an unwanted pregnancy to occur besides accidents. Becoming pregnant has complex meanings that may be only partly related or actually unrelated to the wish for a child. It is one way of establishing one's fertility, of indicating potential creative productivity, or of confirming femininity. Our data and the work of others indicate that even women who actively and unambivalently seek abortions sometimes feel pleasure at the idea of having become pregnant. Six months after the abortions, many women feel that the whole experience has increased their view of themselves as women. Most of the women in the study did not feel that their wish for the abortion was connected with any serious doubts about their capacity to be mothers, but to the undesirability of a particular pregnancy at a particular time.

Becoming pregnant, deliberately or inadvertantly, may be a way of avoiding difficulties within a career, or an expression of the anxiety a woman faces at the point where she is about to make an important move. It is not uncommon to encounter women who were about to return to graduate school or start work on a long-delayed book or other project, who then become pregnant. Some women want to change their direction when their youngest child is in school. Having no clear training, or being frightened about how to catch up with years missed, they may find themselves pregnant, which leads to a more familiar role. (Twenty-eight percent of our patients had as their youngest child one who was older than seven years. Thus the pregnancy would have brought them back into a new period of motherhood of young infants when this period had already once been passed). They thus can escape the strains of competition and the complexities of resolving the family-career dilemma, the frustrations of difficult work, or the problems of dealing with one's ambiguous status in a largely masculine field.

Conscious or unconscious ambivalence about her career which might have led a woman to an unwanted pregnancy does not then present the same barrier to further career development as it might if abortion were unavailable. A woman who feels unready or unwilling to have a child at a particular time does not have to live with the results of only one part of her ambivalence.

Where abortion laws are restrictive, . . . the woman must convincingly present herself as ill and threatened in order to qualify. This situation rewards illness and weakness, and supports willingness to manipulate and pretend in order to secure the assistance a woman feels she desperately needs. We saw the dilemmas resulting from this approach when the requirements were more strictly enforced in Massachusetts and there was no legal abortion nearby. Some women faced enormous difficulty in presenting themselves as weak or desperate, particularly those whose successful adaptations included pride and strength in their academic or career roles. This posture runs counter to those personal resources which had been important in their previous responses to critical experiences. Consequently, they then exposed themselves to the risks and embarrassments of illegal abortions.

Students looking for ways to solve the problems of integrating family and career, or of simply developing their own patterns of functioning in the professional world, look to models of other successful women in their fields. Just as with the other aspects of professional experience, they want to see "how it's done." To see that a respected colleague or friend makes a decision to have an abortion and that this is a manageable experience, although this may not be public information, is important in the student's awareness of alternatives that might be available to her at a time she might be in a similar dilemma.

The possibility of a safe, dignified abortion openly chosen confirms a woman's self-image as someone who is valued not only for her childbearing role. Whether a particular woman ever has an abortion is not as crucial as her awareness of the possibility of having one. The existence of a choice supports the validity of other priorities. If a pregnancy does interrupt another set of priorities, and if it is clearly possible to abort it safely, thus providing a real alternative to proceeding with it, this weakens the expectation that women's only true fulfillment leads to once again putting the "mother" role first. In my experience, this alternative self-image as a person with other legitimate activities can be very supportive in lessening the guilt women feel when they do place nonfamily commitments high. The concept that a woman's role is not necessarily the home, although she may enjoy her home and care deeply about her family, is reinforced by the awareness of having made an active choice to be there. Those women who do not feel they are suitable or optimal for motherhood do not then feel so downgraded and unacceptable.

Many of our patients who seek abortions have described the change in their relationships with their husbands and children afterwards. Most marked is the improvement in relation to children when the crisis precipitated by the possibility of having to meet a new set of demands is relieved. They value the existing children, and they can deal with them more effectively when there is some support for other aspects of their lives. The legitimacy of the abortion can be important here. The hospital or other respectable institution lends sanction to the decision. . . . Anxiety as to whether the abortion will create some permanent physical damage can be an expression of guilt about the abortion and can be experienced as a punishment for doing a wrong. This anxiety can be reduced by the safety of the setting or even by its ordinariness and the acceptance and understanding of professional people in the environment.

It is interesting that many women, particularly those who are well educated, may feel guilty and ashamed over the pregnancy rather than the abortion. They feel, "How could I have gotten myself into this?" They nevertheless do act impulsively sometimes, irrationally at others, and have accidents as well.

Our preliminary data indicate that many variables are related to the balance of the outcome. Social and situational variables are perhaps as important in determining the result as is the personality of the woman.

There is evidence, furthermore, that an abortion may have a specifically positive effect on the resolution of the crisis of unwanted pregnancy. This positive outcome is not only due to the relief of immediate pressure, but can be maturational in the long run. This maturational potential is probably related to the experience of making the decision. Many women, in looking back on this period, feel that this is a highly significant decision, often the first major decision they made autonomously. Participation and support from lover, husband, counselors, or friends are helpful, as is the possibility for carrying out the decision in an atmosphere of safety and acceptance. But the responsibility lies with the woman herself. Handling it successfully has an important long-range effect. Career decisions usually involve a high degree of independence and self-determination. . . . Actions that are personally appropriate may be considered very deviant socially. Among certain groups of women, decisions such as having an abortion are accepted and, in fact, the rule, but not for everyone. The abortion experience may increase the capacity of the woman to deal with other decisions, leading to increased autonomy and individuation. The decision often seems to be a pivotal point in the move away from a dependent relationship with parents, even though we also have evidence that those women who have troubled relationships with their mothers have more distress, shame, and defense afterward than those who do not. Obviously it does not always work that way. An abortion may represent a conflicted, regressed, guilt-laden experience. Or one may need to repeat the expression of the underlying conflict and become pregnant again—only to wish to undo again. Our experience is that the intensely disturbing experience is rare. There have been few serious reactions, except in disturbed patients. Repetition probably is most frequent when there are defenses preventing a conscious confrontation with the issues involved—a problem not unique to abortion.

Perhaps the most important effect of the availability of abortion is the control of a woman's reproductive life, which it makes possible for her. Obviously this is provided by contraception in a more sound, sensible, rational, preventive form. But people are not all rational nor are they all single-minded. Not everyone uses contraception effectively at all times. The possibility of another point of decision-making permits a multiplicity of solutions for optimal development of the individual needs of everyone: mother, father, and children.

SUGGESTED READING

Bibring, G. L. 1959. Some Considerations of the Psychological Processes in Pregnancy. The Psychoanalytic Study of the Child 14: 113–121. International Universities Press. New York, N.Y.

Nadelson, C. & M. Notman. 1972. The woman physician. J. Med. Ed. 47: 176–183. March.

Notman, M., A. Kravitz, E. Payne & J. Russell. 1972. Psychological outcome in patients having therapeutic abortions. In Proc. Third Internat. Cong. Psychosomatic Problems Obstet. Gynecol. : 552–554.

Payne, E., A. Kravitz, M. Notman & J. Russell. 1972. Therapeutic Abortions: Outcome Study of 100 Cases. Presented at 125th Annual Meeting of American Psychiatric Assoc. May. Dallas, Tex.

Rapoport, R., R. Rapoport & M. Fogarty. 1971. Sex, Career and Family. P.E.P. Monograph. George Allen & Unwin Ltd. London, England.

19

Some Specific Psychological Tasks in Pregnancy and Motherhood

GRETE L. BIBRING

. . . Much attention has been given by modern medicine to the ever increasing knowledge of the physiological and physiopathological events in pregnancy and delivery and to faultless prenatal and obstetrical care. From the time when this biological process was viewed as a most secretive and private experience which must not be invaded by an open and direct scientific approach to the present achievements of obstetrics, a long distance has been covered. However, pregnancy, delivery and the period of early infant care should by no means be viewed as an exclusively or even predominantly somatic condition. Pregnancy, like puberty and menopause, is an intrinsically psychosomatic developmental step in which the somatic shift in no way surpasses in effect and significance the psychological thrust, but more than that, in which both the somatic and the psychological growth are intensely interdependent, supporting or interfering with each other, as the case may be, and in which they are in equal measure responsible for the success or failure of this maturational phase.

. . . In the smooth and successful physiologic course alone, our expectations as to the desirable outcome are not yet guaranteed. What we have to consider is the parallel

SOURCE: From "Some Specific Psychological Tasks in Pregnancy and Motherhood" by Grete L. Bibring, M.D., in *Premier Congrès International de Médecine Psychosomatique et Maternité, Paris, 8–12 Juillet 1962*, edited by L. Chertok (Paris, Gauthier-Villars, 1965). Reprinted by permission of Gauthier-Villars and the author.

psychological process of maturation in the girl, leading to the position of a mother not only in fact, corroborated by the material data, but also in spirit and in terms of emotional growth. Much too often do we find a disregard of this vital aspect as if every pregnancy leading to successful delivery guaranteed not only the birth of a child but also that of a mother. Most of us know only too well that this is not always the case.

Though there is a growing awareness of the significance of this interrelatedness among experienced obstetricians, the prevalent tendency still remains to disregard the psychological aspects of pregnancy as less important and not part of our medical concern. As the result, this area is still viewed predominantly by many doctors, as it is by laymen, in terms of prescientific, culturally determined prejudices and biases. There are in our modern world fewer clearly animistic and magic concepts concerning the state of the pregnant woman as a mysterious, even ominous condition which has to be dealt with by ceremonial procedures, yet we find that this fearful superstition has only been replaced by a different type of dogma. Our leading bias today is of the opposite nature —that pregnancy is a state of bliss and beautiful harmony, free from and untouched by inner struggles and conflicts if the woman deserves to be called healthy and normal. This modern concept has in common with the ancient and primitive ideas the fact that both are not based on scientific studies and findings concerning this important period in the life of the woman, but on culturally determined patterns of thoughts.

To learn more about this process in its normal course, I set up with a group of investigators at the Beth Israel Hospital in Boston a research project[1] that has been going on for more than ten years; we come from different

[1] Supported by a grant from the Filene Foundation, Boston, Mass.; by grant M-1393, United States Public Health Service, National Institutes of Mental Health, and by grant 57-155 from the Foundations' Fund for Research in Psychiatry.

professions—medicine, psychology and social science, and from different medical specialties—psychiatry, gynecology, pediatrics. All of us are experienced in psychoanalytic personality theory which we chose as the framework for our study. . . .

It is our main thesis that pregnancy—this means every pregnancy—includes intrinsically an element of crisis as an indispensable factor of the process that leads from the condition of childlessness to the significantly different state of parenthood.

Crisis has to be understood here not as denoting pathology but in its true general sense as a decisive stage in the course of events—a turning-point that brings with it the unsettling and dislodging of old habitual solutions. These solutions may have been quite adequate for the preceding life constellation but prove insufficient or even inappropriate for the approaching new and essential tasks. This crisis brings in its wake the revival and intensification of old, even dormant, conflicts, often pitching quite opposite tendencies against each other. Crisis is a juncture between health and illness, between normality and pathology, or between maturation and regressive fixation. All this does by no means imply that this crisis of pregnancy has to present itself outwardly in a dramatic and alarming form; it may go on rather silently, may be difficult to observe directly but only in some of its derivatives, in attitudes and behavior, in signs which in their significance may not be easily recognized by the untrained observer.

However, it is this crisis, hidden or in the open, as the case may be, which has to be resolved to permit the healthy maturational growth of the woman.

What then is the crisis mainly concerned with, what are the central conflicts of general significance which are created or intensified by pregnancy and which await resolution so as not to interfere with the vital experience and function of a mother in her new family role? It has to be said here that the two conditions, gestation and motherhood, are not and cannot be separated in our presentation because they are not only biologically but also psychologically an inseparable unit. What is of importance for us here is the fact that it is during this preparatory period of pregnancy that the awareness and anxiety emerges in the woman about what happens in her body and in her as a person, about the changes which take place at this time, anticipating the even greater changes of the future, the stress of the new orientation towards herself and towards others—all this, with its stimulating and disturbing effect on her equanimity, preoccupy and influence the woman deeply at this time.

In two articles published in *The Psychoanalytic Study of the Child*[2] we concentrated our attention on one of these areas: its specific task consists in the shift from the girl's psychological position of being a single, self-contained organism, whose self-image coincides normally with the boundaries of her own individual existence, to the position of a mother, i.e., an individual who has carried another organism within herself and as part of herself; an organism which finally will separate from her to become another person. This individual will from then on remain outside of her, and yet will never quite lose for her the imprint of his origin. This then introduces into the life of the woman a very special and unprecedented relationship: the child will be experienced partly as a person in his own right with all the implications of supporting his growing independence and separateness, and yet the child will continue partly to be herself or an extension of herself with all the implications of her wanting to be reunited with him, or not to lose him to strangers, to the world.

[2] Bibring, G. L. "Some Considerations of the Psychological Processes in Pregnancy," *The Psychoanalytic Study of the Child*, Vol. XIV (New York: International Universities Press, 1959) ; Bibring, G. L., Dwyer, T. F., Huntington, D. S. and Valenstein, A. F.: "A Study of the Psychological Processes in Pregnancy and of the Earliest Mother-Child Relationship: I. Some Propositions and Comments," *The Psychoanalytic Study of the Child*, Vol. XVI (New York: International Universities Press, 1961).

What I describe here is the well-known struggle in the
mother for a harmonious equilibrium between the wish
and the necessity to let this child mature according to his
own needs, without neglecting or withdrawing from him
and the wish and the necessity to let the child be close
and feel that he belongs, without possessing him and
without smothering him. I believe that I do not have to
point out how often we see a woman fail to achieve this
mature balance of good parenthood and instead either cut
herself off from the child as if he represented an intrusion
into her autonomy and her freedom as an individual or,
on the other hand, cling to the child and tie him to herself
as if she could not be a whole person without him.

A second area of significance which may affect pregnancy and its healthy outcome is the relation of the
woman to her male partner, her husband. Did she reach a
mature sexual relationship to him? Can she accept receiving him and carrying this child for him without feeling
abused and taken advantage of as a woman? Furthermore, is she willing and able to share her husband's love
with the child or does she want to be his child herself? . . .
Finally, does her love for her husband persist as a
strong and sustaining force or does it recede into the
background, replaced almost completely by her devotion
to the child, as if the husband had fulfilled his function
in her life with the arrival of the baby? All this, petty
and superficial as it may seem to the casual observer, can
be the sign of the woman's failure to achieve the maturational move towards motherhood, for this state does
neither thrive on self-centeredness and competition with
the child nor on disclaiming her role and function as a
wife.

There is a last, third point which I would like to bring
into focus because in general importance it equals those
mentioned before. It concerns itself with the girl's relationship to her own mother. Shifts and modification in
this particular bond with mother take place continuously
in the girl from the moment she is born to the time when

she reaches adulthood. The symbiotic co-existence of infancy turns into the close dependency of the first years of childhood, followed by the growing self-reliance of preadolescence until puberty introduces in an often quite explosive form an intense struggle in the daughter for outer as well as inner independence, leading finally to her position as an adult. None of these phases bring into existence a completely new kind of relationship. They all carry within them the vestiges of the preceding experiences shaped and transformed under the impact of new and vital events.

In general we assume that this process comes to a relative halt, to a rather stable and definite equilibrium in adulthood, short of the slow working but never ending influence of maturing and aging, yet intensely affected only by rather traumatic episodes like sickness, loss, dramatic changes in the circumstances of life.

However, in our study of pregnancy we have found strong indications that this period represents for the young woman (all our research cases were primiparae) an additional and probably indispensable chapter in arriving at a fully mature relationship with her parents, especially with her mother.

From the beginning of pregnancy on we observed that the majority of our women spontaneously referred to such changes in their reactions towards their mothers. We may present this in a simplified form of classification by the two end points of a spectrum: On the one hand, many of our pregnant women impressed us at the beginning of their pregnancy as dependent above average, turning to mother for every answer, listening to her advice before anybody else's—even the expert's—being still overinvolved in mother's attention to them, in competition with other members of the family. Among this group we observed frequently a beginning disengagement, a growing self-esteem and a feeling of independence, a pleasure in trying to make decisions on their own without mother.

In contrast to this group there was an equally familiar picture to be seen in other girls who carried some kind of grievance of long standing against their mothers; an estrangement and a determination not to let mother participate too closely in this important event or in the life of the expected baby, a somewhat belligerent independence as if mother had not done too well by them in the past and thus should at least not interfere with their baby in the future. We learned to expect and predict in most of these cases that at one point or another during pregnancy there will be a softening in the girl's attitude, a remark will occur such as "I understand mother much better now," "after all she meant well . . ." and a greater tolerance and acceptance develops. It is as if in the normal pregnancy this step towards becoming a mother herself is essential in solving the remainders of childhood conflicts which either have kept the daughter in an anxious infantile obedience or pushed her into a somewhat rebellious and defiant independence. In the case of successful maturation through pregnancy these half-way solutions are replaced by an adult and comfortable awareness of becoming a co-equal partner of mother, a friend and companion in this unique experience of parenthood.

This chapter of her life history, like those mentioned before, has equal import for the woman's general well being and healthy enjoyment of pregnancy as it is of immense significance for her freedom and fitness to become a good mother. Time does not permit me even to sketch the complications and failures which can enter into the relationship with the baby if these solutions are not reached adequately. I will only mention here that an unexpectedly large part of the by-now-famous disturbances in the early mother-child relationship, which then so frequently lead to increasing complications and finally to the so-called problem child, have their roots in the woman's neurotic entanglement with her own mother, be it in a fearful inner submissiveness or in a belligerent defiance—both of them leading to an unhealthily rigid attitude toward the child, so very different from the free give-and-take, from being tuned in on the needs and need fulfillment of the baby and of herself as a happy mother.

To summarize:

1. To be able to love the child as an independent being with his own individual personality though there will exist a deeper bond with him as he remains forever part of herself . . .

2. To accept and fulfill her changing role vis-a-vis her husband, maintaining her sexual attachment to him and growing into the position of the mother of his child . . .

3. And, finally, to solve her relationship to her own mother, from being mainly her mother's little daughter to becoming a co-equal to her mother in function and stature . . .

these are the ubiquitous psychological tasks of pregnancy and motherhood. . . .

20

Delivery

HELENE DEUTSCH

For many years psychiatrists have been interested in the
mental states of the newborn child, its traumatic experiences and fears. The first anxiety state arising from its
separation from the mother is considered the prototype
and cause of all its later anxieties. Strikingly, less attention has been given to the simultaneous processes in the
mother. The development of modern obstetrics seems increasingly to reduce the mother's active participation in
the process of birth, and the observations recorded in the
following paragraphs may appear anachronistic in the
near future.

It is valuable therefore to gain an insight into the
psychologic reactions of a woman who is delivered spontaneously, that is, into the greatest of all female pleasure-
pain experiences, and its accompanying psychologically
determined disturbances, before modern technic has
deprived psychiatrists of the possibility of doing so.
Obstetricians and midwives are too much concerned with
physical processes to bother about their patients' psychic
experiences. They are usually tired and exhausted, and
because they concentrate on the somatic factors, their
interest is awakened only when active intervention seems
necessary. The obstetrician considers his task completed
when the child has emerged unharmed from the mother's
body and the mother shows no pathologic symptoms.

Further, modern obstetrics does not wait for an ab-

SOURCE: From *The Psychology of Women*, Vol. II, by Helene
Deutsch, M.D. (New York, Grune & Stratton, 1945), pp. 210–
217, 222–229, 247–249. Reprinted by permission of Grune &
Stratton, Inc. and the author.

normal difficulty in delivery before intervening actively. The hastening of birth by the physician, at the moment when in all probability the child is ready to face all the hardships of extrauterine existence, is increasingly accepted, and it seems that soon there will be no spontaneous biologic process of birth at all.

The following observations are referable in part to a period in obstetric science when the spontaneous process was interfered with only in cases of special necessity. Thus it was possible not only to follow the psychic accompaniments of the physiologic process, but also to track down the psychologic factors of an incipient disturbance. I should like to emphasize the fact that, except when the contrary is indicated, all this material relates to first deliveries. Later deliveries either are repetitions of the first, or have a more individual character determined by the life situation. The typical factors seem most pronounced in the first delivery.

To understand the psychologic situation at the time of birth, we must go back to the last phase of pregnancy. The approach of childbirth is indicated by certain harbingers. Several weeks before the event the uterus drops. At the slightest outside excitation, or altogether spontaneously, it contracts—as though practicing for the labor pains to come. This lowered position of the uterus results in pressures, feelings of tension, and respiratory difficulties, and even the healthiest woman now finds her somatic condition burdensome and uncomfortable. In addition there is a psychic impatience; the harmony between mother and child is disturbed. It is as though nature were seeing to it in advance that the imminent separation from the child should not be too painful (psychologically) for the mother.

We know from numerous experiences that there is hardly any biologic process that is not accompanied and influenced by psychic processes. In the last weeks of pregnancy the mother-child union is disturbed by physiologic factors, and the organic changes produce increasing feelings of discomfort. The physical burden becomes a background for emotional impulses that assume a hostile character with regard to the unity with the child. The mother's inner perception of a pull on her body increasingly transforms the fetus into an alien body, just as it did in the first phase of pregnancy. With the increase of bodily discomfort, the ego of a psychically healthy woman becomes gradually weary of the shrinking of her life contents produced by pregnancy and of her exceptional physical and psychic situation. Apparently the merger of extremes—ego and species—cannot be tolerated for a very long time. The relationship with the child is split: the being in the uterus already has his double, who is the subject of all expectations and fantasied with fulfillments and whose real existence as a distinct person is gradually approaching. With the end of pregnancy the I-you polarity is simultaneously strengthened, and the psychic management of loving and hostile impulses uses this duality: the enemy must get out in order to reappear as a precious friend in the outside world.

Thus during these last weeks there begins the conflict between the will to retain and the will to expel, and normally it takes place only psychically. The will to retain is above all the expression of narcissistic self-sufficiency that has developed during pregnancy and that refuses to renounce the established unity. The realization, through bodily sensations, of the imminent destruction of this unity, manifests itself in the mother's heightened identification with the child and opposes the expulsive tendencies. On the other hand, the fantasy of the child as an external love object of the very near future has been developed during the whole period of pregnancy and it now joins with the negative emotions of the expulsive tendencies (by negative emotions we mean the effects of the physiologic discomfort). If the conflict between the two tendencies assumes a pathologic character and the expulsive forces win the upper hand, the result may be a premature delivery. But if, in addition to the narcissistic

DELIVERY   265

sense of unity, the mother feels concern about the fate
threatening the child after it is expelled from its secure
shelter, and fears her new responsibility, the retentive
tendencies and with them the tendency to prolong pregnancy are intensified. Conservative clinging to the status
quo, horror at the idea of splitting a unity woven by
many emotional and physical threads, and fear of the
pains and dangers of delivery, create resistance to the
termination of the condition. The chemically and physiologically determined disharmony between mother and
child that manifests itself in the last weeks of pregnancy,
is the prelude to the imminent separation that normally
marks the victory of the physiologic over the psychic
element. It is interesting to note that the sharpening of
the two tendencies is revealed in the dream life of the last
phase of pregnancy, when the typical pregnancy dreams,
in which the expectant mother identifies herself with her
future child (the so-called mother-womb fantasy), are
increasingly frequent. The mother, who in the dreams of
the previous phases of pregnancy often appeared as a
little girl swimming in water, now sees herself slipping
through narrow cracks, falling from a height, laboriously
climbing out of water, striving to reach a far-off goal, etc.
In these dreams her own personality can be recognized
directly or through associations. Since the question of
boy or girl is now more acute, and curiosity about it
greatly contributes to the mother's impatient waiting, the
child's sex is particularly emphasized in the dreams: the
child of the dream is specifically a boy or a girl.

On this point the mother's conscious and unconscious
wishes are usually in conflict, and sometimes the wish-
fulfilling tendency of the dream adapts itself to hypocriti-
cal consciousness, and sometimes to unconscious sin-
cerity. Consciously, very many women, masculine as well
as feminine ones, wish for a boy as their first-born. . . .
Deep beneath this wish, deriving from object love, is
concealed a feminine-narcissistic aspiration: the woman
wishes for a daughter in order to be reborn in her, en-

dowed with all the charm of the new being.[1] It is striking
how often the boy in the dream appears as ugly and the
girl as beautiful. Thus the woman's ambivalent relationship to her husband is expressed: "Here is your boy—he
is ugly as you are." But the dreamer's own image always
appears in the full beauty that she desires for herself and
her daughter.

Very often the child in the dream appears not only as
already born, but as far advanced in his development,
speaking, walking, etc. In this dream the mother fulfills
her wish to see her child in the outside world, already
freed from the dangers that she herself fears. The dreams
are not always so optimistic: the fear of giving birth to a
monster is intensified in the last weeks of pregnancy, and
cripples, idiots, monsters appear in the pregnant woman's dreams just as in her daytime anxieties. . . .

On the eve of her definitive initiation into real motherhood, even the most mature woman is regressively transformed into a child. Just as in puberty we are confronted
here with the peculiar fact that a tremendous advance in
existence mobilizes regressive forces. The woman's impatient curiosity in the last weeks of pregnancy reminds us
of the childish urge to explore things, which usually expresses sexual curiosity: "How will the child get out?"
The adult woman trembles with anxiety just like the
child: "How will anything as big as a child get through
that little opening?" And repeating her old unconscious
desire to look inside the body of her pregnant mother, she
is filled with the ardent wish: "If only I could look inside
myself once—then I would not mind if the pregnancy
lasted longer." The fear that she had during the first
phases of pregnancy—"Am I really pregnant?"—again
comes to the fore: "Is it really a baby?" If the fetus
moves less than before, then something bad must be hap-

---

[1] It is this insight into the psyche of the civilized mother that
led me to suspect that the Marquesas women devour their newborn
girls in order to absorb their youth and charm. This motive is also
familiar to us from folklore.

pening; if it is lively, then something else is wrong—"it is
so restless." The feeling that her possession is insecure,
which accompanies woman during her entire pregnancy,
is now intensified, and she fears not only for her own life,
but even more for that of the child: "Is it there at all?
Will it live? Is it normal? How does it look? What is its
sex?" She is obsessed by worries and doubts amid her
great joy and anticipation.

In all women—the happy and the disappointed, the
strong and the weak, the loving and the hating—the
doubts, restlessness, impatience, and joyful expectation
all conceal the fear of delivery, which is increasingly intensified with the approach of term. What are the sources
of this fear? To what extent is it justified?

Although childbirth is a physiologic phenomenon, a
number of its manifestations border on the pathologic.
Even under the most normal conditions, it is characterized by pain and bleeding, which otherwise mark only
morbid states. Certainly nature did not intend to make
the normal process so difficult, yet the higher the species
in the animal series, the more complicated is the reproductive function, the graver the dangers, and the worse
the pain.

Today we have effective methods of overcoming the
dangers of the birth process. Surgery triumphs over the
anatomic anomalies and chemistry over the powerful
physiologic disturbances. . . .

However, woman's fear of death has not been eliminated with the real dangers. She has merely transferred
her motivation from reality to psychic life. Analytic science can discover only those determinants of fear that
spring from the woman's individual life. But we assume
that all these fears are only provocations or intensifica-
tions of a deep hereditary fear of death that accompanies
the new life awakening in the mother's body. Its deepest
sources are inaccessible to us. But we know that the fear
of separation is one of its chief representatives.

Because of the identification with the child that takes

place during pregnancy, the fear of separation is not only
that of "I am losing the child," but also that of "The
child is losing me." In other words, in birth the child
loses the condition of absolute protection and security,
that primitive condition of bliss for which all of us
yearn. . . .

Another important source of the fear of death in childbirth lies in an unresolved and guilt-laden relation of the
woman to her own mother. We have seen that in all the
phases of development toward femininity, in all her love
and in all the activities of reproduction that bring woman
closer to motherhood, her greatest danger lies in her unresolved guilt feeling toward her own mother. For this
makes her incapable of becoming herself a happy mother,
free from anxiety. It is clear that this guilt feeling and the
anxious tension connected with it are particularly mobilized at childbirth. . . .

*   *   *

In many women the restlessness of the last weeks of
pregnancy is expressed by intensified activity: they can
barely keep quiet, and have a continual urge to do something, by which they betray anxious uneasiness even if
they are free of conscious fear. The subjectively strengthened sensation of the uterine contractions induces the
woman to go to the hospital prematurely, while her dis-
appointment at its turning out a false alarm may make
her swing to the opposite extreme, and . . . her term is
delayed by an inhibiting process. Such subjectively
caused disturbances in the last phases of pregnancy can
greatly influence the later process of delivery.

To clarify the psychologic accompaniments of this
process, we shall briefly sketch the physiologic phenomena. We distinguish three stages in a normal birth: those
of the dilatation, the expulsion, and the afterbirth. The
dilatation stage often lasts for several days and is marked
by slight contractions of the uterine muscles, associated
with mild drawing pains. For a woman having her first
child they are a signal for preparation, and almost all

women develop a striking activity in this phase. Only when they are paralyzed by fear do they yield to fate and let others act for them. Normally this fear is, if not mastered, at least outweighed by euphoric anticipation: "I shall soon have a baby."

Naturally, the woman's attitude will from the beginning be determined by her readiness, by the extent to which she has prepared herself, during the last period of pregnancy, for the trauma of separation, or, in other cases, by the extent to which her impatience to get rid of her burden has disturbed the normal process.

This more or less protracted preparatory phase is followed by the first delivery stage, the actual dilatation, so named because the mouth of the uterus is gradually dilated by the violent contractions of the uterine muscles. These contractions draw the neck of the uterus so far upward that its orifice is opened, thus allowing of the passage of the child. While the opening is gradually enlarged, the membranes surrounding the fetus push through, pressing against the orifice, and are ruptured, permitting escape of some of the amniotic fluid.

During the second or expulsion stage of delivery the contractions of the uterus continue; that is to say, the muscles in the neck of the uterus are contracted in a longitudinal direction, then the adjoining section of the muscles contracts in a circular direction. This circular contraction moves constantly higher, and the lower section of the uterus and the vagina become a soft sac through which the child, partly through the driving force of the rhythmic uterine contractions and partly by abdominal pressure, is pushed until its head is protruded through the vagina.

The third stage of parturition, the afterbirth period, usually follows from fifteen to thirty minutes after the birth of the child. In this phase the remaining products of gestation (the placenta) are expelled.

Only the first two stages of delivery are psychologically interesting. The functioning of the uterine muscles, the

contractions and dilations, depend upon the innervation
[nervous excitation]. The innervation has three sources:
the sympathetic nervous system, which inhibits the expulsion of the fetus; the parasympathetic system, which
stimulates the muscles of expulsion; and a local innervation of ganglia within the uterine muscles that participate
in expulsive contractions. The normal process of parturition depends upon the harmonious interaction of the
various muscles and their innervations. The latter in turn
are very much dependent upon internal and external influences. Psychosomatic medicine is familiar with the extraordinary dependence of the sympathetic and the parasympathetic nervous system upon emotional influences;
other organs likewise can fail in their functioning under
the influence of psychogenically disturbed innervation
processes. The task of delivery is thus based upon the
antagonistic effects of specific innervations. These effects
are automatically regulated: an excessive hastening of the
process is opposed by corresponding innervational inhibitions, and vice versa. What is true of the organic processes is also true of the psychic processes. They too, as
we have seen, are full of antagonisms; various psychic
tendencies and emotional impulses are offset by counter-
reactions and inhibitions. The autonomic nervous system,
which assumes direction of the physiologic process of
birth, and likewise the unconscious psychic life, are independent of the conscious will of the woman in labor. The
functioning of the autonomic nervous system can be modified by drugs; the psychic unconscious can be influenced
more or less indirectly through consciousness. Moreover,
the two spheres can enter into a direct but unconscious
relationship.

The process of birth, with its boundless anxiety stem-
ming from various sources, offers a particularly propi-
tious soil for the action of psychogenic influences. The
mother's attitude toward her child, her readiness for
motherhood, the events of her pregnancy, her whole life
situation, certainly contribute to the psychic atmosphere

of delivery. However, it is striking how many deliveries
follow their normal biologic course despite a miserable
life situation, despite poverty and worry, fear of social
consequences (illegitimacy), an unhappy marriage, etc.
Conversely, there are disturbances that cannot be explained either physiologically or psychologically. Their
causation lies in the unconscious, and subsequent psychoanalytic reconstruction of such disturbances has given
us much insight into the birth process as a whole. . . .

. . . Many women from the beginning take a completely passive attitude: the physician has promised them
that they will not feel anything, that they need not worry
about anything, and they base their behavior on that.
When seized by sharper pains, they grow very angry and
impatient, call for a doctor, demand narcotics, and refuse
to give any active cooperation.

As a whole, however, the activity that manifests itself
in the final phase of pregnancy is a mechanism of defense
against fear. The driving unrest, the urge to activity, is
usually rationalized as a method of making the waiting
period seem shorter. In actual fact it is a preparation for
the active process of birth, produced by the inner urge.
Woman's contribution in delivery is manifested not only
by the product—the child—but above all by her active
participation in the birth. Whether she behaves more actively or more passively is usually, though not always,
determined by the nature of her personality as a whole.
Some women have turned all their psychic activity to
other goals, so that the process of birth is for them only a
biologic process to which they submit passively. Conversely, women otherwise more passively disposed are
thrown by the first pains into a joyful excited state that
spurs them to the greatest activity.

Some women display particularly intense activity at the
beginning of childbirth. Mrs. N., whom I observed immediately after her arrival in the hospital, gave me a
direct description of the beginning of her delivery. She
was a chemist by profession; during her pregnancy she

felt very well and continued to perform all her professional duties. The pains began a few days earlier than expected and surprised her while she was engaged in making an important chemical experiment and demonstrating it, with her superior, to a group of students. She worked eagerly while her pains grew increasingly frequent, thinking: "If only we can finish the experiment!" When I asked her why she did not-interrupt her work, she said that she did not have the feeling of two separate actions taking place; she felt as though the two were somehow connected and as though her task was to carry them both through to the end. Fortunately, she was delivered only two hours later; she herself was fully convinced that she had herself in hand, and that the birth would come at the right time. Mrs. N. was not a masculine woman, but she fully possessed the degree of activity trend that a woman needs to banish her fear and actually to participate in the birth of her child.

Mrs. N. is naturally only an exaggerated example of predelivery activity. In most women this activity is devoted to intensified preparations, in many others it has a more steady character, in still others it constitutes only a short temporary break-through that soon subsides. . . .

The activity of the average normally active woman at the onset of the first pains is somewhat as follows. She herself packs her suitcase, casts a last glance over the nursery to see that everything is in order, wants to have telephone conversations, mostly with her women friends, and often insists upon personally informing her physician, hospital, etc., that her labor has begun. The negation of fear underlying this outbreak of activity is often quite conscious.

Many women fall into a joyful excitation with the beginning of the pains, especially when the pregnancy has been protracted—"I thought I would never have a child." The child has gradually assumed an unreal character, the idea of its existence has become blurred. In others, on the contrary, the reality of the child is so strong at the end of pregnancy that the woman feels as though she were separated from it only by the "curtain" of the abdominal casing, and in her impatient excitement she wants to see it as soon as possible.

During the first stage of childbirth (the dilatation stage), even the most active woman should entirely subordinate herself to the inner forces—a passive, cooperative, patient endurance of the process is her only task. There are women who cannot tolerate this behavior. They want to take the birth into their own hands at once, they want to do something, and refuse to subordinate themselves either to inner forces or to external advice. Like any other manifestation of excessive activity, this behavior may express a primary tendency or a defense against fear. If the innervation processes of the first phase are marked by excessive tension, if the impulses are influenced by fear or an excessive propensity to active participation, the phenomena of labor lose their normal spontaneity, and the process is disturbed. On the other hand, an overpassively submissive attitude toward the innervation forces can prolong the dilatation phase, so that the progressive contractions take place slowly, lazily, or not at all: the birth is stalemated.

In this phase external influence can be very potent. I recall one defiant woman who, upon discovering that she was serving as an object of study for some medical students, immediately interrupted her labor pains, and did it again each time a student approached her....

The situation is different in the second or expulsion phase. Now the woman in labor must perform a great physical and psychic task. Abdominal pressure in childbirth is secured only with great effort, and the pain grows steadily worse. The pressure begins rhythmically with the pains; carried forward by the internal physical contractions, her own will power, and external encouragement, the woman in labor consummates her individual act in the service of the species.

Direct observation of women in labor leaves no doubt that childbirth is experienced as a strenuous act of accomplishment and that it requires tremendous mastery over fear and suffering. The shock of the pains and the excitation of the motor apparatus obviously reduce the capacity for receiving external impressions. All former joys and mortifications become pale and unimportant, communication between the ego of the woman in labor and the environment is reduced solely to matters directly connected with the birth process. Her activity is fully taxed, her accomplishment is connected with a tense "listening" to the innervation processes, and everything else, present, past, and future, seems to vanish. Nevertheless, sometimes the sense impressions directly connected with the delivery seem to be excessively sharp, almost paranoic, and the woman in travail has a tendency to misinterpret, mishear, etc. . . .

The psychoanalyst's contribution to knowledge of the birth process in this respect is the observation that unconscious psychic influences have free access to the above mentioned concentration on an active accomplishment. During this period of reduced consciousness their influence can be even stronger than in normal states. It is usually because of them that a well initiated labor stops, that the contractions become too strong or too weak, that they do not function at the right moment, or that they function in a paradoxic way. Instead of relaxation there is contraction, instead of a pushing forward there is a closing, barring movement, etc. In some cases one can observe a sudden cessation of the woman's participation: she protects herself from the rising fear and the pains by letting herself slip into passivity. Other women want to preserve their active control to such an extent that they free themselves from the normal rhythm of the process and cause a kind of confusion of the contracting activity. . . .

*   *   *

Medical science does not content itself with intervening in pathologic phenomena, but is rapidly extending its mastery to the normal physiologic processes. Science endeavors to conquer nature and its imperfections, and to correct whatever damage civilization has done to nature. Even in normal cases, the duration of delivery now depends upon the obstetric technic used, pain is mastered with the help of drugs, and fear is conquered by gradual lessening of the mother's active participation in the process. Her role as birth giver is growing ever more passive.

I question the desirability of this development. Woman's active part in the delivery process, her lasting pride in her accomplishment, the possibility of rapid reunion with her child, and some degree of gratification of that primary feminine quality that assigns pain a place among pleasure experiences in the psychic economy, are precious components of motherhood, and an effort should be made to preserve them.

The psychiatrist and the obstetrician must combine to help nature to the best of their abilities. The obstetrician is usually unable to use his psychologic acuteness and possible interest in psychologic observation. He rarely has the time or the patience to listen to the woman's fragmentary and often irrelevant utterances before, during, and after delivery. He pays little attention to them as a human being and even less as a scientist. He dashes from one delivery to another, often manages his cases so that they coincide in term, in order to be able to let as many women as possible profit from his expert help within a short time, and considers his task well done if everything goes smoothly. An important obstetrician, one of the few who admit the fact of psychologic influences in somatic processes, told me that in the course of his practice he had known only one woman who, upon awakening from her narcosis, refused to acknowledge her child as her own. Yet I knew that four of his patients had had that feeling but had never had the opportunity to communicate the fact to him. . . .

If the disturbing elements within and without are well mastered, if the delivery follows a normal, natural course, and if by direct emotional influence or other means the excess of fear and pain is successfully reduced, childbirth is the greatest and most gratifying experience of woman, perhaps of human beings. Two powerful factors make it so: first, the joy in accomplishment that is connected with the mastering of fear and pain and with the woman's own activity; second, the happy relation with the child that begins immediately after delivery. The dynamism of this relationship is clear: the whole psychic energy tied to the labor and withdrawn from the outside world streams toward the child in the moment of delivery, and the newly achieved freedom from pain and fear creates a feeling of triumph and endows the first moment of motherhood with real ecstasy. It is not yet motherliness that characterizes the mother-child relationship—it is only the first foundation stone, perhaps even a reservoir from which springs the gradually developing love for the child.

21

Childbirth in America

ANDREA OSTRUM

PSYCHOLOGICAL THEORIES OF CHILDBIRTH

The body of theory that might be said to comprise a psychology of childbirth is varied and far-flung. It can be subsumed, however, under three main theoretical orientations, each of which has attempted to explain the psychological underpinnings of the childbirth experience.

Psychoanalytic Theory

The most definitive psychoanalytic theory of childbirth has been articulated by Helene Deutsch in her two-volume work, *The Psychology of Women* (1945). For Deutsch, the childbirth experience is inextricably linked with the female personality structure, which, in her view, is inborn, fundamentally unchangeable, and determined by the anatomical and functional characteristics of female sexuality. Childbirth is viewed as part of a natural physiological continuum involving intercourse, fecundation, and parturition. All three of these female sexual functions, according to Deutsch, require postponement of gratification, abandonment of activity, and the union of pleasure and pain. These requirements in turn constitute the basis of the female personality structure which is characterized by eroticism, passivity, and masochism. Individuals differ in terms of varying degrees, manifesta-

SOURCE: From an unpublished Ph.D. dissertation, "Psychological Factors Influencing Women's Choice of Childbirth Procedure," by Andrea Ellen Ostrum, Columbia University, New York, 1972. Copyright © 1975 by Andrea Ellen Ostrum. Printed by permission of the author. Edited in cooperation with the author.

tions, and combinations of these three basic constitutional factors.

Deutsch, in line with her deterministic view of female psychology, sees the individual's experience of childbirth as varying only inasmuch as women react differently to certain given and unchanging parameters of the experience. Chief among these parameters is a deep primal fear of death, which is aroused by the uncontrollable and unknown nature of birth and by fear of separation from the fetus, which during pregnancy has been experienced as part of oneself (Deutsch, 1945; Kroger and Fried, 1962). This fear can be intensified by former genital anxiety (castration and defloration), old anal and urethral fears, and by guilt over death wishes towards one's own mother. The individual delivery experience, according to Deutsch, is determined by each woman's disposition to passivity and to activity, the quantitative degree to which each of these dispositions is present, and the form in which they are manifested. Within this framework, the gratification of labor and delivery depends upon the woman's ability to regulate her passive and active responses appropriately to each phase of childbirth.

Given Deutsch's belief in the essential female ingredients of passivity and masochism, it is interesting to note her emphasis on activity in childbirth. She wrote, "Direct observation of women in labor leaves no doubt that childbirth is experienced as a strenuous act of accomplishment and that it requires tremendous mastery over fear and suffering" (1945, p. 228). Deutsch goes on to say that childbirth is the "greatest and most gratifying experience of woman, perhaps of human beings" because of two powerful factors: "first, the joy and accomplishment that is connected with the mastering of fear and pain and with woman's own activity; second, the happy relationship with the child that begins immediately after delivery" (1945, p. 248). Deutsch questioned the increasing use of obstetrical anesthesia because it interferes with precisely the two factors that make birth most gratifying. Anesthesia makes woman's role as birth-giver "even more passive" and creates a "barrier of separation" between her and the child (1945, p. 253).

While Deutsch herself did not develop a theoretical program of childbirth procedure to implement her views, she had a profound influence on Herbert Thoms, professor of obstetrics and gynecology, who in 1947 began one of the earliest American programs of natural childbirth at Grace–New Haven Hospital in Connecticut (Chertok, 1959). Thoms was primarily affected by Deutsch's psychodynamic view of childbirth and by her opinion that physicians ought to attempt to gain insight into the psychological reactions of women delivered spontaneously. He attempted in clinic-wide research to study factors such as pain, anxiety, and conflict in women giving birth. In the implementation of his obstetric program, Thoms, influenced by Deutsch's "therapeutic" approach, insisted that "the key to success in any childbirth programme is skilled and sympathetic attendance for the woman in active labor" (Chertok, 1959, p. 66). The Grace–New Haven program, accordingly, included prenatal instruction on pregnancy and birth processes, support and guidance by staff during labor, and provision for hospitalizing the mother and baby together if desired (Thoms and Roth, 1950). Thoms did not insist, however, on a nonmedicated birth, leaving this up to the decision of the woman herself. The aim of his program was to eliminate sources of anxiety for the expectant mother, primarily through the closest possible understanding and cooperation between the mother and her attendants. In so doing, he clearly hoped that women would be better able to elect a spontaneous childbirth and to experience the gratification that he and Deutsch believed was being eliminated by modern obstetric techniques.

Anthropological Theories

UNIVERSALISTIC SCHOOL: LAWRENCE FREEDMAN. Anthropological evidence has been used to buttress two con-

flicting theories about childbirth. Lawrence Freedman, an
associate of Thoms', believed that childbirth was characterized by a universal terror and apprehension of the unknown, and of complications and death (Freedman and
Ferguson, 1950, p. 368). Furthermore, he felt cultural
evidence indicated that the overwhelming majority of
tribes had pain in childbirth comparable to ours, and
that, contrary to some theories, pain in childbirth had not
been introduced and fostered by civilization. Freedman
based his conclusions on a cross-cultural study that examined anthropological descriptions of the childbirth
rituals of primitive tribes. He and Ferguson found that
"there is hardly a group anywhere that does not have
quite extensive, and in some cases extremely ingenious,
therapeutic procedures aimed at easing and hastening the
birth of the child" (1950, p. 365). They felt that an
almost universal presence of taboos, magical and propiti-
atory ceremonies accompanying pregnancy and delivery,
indicated a fear of childbirth common to all people regardless of cultural variation. Freedman approached
childbirth with a psychoanalytic orientation. A psychiatrist and a former associate of Thoms', he placed primary
importance on psychiatric participation in obstetric management, in order to understand the memories and fantasies of childbearing women. He initiated a program
whereby medical personnel are trained by psychiatrists in
understanding nonverbal communication in order better
to deal with observed behavior during birth. Freedman
also advocated a prenatal educational training program
to decrease the element of the unknown and to provide
women with adaptive behavior that they can use to cope
with both anxiety and fear during childbirth.

RELATIVISTIC SCHOOL: MARGARET MEAD. Mead, with
her own anthropological orientation, came to conclusions
about childbirth completely different from those of
Freedman. She felt that childbirth is experienced "according to the phrasing given it by the culture, as an experience that is dangerous and painful, interesting and en-

grossing, matter-of-fact and mildly hazardous, or accompanied by enormous supernatural hazards" (1949, p. 243). Mead based her conclusions on both her own observations in anthropological field work and a review of cross-cultural patterns in childbearing drawn from information recorded in the Human Relations Area File. The material reviewed by Mead and Newton (1967) included, in addition to childbirth rituals, descriptions of actual practices of childbirth of present-day tribes, some of which were directly observed by anthropologists. Mead and Newton found different patterns of birth from culture to culture, with some cultures seeing pregnancy and birth as a time of fear and anxiety, and others as an easy, open process. There were indications that the time of labor varied markedly from one society to another, with lengthy labors being associated with frightening birth rituals and quick labors being associated with relaxed, casually treated births. Mead concluded (1949, p. 237):

> It cannot be argued that childbirth is both an unbearable pain and a bearable pain, both a situation from which all women naturally shrink in dread and a situation towards which all women move readily and happily, both as a danger to be avoided and consumation devoutly to be desired. At least one aspect must be regarded as learned, and it seems simpler, in the light of present knowledge to assume that women's attitude towards childbearing and men's attitudes towards childbearing have complex and contradictory elements in them and that a society may pick up and elaborate any one or sometimes even a contradictory set of such attitudes.

Mead felt that women's experiences of childbirth were strongly influenced by male attitudes and expectations about birth. "Male imagination, undisciplined and uninformed by immediate bodily cues or immediate bodily experience, may have contributed disproportionately to the cultural superstructure of belief and practice regarding childbearing" (1949, p. 238). In the United States

today, male influence on childbirth is channeled most
directly through the medical profession, which consists,
according to Mead, of "males strongly influenced by their
conceptions of what a female role is and a minority of
females whose interest in medicine has been defined as
male and who are strongly repelled by their conceptions
of the limitations of the female role" (1949, p. 376). Mead
concluded that "together they may shape medical practice into strange forms in which the women who might
make a contribution from a first hand knowledge of
femininity are silent and the men are left freer to follow
their fantasies than they would have been had there been
no women among them" (1949, p. 376). While Mead
has not directly presented a childbirth program, she has
suggested that childbirth practices no longer stem from or
reflect the knowledge of the childbearing woman. The
professionalism of medicine, rather, has resulted in
women being "indoctrinated" either into medicated childbirth, which takes away from women "the simple power
of bearing their own children," or, more lately, into natural childbirth, which seems to restore this act to women.
While not stated directly, there seems to be an implication in Mead's writing that the specific childbirth procedure of the moment may be less important than restoring
the direction and control of the birth process to women,
who have the most direct perception of what it is like to
give birth. Natural childbirth, while presented by Mead as
preferable, can be as much of an "indoctrination" as
medicated childbirth if it does not stem directly from the
felt needs and wishes of childbearing women themselves.

Neurophysiological Theories

READ METHOD. The theoretical foundation of Grantly
Dick-Read's method, "childbirth without fear," is the vicious circle of fear-tension-pain-fear. Fears and anxiety
about labor, Read believed, were introduced by superstition, civilization, and culture. Fear and anticipation of
pain lead to sympathetic nervous system activity, which,

in turn, causes a contraction of the uterine muscles. Muscular contraction creates a resistance at the outlet of the womb to the expulsive activities of labor, which, in turn, leads to muscular tension. This tension is interpreted, according to Read, by the sensitive nerve endings in the uterus as pain. Therefore, "if fear, tension, and pain go hand in hand, then it must be necessary to relieve tension and to overcome fear in order to eliminate pain" (1944, p. 24). The Read method involves a two-pronged attack on fear and tension. Education in the phenomenon of pregnancy, labor, and delivery is designed to counteract the culturally induced "unreal" roots of anticipatory fear. Physical relaxation during labor is designed physiologically to prevent muscular tension. The importance of trained muscular relaxation is based on the theoretical assumption that "it is physically impossible to be nervous in any part of your body if in that part you are completely relaxed" (1944, p. 299). Read felt that relaxation during labor required an alienation of the mind from any active interest in the uterine function. Control of respiration, primarily through deep chest breathing, was the main tool to accomplish relaxation during labor. Relaxation must be taught before delivery and, in the Read method, is begun in the forth or fifth month of pregnancy. Read himself emphasized the educative and therapeutic aspects of training for childbirth. He believed that women with education, without exercises, do better during labor than those meticulously prepared and skilled in physical culture but without education in childbirth. The central aim of the Read method is, by the alleviation of fear, to permit the complete relaxation and elasticity of the uterus and, thereby, to allow the free painless delivery of the child.

"Childbirth without fear" was introduced into the United States in 1946 and was adopted as basic policy by the Maternity Center Association of New York in 1947. The first mass application of the Read method in the United States was at Grace–New Haven Hospital where

Dr. Herbert Thoms in 1947 began a program of "educated childbirth." The Read method never achieved organized mass application in the United States. Rather, it was taken up by individual doctors or occasional hospitals and was primarily advanced by several private associations throughout the country that, like the New York Maternity Center, offered programs of prenatal training for parturient women and nursing personnel.

PSYCHOPROPHYLACTIC METHOD. The psychoprophylactic method of childbirth (hereafter referred to as the PPM) was developed in the Soviet Union in the late 1940s and 1950s. The PPM, like the Read method, is based on the premise that pain is not a necessary accompaniment of childbirth and can be prevented from occurring by verbal analgesia. Like acupuncture in China, however, the practice of the PPM is far more advanced than the theoretical understanding of how or why it works. There are, in the Soviet Union, theoretical disagreements about the physical versus cultural origins of pain in childbirth, the state of the cortex during childbirth, and individual differences among women in receptivity to the method. Certain principles and practices, however, are accepted by all workers (Chertok, 1959): (1) that uterine function can be influenced by excitation of the cortex; (2) that pain is undoubtedly the result of cortical function; and (3) that speech can serve as a real conditioning stimulus to cortical excitation. The PPM is based on the Pavlovian theory of reflex-conditioned activity, according to which one set of reflexes (termed "conditioned") are acquired, temporary, and characteristic of the individual. . . . Russian research has established that it is possible to alter the sensation of pain by speech as well as by physical or chemical agents. The key to preventing pain in labor, without medication, therefore, lies in altering the activity of the cortex through the second signaling system of speech. The primary means of accomplishing this result, according to the PPM, is a total re-educative effort and complete "asepsis of behavior and speech" (Chertok, 1959, p. 128). All phrases making allusions to pain or possible complications of childbirth are avoided. Women are educated both in the physiology of labor and delivery, and in the Pavlovian interpretation of pain in childbirth, with the aim of removing the idea that organic changes of pregnancy and birth are accompanied by pain. In addition, certain physiological activities are taught, with the aim of creating new conditioned reflexes to labor that will alter cortical activity and prevent pain. Some of these procedures are rythmical respiration and abdominal effleurage. Other procedures are also taught that directly effect obstetric activity, such as relaxation of smooth muscles and active collaboration in expulsion of the baby. The PPM trains women to be accurately aware of their bodily sensations during the process of labor and delivery and to adjust their activities (breathing, pushing, and so on) accordingly. The PPM differs from the Read method in that it encourages activity and active participation in labor rather than dissociation and relaxation. The aim of the PPM is, through active intervention, to affect pain directly at its source (the cortex) and, by so doing, to prevent it from ever occurring during childbirth.

The PPM was first presented at a national conference in the Soviet Union in 1951. That same year the Soviet government ordered that the method be applied to the entire country. Mass application was achieved through the government-regulated medical system, with teaching being done in groups and primarily by trained midwives. In 1952 Dr. Ferdinand Lamaze returned from a study trip to Russia and introduced the PPM to France, where the original users were a small group of women involved in leftist organizations and activated by powerful ideological motives. General public acceptance in Western Europe and Latin America was guaranteed when in 1956 the PPM was endorsed by Pope Pius XII. China followed soon after France in acceptance of the method and, like the Soviet Union, ordered it to be applied to the entire

country. Throughout the 1950s the PPM spread to 44
countries in Western Europe and Latin America. By
1969, 50 per cent of the women in France were using the
PPM. The PPM was introduced to the United States in
1959 by Marjorie Karmel in her best-selling book, *Thank
You Dr. Lamaze*. It has been advanced by the American
Society for Psychoprophylaxis in Obstetrics (ASPO), a
New York–based national organization with physician,
teacher, and parent divisions. ASPO is devoted to the
prepagation of the PPM by educating the medical profession, hospital administrations, and the general public
about the method; by offering prenatal training course;
and by training new teachers, who in the United States
are usually nurses, physiotherapists, or former PPM
users.

CURRENT AMERICAN PATTERNS IN
OBSTETRICAL ANESTHESIA

It is difficult to establish concretely nation-wide trends
in obstetrical anesthesia because no national surveys have
been published. From isolated findings, however, certain
signs do emerge. Primary emphasis by the medical profession in the United States is given to medical rather
than nonmedical anesthesia for childbirth. The 1970
Index Medicus contains two fine-print columns of references to American research on medical obstetric anesthesia; American research on nonmedicated obstetric
anesthesia comprised three articles, all descriptive in nature. In practice as well, nonmedicated anesthesia appears to be the least used form of obstetric management in
this country. In the absence of national surveys, the best
demographic information abut the practice of nonmedicated childbirth can be found in the figures published by
ASPO, the largest organized group actively promoting
nonmedicated deliveries. ASPO's national coordinating
office gives a total membership figure for 1971 of about
2100. Of these, 250 are physicians, 850 are teachers,

and 1000 are parents. The ASPO annual report for 1970 records 36 chapters cross-country. Of these, 21 are on the East Coast, 4 are in California, 9 are in the Midwest, and 2 are in the North and Southwest. The majority of the ASPO chapters are in urban areas or suburban areas near large metropolitan centers. While the membership figures of ASPO represent only those actively supporting or working with the PPM, and as such are an underestimation of the users and practitioners of even this one particular method, they do give some idea of the availability of nonmedicated childbirth on a cross-country scale. In Brooklyn, where the present study was executed, there were, as of 1970, out of 78 practicing obstetricians three physicians formally listed as members of ASPO. Five hospitals offered some preparatory course for childbirth. These, plus one additional hospital, allowed husbands to be present for the delivery. (There were, at this time, 23 hospitals in Brooklyn which offered obstetric care.)

It is widely known and accepted that American users of the PPM have tended to be almost exclusively middle- and upper-middle-class private obstetric patients. (The author knows of no currently operating program of preparation for birth designed for nonprivate ward patients.) The original patient population that used nonmedicated childbirth was expanded during the second half of the 1960s with the growth of the hippie-communal movement. In the counterculture, nonmedicated childbirth is part of a total value system based on a return to nature and a rejection of modern technological society. The counterculture itself, however, consists primarily of children with a middle-class white background. Nonmedicated childbirth in the United States, therefore, continues to be practiced on a limited scale, primarily in eastern and urban areas, and by a narrow segment of the total population centered in the affluent middle class or its counterculture dropouts.

Regional anesthesia depends for its administration on

specially trained and skilled anesthesiologists, who are
currently in great shortage. Thus, despite the preference
of the medical profession for this type of anesthesia (as
of 1969, 80 percent of all obstetrical anesthesia in certain West Coast maternity units was epidural anesthesia),
its usage is limited by the shortage of trained personnel.
As of the last reported survey in 1959, only 15 percent
of all vaginal deliveries used a trained anesthesiologist
(Shnider, 1969). In other cases, anesthesia was administered by obstetricians, nurses, and untrained personnel.
The shortage is especially acute in small hospitals in rural
states. It is safe to assume, therefore, that regional anesthesia is not commonly available in rural areas, small
cities, or small hospitals. In urban areas, the availability
of regional anesthesia will depend on whether or not
there is an anesthesiologist trained in its administration
in the particular hospital attended, and even (as reported
by one consultant obstetrician) on which resident happens
to be on duty at the time of delivery.

Most women in the United States, therefore, especially
those outside of large urban centers, receive general
anesthesia for childbirth, most often administered by
nonanesthesiologists.

THE PSYCHO–POLITICS OF CHILDBIRTH

Childbirth patterns tend to be self-perpetuating. In the
United States, where women have traditionally been
heavily sedated, the elimination of both the sensation and
memory of pain has removed from women the incentive
to seek alternative methods of nonmedicated anesthesia.
In Western Europe, where Church doctrine at one time
deemed childbirth pain to be ordained by God, women
accepted their lot with resignation. In all countries, however, childbirth patterns are shaped primarily by the priorities and decisions of those who control institutionalized power, whether on a national, local, cultural, or professional level. Once the individual woman has aban-

doned birth as a private act and placed herself in the care and confines of a public medical system, her choices are limited by those who run the system. In a country where drugs are to be conserved, a woman demands medication to no avail. In a hospital where husbands and relatives are barred by fiat from the labor room, a woman remains alone. In a town where all doctors routinely administer medication for birth, a woman will be asleep. And in all cases, the determination of such priorities is primarily in the hands of men. Those who control the decision-making, funding, and implementation of medical research and health care practice (doctors, scientists, hospital administrators, governmental agencies) are almost exclusively male. Hence, those factors that determine how women will give birth are essentially outside their control. Women cannot mold the circumstances of childbirth to suit their needs because they have no power within the system that regulates these circumstances.

This fact has long been recognized by female social scientists. Margaret Mead (1949, p. 268) has described aspects of the birth procedure as designed "primarily to facilitate the ministrations of the obstetricians." Helene Deutsch went even further (1945, p. 258). "Modern obstetrics, a masterpiece of masculine efficiency, deprives woman of her active monopoly in this field." It seems peculiarly ironic that women in modern societies must accomplish the exclusively female act of childbirth in circumstances designed and streamlined by men. And, in fact, male direction of the childbirth process runs counter to practices common in most nondeveloped societies. In primitive cultures all over the world, the elderly woman, rather than the skilled man, is the predominant attendant at normal labor (Mead and Newton, 1967). Moreover, in primitive cultures the midwife was chosen according to specific personality and experiential characteristics judged to be important to that position. An additional note is that out of 64 primitive peoples whose childbearing practices were recorded for an anthropological survey, 31 excluded men from even witnessing normal delivery (Mead and Newton, 1967). Putting aside the thorny question of self-determination, this author believes that the male domination of childbirth management has, and must, of necessity, work against the best interests of women. Clara Thompson has written (1964, p. 249): "In the case of sexual experiences . . . one sex has no adequate means of identifying with the experience of the other sex . . . nor can a man identify with the tension and sensations of menstruation, female genital excitement, or childbirth."

The modern male-dominated health care system has, in fact, produced innovations in childbirth procedures that have made birth more difficult for women—chiefly the isolation of women from their female kin and community, the prone position of hospital deliveries, and the desexualization of childbirth. The isolation of women in impersonally run obstetric wards has been written about and agitated against extensively (Read, 1944; Thoms and Roth, 1950; Freedman and Ferguson, 1950; Lesser and Keane, 1956; Zussman, 1969). And yet, family-centered childbirth remains the exception rather than the rule; and most women remain, because of hospital rules, separated from both close relatives and female friends, who in primitive tribes have traditionally formed the social network within which childbirth took place.

Anthropological research has also shown that in an overwhelming majority of non-European societies (62 out of 76 surveyed) women use the upright position for delivery, according to which the expulsion of the baby is helped by the force of gravity. This position was maintained by means of a "delivery chair" in medieval times, when deliveries were attended by midwives and men were not allowed contact with the woman in labor. The prone position of traditional obstetric deliveries represents an assimilation to surgical procedure introduced where obstetric care has been taken over by the medical profession. The treatment of childbirth as a disease is also antithetical to what might once have been a source of gratification for women in labor—namely, sexual pleasure connected with the descent of the fetus down the vaginal canal. Childbirth rituals of some primitive tribes show a strong relationship between birth and sexuality (Mead and Newton, 1967). And some modern psychotherapists have commented on orgasmic gratification occasionally experienced by women during the final stage of birth. Such gratification is understandably rarely experienced in the modern hospital setting, where childbirth is treated as a physical affliction. Nor is the possibility of sexual pleasure even recognized or explored in most medical and psychological research.

This author would agree with Margaret Mead that "Since women's physiology is exceedingly different from that of men, it is necessary for women to have more of a role in controlling it . . . not because she wants to replace men with women, but because she believes that actual experience is an essential element in education" (quoted in Frankfort, 1971, p. 29). Mead's solution of replacing obstetricians with midwives appears to this author to be an unrealistic means of achieving her goal. As long as women do not have an adequate share of the decision-making power in health care institutions, midwives (if indeed they can be instituted) can do little more than offer a more sympathetic and knowledgeable presence to women. While this, in itself, is an innovation to be desired, the goal of making childbirth practices responsive in every aspect to women's needs can be fulfilled only if women, acutely aware of their own needs in this area, formulate and implement the childbirth policies and programs of the institutions in which they give birth. Until that time, women will continue to give birth in an alien place; and the act of childbirth will never be wholly their own.

REFERENCES

Chertok, Leon. *Psychosomatic Methods of Painless Child-birth*. London, New York, Paris, Los Angeles: Pergamon Press, 1959.

Deutsch, Helene. *The Psychology of Women*. 2 vols. New York: Grune & Stratton, 1945.

Dick-Read, Grantly. *Childbirth without Fear*. New York: Harper & Brothers, 1944.

Frankfort, Ellen. "Vaginal Politics." *The Village Voice*, December 19, 1971, pp. 21–22, 29.

Freedman, Lawrence A., and Ferguson, Vera. "The Question of Painless Childbirth in Primitive Cultures." *American Journal of Orthopsychiatry* 20:363–72, 1950.

Kroger, William S., and Fried, Samuel C. *Psychosomatic Gynecology*. Hollywood: Wilshire Book Company, 1962.

Lesser, M., and Keane, V. R. *Nurse-Patient Relationships in a Hospital Maternity Service*. St. Louis: C. V. Mosby Co., 1956.

Mead, Margaret. *Male and Female*. New York: William Morrow, 1949.

——, and Newton, Niles. "Pregnancy, Childbirth, and Outcome: A Review of Patterns of Culture and Future Research Needs." In *Childbearing, Its Social and Psychological Aspects*, edited by Samuel Richardson and Alan Guttmacher. New York: Williams & Wilkins, 1967.

Shnider, Sol M. "Obstetric Anesthesia Coverage: Problems and Solutions." *Obstetrics and Gynecology* 34:615–20, 1969.

Thompson, Clara. *International Psychoanalysis*, edited by Maurice R. Green. New York: Basic Books, 1964.

Thoms, Herbert, and Roth, Lawrence. *Understanding Natural Childbirth*. New York: McGraw-Hill, 1950.

Zussman, Shirley. "A Study of Certain Social, Psychological, and Cultural Factors Influencing Husbands' Participation in Their Wives' Labor." Ph.D. dissertation, Teachers College, New York, 1969.

22

The Acceptance of the Concept of the Maternal Role by Behavioral Scientists: Its Effects on Women

ROCHELLE PAUL WORTIS

The maternal "instinct" is a comfortable male myth; a woman can only give freely if she is in a position where she does not feel deprived herself.[12]

The purpose of this review is to reexamine critically the importance of the concept of "mothering" and to suggest that much of the evidence employed in psychological studies of the importance of the mother for the development of infants and children is based on assumptions that are scientifically inadequate. Furthermore, modern psychology, with its emphasis on individual advancement, individual achievement, and individual development, has encouraged the isolation of the adult woman, particularly the mother, and the domestication and subordination of females in society.

I am here challenging a concept that has for generations been viewed as a biological and social necessity. It is important, however, to discuss some of the contradictions inherent in our system of child-rearing that have overwhelming negative, oppressive effects on half the population (women) and on all infants who develop in

SOURCE: "The Acceptance of the Concept of the Maternal Role by Behavioral Scientists" by Rochelle Paul Wortis, Ph.D., in *American Journal of Orthopsychiatry*, 41, no. 5 (October, 1971), pp. 733–746. Copyright © 1971 the American Orthopsychiatric Association, Inc. Reproduced by permission of the *American Journal of Orthopsychiatry* and the author.

the environment of the nuclear family, with its prevailing emphasis on the mother-infant socialization process.

There are four basic questions to bear in mind when reading the literature on mother-infant interaction:

1. Is it a biological fact that, in the human species, the mother is the most capable person to socialize the infant?

2. Is it a biological fact that the human newborn seeks out the mother (rather than the father) or a female (rather than a male) as the figure to which it naturally relates best, needs most, and attaches itself to socially?

3. Socially, what criteria should we employ to define whether it is beneficial for the infant to form a strong bond of attachment to one woman?

4. Is it beneficial for the mother to assume the principal responsibility for the care and socialization of the young child?

We must begin with the understanding that we all have a strong prejudice about the need for "mothering" because we were all mothered. In a society such as ours, in which mothering is the principal mode of rearing children, any variant pattern that occurs (such as "multiple mothering," infants being raised by their fathers, or group rearing of infants) is considered abnormal. Participants in such variant patterns are constantly reminded of the "fact" that what they are doing is an exceptional alternative, a poor substitute for the "normal" pattern. This implies that they could never equal or improve upon the norm.

Margaret Mead has long been questioning the provincialism of studies of mother-infant interaction by Western psychologists and psychiatrists. In particular, Mead criticized the emphasis on the exclusive mother-infant bond. She emphasized that the conscious care of the infant is a cultural, not a biological invention. Therefore, whether or not the mother is the principal figure in the developing child's environment is a socio-cultural question and not a biological one. According to Mead, diversified kinds of attachment relationships have been successful in other cultures.[24] In our society, on the other hand, the vast majority of women are conditioned to expect that the child-rearing function will be their major individual responsibility.

ATTACHMENT

The "Attachment Function," as defined and elaborated by John Bowlby,[7] is a dual process through which the infant develops a strong psychobiological need to maintain proximity with the mother while the mother has a strong psychobiological need to maintain proximity with the infant. Attachment behavior usually begins to appear at around four to six months and, during the first year of life, a strong affectional bond develops.[1, 7] An "autonomous propensity" by the mother and infant to develop attachment toward each other is assumed by Bowlby's theory. This aspect of the theory will be discussed later in this paper.

The primacy of the mother-infant attachment bond is contradicted by Schaffer and Emerson's[35] study of attachment. They described three different stages in the development of attachment behavior: an "asocial" stage, in which the infant actively seeks optimal stimulation from *all* aspects of the environment; a "presocial" stage, in which the infant indiscriminately seeks proximity to objects that give it satisfaction; and, finally, a "social" stage, in which attachments to specific individual occurs. Schaffer and Emerson concluded that:

> To focus one's enquiry on the child's relationship with the mother alone would therefore give a misleading impression of the attachment function. . . . In certain societies multiple object relationships are the norm from the first year on: the relevant stimuli which evoke attach-

ment behaviour are offered by a number of individuals
and not exclusively one person, and a much more diversified system of attachments is thus fostered in the infant.
[pp. 70–71]

That there is no evidence for the assumption that attachments must be confined to only one object, the mother,
nor that all other attachments are subsidiary to the
mother-infant bond, was one of the findings of their
study. They concluded that:

Whom an infant chooses as his attachment object and
how many objects he selects depends, we believe, primarily on the nature of the social setting in which he
is reared and not on some intrinsic characteristic of
the attachment function itself. [p. 71]

Finally, Schaffer and Emerson suggested that while the
mother tends to be present in the child's environment for
most of the time, this does not guarantee that she will
provide the quantity and quality of stimulation necessary
for optimal development of the infant. A recent experi-
mental-observational study by Kotelchuck,[20] one of the
few studies on father-infant interaction, demonstrated
that one-to-two year old infants are equally attached to
their fathers and mothers. Furthermore, the strength of
attachment to fathers correlated with the degree to which
the fathers cared for their children during their development.

SEPARATION

The principal argument used to encourage women to
devote their constant attention to newborns is based on
the suggested deleterious effects of mother-child separation (the "Bowlby-"[5] or "Spitz-hypothesis"[38, 39]). Most of
the studies of mother-child separation have been based,
however, not on normal separation of infants from their
parents, but on institutionalized children. Because of the

physical and social sterility of many hospitals and orphanages, these children often suffered from inadequate environmental and human stimulation.[10, 44] The mother-child separation studies have not provided an adequate history of "the reasons which led to the children studied being uprooted from their homes or about the conditions in which they lived before this happened," according to Barbara Wootten.[45]

> One can hardly assume that the boys and girls found in a Children's Home constitute a fair sample of the child population generally: something unusual either in themselves or their environment must have happened to account for their being deprived of ordinary family life.[43] [p. 146]

Yarrow's[44] review of studies published between 1937 and 1955 concluded that most of the studies of institutionalized infants selected subjects who were already under treatment for emotional or personality disturbances. Furthermore, they were lacking in data on the early conditions of maternal care. In addition, Yarrow wrote,

> The dramatic character of these changes [i.e., reactions of infants to separation from the mother] has overshadowed the significant fact that a substantial portion of the children in each study did not show severe reactions to separation. [p. 474]

Casler[10] concluded that,

> none of the clinical or institutional studies ostensibly supporting the "Spitz-Ribble hypothesis" really does so, simply because none is able to demonstrate that probable causes of the adverse effects of institutionalization, other than maternal deprivation, are inoperative. [p. 12]

Casler further described several studies in which institutionalized babies showed no ill effects. Pinneau, who published several articles[30, 31, 32] dissecting methodological inadequacies of the Spitz and Ribble studies, concluded that

> It may well be that the burden of blame for the uncritical
> acceptance of his work does not rest with Spitz, who has
> published his results as he sees them, but rather with
> those who have acclaimed his work, and whose research
> training should enable them to make a critical evalua-
> tion of such research reports.[32] [p. 462]

Positive alternatives to traumatic separation of infant
and mother have not been sufficiently discussed in the
psychological literature. In fact, there seems to have occurred a dangerously unscientific extrapolation of assumptions from studies of institutionalized infants to the
much more common situation in which infants leave their
homes for part of the day, are cared for by other responsible individuals, and are returned again to their homes.
As a result, women are taught to believe that infants
require their undivided attention during the first two or
three years of life, at least. The way our society is structured, this attitude functions to confine the woman physically (to her home) and socially (to her family unit).
Neil O'Connor[28] observed:

> There is some danger that by analysing one source of
> emotional disturbance, such as mother-child separation,
> the interaction of the society and the family may be
> neglected, and the family considered as if it were an
> isolated unit, which alone determines the behaviour of
> individuals in all their social relations. [p. 188]

On this matter, Margaret Mead[23] wrote:

> At present, the specific biological situation of the con-
> tinuing relationship of the child to its biological mother
> and its need for care by human beings are being hope-
> lessly confused in the growing insistence that child and
> biological mother, or mother surrogate, must never be
> separated, that all separation, even for a few days is

inevitably damaging, and that if long enough it does irreversible damage. This . . . is a new and subtle form of antifeminism in which men—under the guise of exalting the importance of maternity—are typing women more tightly to their children than has been thought necessary since the invention of bottle feeding and baby carriages. Actually, anthropological evidence gives no support at present to the value of such an accentuation of the tie between mother and child. . . . On the contrary, cross-cultural studies suggest that adjustment is most facilitated if the child is cared for by many warm friendly people. [p. 477]

Finally, returning to the experience of natural separation between parents and children, none of the studies of children of working mothers has demonstrated systematic differences between children who are home all the time and children whose mothers work.[45, 46] However, because the Bowlby-Spitz hypothesis has had such a profound impact on child-rearing practice, legislators, employers and educators have refused to provide sufficient adequate free child-care for working women.[46] Consequently, working women are usually forced to find their own, individual solutions to the child-care problem. Even in "dual-career" families (families in which the mother and father both have professional careers), the men and women tend to accept as inevitable that women should take on the major responsibility for the organization of child-care and the household in addition to their career responsibilities.[33] The consequence is that the women in such families carry the strain of both career and family problems. Apparently this is a major problem in Eastern European socialist countries as well as in Western society.[33, 46]

The excellent reviews mentioned above, on the subject of separation and institutionalization, share in criticizing overgeneralizations that have been drawn from separation studies. Several reviewers[10, 44] attempted to ana-

lyze the objective variables that the mothering function
provides for the healthy growth and emotional security of
the developing infant. However, none has sufficiently
questioned the concept that the mother must be the one
who does the mothering. Yudkin and Holme[46] wrote:

> Most of the literature, however, tends to stress the value
> of the exclusive mother-child relationship and to ignore
> the possibility or even the need, for its dilution. This is
> to attempt to justify a particular, local and almost cer-
> tainly, temporary, economic and cultural pattern as an
> eternal biological law. This can only do a disservice to
> both the mothers and the children. [p. 138]

NATURALISM AND INSTINCT THEORY

The assumption that the biological mother must be the
major responsible adult in the infant's life is intimately
related to the theory that women have an instinct to
mother. The assumption is based on observations, from
the earliest recorded history, that confirm that women are
usually the ones who nurture and raise children, specifically their own children.* It remains an assumption, or
hypothesis, however, that what we observe and describe
naturalistically is what is biologically correct or socially
optimal. John Stuart Mill wrote:

> the unnatural generally means only uncustomary, and
> . . . everything which is usual appears natural. The sub-
> jection of women to men being a universal custom, any
> departure from it quite naturally appears unnatural.
> [quoted in Millett,[25] p. 94]

* An entertaining and informative article by Una Stannard[40]
attempts to document that "Women have the babies, but men have
the maternal instinct." In her historical paper, Stannard reminds
us that the major books and manuals telling women how to be
good mothers have been written by men.

In the words of one reviewer,

> While most of us will continue to believe in the impor-
> tance of mothering during infancy, we must recognize
> that this belief has more the characteristics of a faith
> and less the basis of demonstrated fact. [Erikson, quoted
> in Casler,[10] p. 9]

Ethology, the study of animals in their natural environments, has had a strong influence on recent practice in
human developmental psychology. Bowlby[6] has been one
of the principal protagonists in the trend to return to
naturalistic observations of human and animal behavior:

> Until recent years, most of the knowledge available about
> mother-infant interaction in humans was either anec-
> dotal or else a result of reconstructions based on data
> derived from older subjects. In the past decade, how-
> ever, enquiries have been begun which have as their
> aim, the systematic descriptive and causal study of what
> actually occurs during a baby's interaction with the
> humans who care for him. [p. xiii]

However, ethologists, carrying out descriptive studies of
behavior, have not approached their observational tasks
bias-free. The discipline of ethology has long been linked
with instinct theory, which attributes the organization of
complex patterns of species-typical behavior to hypothet-
ical, pre-formed biological models.[22, 42] On the human
level, instinct theory emphasizes the biological pre-desti-
nation of psychological characteristics:

> The Freudian view of man's nature starts from the as-
> sumption that he is really a nonsocial or even an anti-
> social creature. His primary needs are not social but
> individual and biological. This means that society is not
> essential to man but is something outside his nature, an
> external force to whose distorting pressures he is victim.[4]
> [p. 96]

Critics of instinct theory have stressed its neglect of
the social and developmental history of the organisms
being observed and its failure to view the organism as one
that both affects and is affected by the biosocial environment in which it develops.[21, 36] Bowlby's theory of attachment behavior[1, 7] is an interactionist one. However,
it assumes that there are certain features of the environment that the infant is biologically structured to be particularly sensitive to. The theory assumes that the environment of the newborn is optimal, and that the infant is
biologically predisposed to adapt to it. As summarized by
Ainsworth,[1]

> ethologists hold that those aspects of the genetic code
> which regulate the development of attachment of infant
> to mother are adapted to an environment in which it is
> a well-nigh universal experience that it is the mother
> (rather than some biologically inappropriate object)
> who will be present under conditions which facilitate
> the infant's becoming attached to her. [pp. 995–996]

Such a theory is conservative because it neglects the
enormous range of socio-cultural environments into
which newborn infants are thrust and idealizes the
mother-infant couple, which, as Orlansky[29] pointed out
long ago, is "one conforming to an ideal-typical norm
held by Western psychiatrists" (p. 15).

It is frequently argued that the human female, like
other mammals, is biologically best equipped to respond
to the needs of a newborn because of her long period of
biological, hormonal and psychological priming during
pregnancy. It has been suggested, for instance, that in the
period immediately after birth, mothers may be particularly sensitive to the needs of their babies.[7] This may
indeed be true. However, it is also true that a woman
who has just had her first child, and who has not previously handled, fed, or cared for an infant, has great difficulty in the first days of the baby's life in establishing
feeding, whether it be by breast or bottle. New mothers

often have to be told how to hold the baby, burp it, bathe it, and dress it. Of course most women learn how to care for their infants quite efficiently within a short period of time, through practice and determination.

Recent studies have demonstrated that infants play an active role, even in the first weeks of life, in getting their needs satisfied. There is now extensive literature on the way in which the infant actively initiates social interaction and is capable of modifying the behavior of the adult who cares for it.[3, 41] This means that the infant helps the adult to develop appropriate responses that will bring about the satisfaction of its needs. This, in turn, means that, given a socially acceptable alternative, the mother need not be the principal caretaker of her own infant, although many women may still want to enjoy this responsibility.

Most evidence today indicates that the factors that are important for healthy infant and child development are: consistent care; sensitivity of the caretaking adult(s) in responding to the infant's needs; a stable environment, the characteristics of which the growing infant can learn to identify; continuity of experience within the infant's environment; and physical and intellectual stimulation, love, and affection. "There is no clear evidence," Yarrow[44] wrote, "that multiple mothering, without associated deprivation or stress, results in personality damage." And Mead[24] wrote,

> The problem remains of how to separate the necessary protection of a child who has been isolated in an exclusive pair relationship with the mother—of a type which cannot be said to be natural at a human level, because it actually does not permit participation by the father, care of the dependent older siblings, and ties with the three-generation family, all of which are human experiences—from advocacy of the artificial perpetuation or intensification or creation of such conditions of exclusive mother-child dependence. [p. 58]

Unlike other reviewers,[17, 27, 46] who advocate reforms
for women that would alleviate the strains of dual or
triple careers, while basically accepting the assumption
that only women can perform the mothering function,
I would like to emphasize that it is scientifically unacceptable to advocate the natural superiority of women as
child-rearers and socializers of children when there have
been so few studies of the effects of male-infant or father-
infant interaction on the subsequent development of the
child.

The acceptance of the concept of mothering by social
scientists reflects their own satisfaction with the status
quo. The inability of social scientists to explore or to
advocate alternatives to current child-rearing practices is
due to their biased conception of what should be studied
and to their unwillingness to advocate social change. As
Myrdal and Klein[27] recognized,

> the sentimental cult of domestic virtues is the cheapest
> method at society's disposal of keeping women quiet
> without seriously considering their grievances or im-
> proving their position. It has been successfully used to
> this day, and has helped to perpetuate some dilemmas
> of home-making women by telling them, on the one hand
> that they are devoted to the most sacred duty, while on
> the other hand keeping them on a level of unpaid drudg-
> ery. [p. 145]

The time has come to evaluate more critically the ways
in which the home and the single mothering figure *fail* to
provide the kind of environment that is optimally stimulating or satisfying to the growing infant.

MOTHERS' FEELINGS AND
THE NEEDS OF WOMEN

A young housewife[12] writes:

I feel it should be more widely recognized that it is in
the very nature of a mother's position, in our society, to

avenge her own frustrations on a small, helpless child; whether this takes the form of tyranny, or of a smothering affection that asks the child to be a substitute for all she has missed. [p. 153]

It is important to recognize that many young mothers have ambivalent feelings about the responsibility of motherhood. Hannah Gavron's[13] survey of women in London showed that

the majority of wives, both working-class and middle-class, appear from the discussion of their own views on home and work to be essentially on the horns of a dilemma. They want to work, feel curiously functionless when not working, but at the same time they sense their great responsibilities towards the children. In both groups those who were at home gave the children as their main reason for being there. [p. 122]

My own experience, studying the development of feeding behavior in infants, corroborates this. I studied mature, healthy, full-term babies, all the products of normal pregnancies and deliveries. The mothers were not tense or unhappy women with unusual medical or psychological histories. Yet, many of the women expressed the same conflicts: boredom, sense of isolation being home alone with the baby, desire to be able to get back to work, and doubts about finding adequate child-care facilities should they have the opportunity of getting employment. Most of the women, whether they wanted to work or not, had the feeling that it would be wrong to go out to work because it might somehow endanger the infant's well-being. The study of Yarrow and her colleagues[45] demonstrated that, "Mothers who prefer to work but out of a sense of 'duty' do not work report the most problems in child rearing" (p. 122).

The negative effects of too intensive a relationship developing between mother and child, leading to a clinical pattern of "overprotection," are discussed by Myrdal and

Klein.[27] Herzog[17] gives passing mention to the fact that "it is no secret that some mothers are not loving, and some who are do not want to devote themselves exclusively to infant or child care" (p. 18). A recent book[11] on child-rearing restates the problem:

> The role in which most contemporary theorists of child development cast the mother makes it hard for her and hard for her children. What's more, the evidence indicates that she has been *mis*cast. No matter how seriously she takes the demand on her for omnipotence, and no matter how omnipotent the performance she turns out, there is no guarantee that the act will come off. All too often the child fails to reflect the best parents' most studious try for perfection. [p. 14]

We must now turn our attention to the home. We are taught that the best environment for the growth and development of a healthy child is provided within the individual home. The home environment, however, is socially sterile because mobility, outside stimulation, exchange of ideas and socially productive relationships are severely limited there:

> The isolated woman at home may well be kept "in touch" with events, but she feels that the events are not in touch with her, that they happen without her participation. The wealth of information which is brought to her without any effort on her part does not lose its vicariousness. It increases rather than allays her sense of isolation and of being left out.[27] [p. 148]

Yudkin and Holme[46] discuss the effects of the physical and social isolation of small families in which:

> a large number of children are tied almost exclusively to their mothers for the first five years of life, having little opportunity to meet any other people or to develop the beginnings of social relationships, let alone to explore the world outside their own home, until the

sudden and dramatic beginning of their school life. Such isolation is obviously likely to increase the closeness and intensity of the relationship between the mother and her young children and may well have an effect on the type of adult personality that results, but whether the effect is good or bad is another matter. [pp. 137–138]

An English housewife[12] wrote:

Housework is housework, whoever does it. It is a waste socially, psychologically, and even economically, to put me in a position where my only means of expressing loyalty to [the baby] is by shopping, dish-washing and sweeping floors. I have trained for teaching literature to university students; it would be far more satisfying to guide a nursery class with Carl in it than it is to feel too harassed by irrelevant jobs to pay his development much attention. [p. 148]

The home, therefore, is physically restrictive and, for many women, is felt to be socially restrictive as well. In the home, one's economic and personal tensions and problems are most pronounced. These factors have a profound affect on the mother and child confined to the home, and are a principal influence on the physical, intellectual, and social development of children coming from different social class backgrounds. Bruner's[8] recent review of studies dealing with the cognitive development of children from different social class backgrounds, is rich in examples of the complex way in which feelings of powerlessness by the mother are conveyed to the children and affect the children's ability to cope with their environment.

Current studies of mother-child interaction in the United States, comparing children of working-class mothers with children of middle-class mothers, have ostensibly demonstrated the "cognitive superiority" of the latter. The conclusions of such research are that working-class mothers have to be taught to behave like middle-class

mothers. The form of implementation recently adopted to
help these women and their children, is to teach working-
class women how to provide optimal maternal stimulation to the child within the home environment. However,
no programs are implemented to provide working-class
women with the advantages of class privilege that middle-
class women enjoy, since it is beyond the power of the
behavioral scientist to effect such changes in the social
and economic status of the people concerned (*How Harvard Rules Women*,[18] pp. 66–74). Hunt's[19] recom-
mendation that parent-child centers become the focus of
intervention programs by professionals to teach "competence" to poverty mothers and their children was aptly
criticized by Gordon,[15] who wrote:

> Hunt is proposing a strategy that, like most formal edu-
> cation, essentially seeks to upgrade black and poor
> people by identifying all those things that are "wrong"
> with them, and changing those things. Such a strategy,
> with its implied criticism and its prescription for the
> adoption of goals and values of the oppressors, should
> hardly be imposed upon a group by outsiders, no matter
> how well intentioned. More effective programs of assist-
> ance are likely to come from among the people them-
> selves. [p. 41]

One might add that the people, in this case working-class
mothers, might feel that other individuals should be involved in the process of child-rearing and that the responsibility for the socialization of children should not
rest on the mothers alone.

In the past and present, day-care programs for children
have been officially encouraged during periods of economic strain, when women's labor was necessary for production. Neither economics nor women's needs to get out
of the home, however, are sufficient justification for child-
care centers. Good day-care programs are a necessity for
infants and children because they encourage the devel-

opment of cooperative social interaction during a period of life in which, in modern Western society, children receive insufficient experience with other trusting, loving, dependable children and adults. In the words of two day-care workers:[16]

> It is well documented that attitudes toward work, race, sex (including male/female roles), initiative, and cooperation are formed during the first five years of life. It follows that we need to be seriously concerned with what happens inside the day care center.

> What goes on between the child and the environment (whether it's a home or a day care center) affects the kind of capacities that the child will have as an adult. The ability to feel deeply and be sensitive toward other people, the ability to trust oneself and use one's initiative, the ability to solve problems in a creative and collective way—these all can be given their foundation or stifled in the first five years.

> By the age of 4 children are taking in the idea that a woman's place is in the home. Three and four year old children are already learning that it's better to be white. They are learning to follow directions and rules without asking why. They are learning how to deny their own feelings and needs in order to win approval from adults.

> These are examples of learning that most commonly result from early childhood experiences. These are elements of the invisible curriculum that usually forms the child's environment in our society. [pp. 27–28]

Recognizing the social needs of mothers and infants, some investigators have begun to encourage entry into day nurseries at much earlier ages than is customary. While these efforts were, at first, strongly criticized by workers in the field, the findings were very encouraging: assessments made at thirty months showed that children from lower-class families who were enrolled in a day-care center from about one year of age did not differ from home-reared children in the strength of attachment to their mothers. Likewise, mothers of day-care infants did not show any differences from home-mothers in intensity of attachment to their infants. The study[9] showed that, while the home-reared group declined in developmental quotient at thirty months, the day-care infants increased in developmental level.

I am convinced that new studies will continue to demonstrate that stable, loving, stimulating group environments can produce healthy, affectionate, bright youngsters, and that, quite early in life, infants can spend a good part of their day away from their homes and parents without adverse consequences. The problem ahead of us is to analyze the relationship between the nuclear family and the functioning of society, and to study and create the conditions under which the home ceases to confine the woman and the child to social and productive isolation. The fact is that, in modern Western society, no other institutions offer the adult the comfort, the emotional security, the loyalty, and the emotional dependability that the modern family provides. Even saying this, it is necessary to recognize the converse, that for many children and women, the modern family is a prison, breeding repression, unequal relationships and authoritarian conformity.* I am cautious, however, not to suggest that we overthrow the family and substitute other institutions as alternative child-rearers. To do this would be impossible at this stage because of the already mentioned positive value of the family, and because we have not consciously experimented sufficiently with alternatives that could successfully replace it.

---

* The evolution of the family and its relationship to societal structure has been the basis for a good deal of study and renewed analysis.[14, 26, 34]

DISCUSSION

The creation of alternative life styles, work patterns, or economic change, cannot be successfully imposed on people or prescribed for them without their cooperation. The creation of any alternative processes, when it involves major changes from historical precedent, is a political problem as well as an educational or psycho-social one. For people to attempt alternatives within this society, they must feel the necessity for change and feel that they are not alone in their efforts to create it. People do not attempt to create even small changes in their lives if they lack the confidence or the ability or the power to make them work. In short, programs that would produce the conscious articulation of goals and criteria for positive social change cannot be undertaken without the initiative of the people who are going to be involved.

Acting on the basis of the common sense of oppression experienced by women in society, the women's liberation movement has begun to analyze the relationship between some transitional and long-range goals which, if won, could significantly change women's status in society. The women's liberation movement will not be satisfied, for example, with equality with men if that equality is defined simply in terms of employment opportunity or work status; in present society, that would mean that they give up one oppressive situation (subjugation in the home) to step into another oppressive situation (exploitation at work). Nonetheless, in order for women to participate in efforts to create more meaningful and rewarding work experiences, they must achieve the transitional goal of shared work with men in the home around the housekeeping and child-rearing functions. This means that ways have to be found in which men can begin to take a more active part in home life and in emotional and social interaction with infants. The encouragement of male participation in early childhood socialization requires, for its success, the transformation of existing social and educa-

tional institutions because men today are not prepared to
assume major shares of responsibility either in home-
making or in child-rearing. As Sweden has already done,
sex-role stereotyping in books (children's and adult's)
and in advertising has to be ended in order to discourage
traditional practices of sex-differentiated behavior. Paid
paternity leaves for men and greater opportunities for
fathers to participate in the care of newborns is recognized as essential. Men have to be involved more in early
education, from day-care to primary schools. Unless
nurseries and schools are staffed by men as well as
women, the responsibility for the socialization of children
will continue to fall upon women and they will continue
to feel that other social responsibilities are not within
their domain. This was apparently the experience of
women in the kibbutzim in Israel. At the beginning,
women were encouraged to share in the heavy work with
men, but men were not similarly encouraged to share in
the care of children. As a result, women became over-
burdened with the strain of both kinds of responsibilities
and gradually dropped out of the productive branches. A
sexual division of labor persists to this day in the kibbutzim. Only women work as nurses and infant's teachers.[37]

For men and women to share in the care of infants
while maintaining jobs, then in their capacity as workers,
both men and women have to be able to work shorter
hours without losing pay. The extra time would be used
for child care either at home or in cooperatively organized day-care centers at work or in the community.
Group day care is considered by the women's liberation
movement to be a more progressive alternative to family
day care because it removes children and adults from the
isolating and non-productive environment of the home,
substituting a social environment in which infants and
adults may interact with each other in large, unrestrictive
spaces with many objects and toys to share. The socialization process, therefore, becomes less individualistic for

the children and more cooperative for the adults. It follows that parental control of the organization and staffing of day-care centers is essential. The new, radical generation of parents do not want dumping grounds for their children, but rather centers of exciting educational activity and play in which children and adults share collectively in the process of growing up. Dissatisfied with the racist, sexist, and middle-class-biased education that children receive in public schools, the radical day-care movement wants day care that is organized and controlled by the people in their communities who wish to create a more democratic, equalitarian society for their children.[16]

A final word needs to be said about alternatives to the nuclear family, in particular the new movement toward communalism. Seen in the most positive of perspectives, a small percentage of the American population is attempting to establish stable communal living arrangements as a way of socializing productive relationships in the living place. Cooking, shopping, cleaning, child-care, and social relationships are being shared by all who live together.

The rennaissance of communalism can be seen to develop out of the women's liberation philosophy. The women's liberation movement helped to convince women that their oppression did not develop from their internal inadequacies, but was the natural outgrowth of problems inherent in the structure of our society. By forming social and political bonds as a group, rather than as individual women, it has been possible for women to experience new and better forms of social relationships and to begin successfully to create some of the changes necessary before all women can, in fact, be liberated. Breaking down alienating forms of social relationships can be seen to be a first step in the process of transforming society. A recent paper on "The Liberation of Children"[2] concludes:

"If we want to change society we can begin by changing the kind of people we are and the kind of children we raise. People who are more loving, more concerned about each other, more secure and less competitive will have attitudes that are contrary to the ones on which our society is based, and while the creation of new attitudes is not in itself a revolution, perhaps it helps create the preconditions."

REFERENCES

1. Ainsworth, M. 1969. Object relations, dependency, and attachment: a theoretical review of the infant-mother relationship. *Child Developm.* 40:969–1025.

2. Babcox, D. 1970. The liberation of children. *Up from Under* 1(1): 43–46 (Up From Under, 339 Lafayette St., New York, N.Y. 10012).

3. Bell, R. 1971. Stimulus control of parent or caretaker behavior by offspring. *Developmental Psychol.* 4:63–72. (Invited address, 1968. Division of Developmental Psychology, 76th Annual Convention, American Psychological Association).

4. Birch, H. 1953. Psychology and culture. *In* Basic Problems in Psychiatry, J. Wortis, ed. Grune & Stratton, New York.

5. Bowlby, J. 1951. Maternal Care and Mental Health. World Health Organization Monogr., Geneva.

6. Bowlby, J. 1961. Foreword. *In* Determinants of Infant Behaviour. B. Foss, ed. Methuen & Co., London.

7. Bowlby, J. 1969. Attachment and Loss. Vol. I. Attachment. The Hogarth Press and the Institute of Psychoanalysis, London.

8. Bruner, J. 1970. Poverty and Childhood. Paper presented at Merrill-Palmer Institute, Detroit.

9. Caldwell, B. et al. 1970. Infant day care and attachment. *Amer. J. Orthopsychiat.* 30:397–412.

10. Casler, L. 1961. Maternal deprivation: a critical review of the literature. Monographs Soc. Res. Child Developm. 26(2) ser. #80:1–64.

11. Chess, S., Thomas, A. and Birch, H. 1965. Your Child Is a Person. Viking Press, New York.

12. Gail, S. 1968. The housewife. *In* Work. R. Fraser, ed. Penguin Books, London.

13. Gavron, H. 1968. The Captive Wife. Penguin Books, London. (first published by Routledge & Kegan Paul, London, 1966).

14. Gordon, L. 1970. Families. New England Free Press, 791 Tremont St., Boston.

15. Gordon, E. 1971. Parent and child centers: their basis in the behavioral and educational sciences. An invited critique. *Amer. J. Orthopsychiat.* 41:39–42.

16. Gross, L. and Macewan, P. 1970. On day care. Women: A Journal of Liberation 1(2):26–29. (Women: A Journal of Liberation, 3011 Guilford Ave., Baltimore, Md. 21218).

17. Herzog, E. 1960. Children of Working Mothers. U.S. Dept. of Health, Education and Welfare, Children's Bureau, Washington, D.C.

18. How Harvard Rules Women. 1970. The Arrogance of social science research: manipulating the lives of black women and their infants. New England Free Press, Boston.

19. Hunt, J. Mc V. 1971. Parent and child centers: Their basis in the behavioral and educational sciences. *Amer. J. Orthopsychiat.* 41:13–38.

20. Kotelchuck, M. 1971. The nature of the child's tie to the father. Unpublished Ph.D. thesis, Harvard University.

21. Lehrman, D. 1953. A critique of Konrad Lorenz's theory of instinctive behavior. *Q. Rev. Biol.* 28:337–363.

22. Lorenz, K. 1935. Companionship in bird life. *In* Instinctive Behavior, C. Schiller, ed., 1957, International Universities Press, New York.

23. Mead, M. 1954. Some theoretical considerations on the problem of mother-child separation. *Amer. J. Orthopsychiat.* 24:471–483.

24. Mead, M. 1962. A cultural anthropologist's approach to maternal deprivation. *In* Deprivation of Maternal Care. A Reassessment of its Effects. Public Health Papers, #14, World Health Org., Geneva.

25. Millett, K. 1970. Sexual Politics. Doubleday & Co., New York.

26. Mitchell, J. 1966. Women: the longest revolution. New Left Review, 40(Nov.–Dec.). (Available as a pamphlet from New England Free Press, Boston).

27. Myrdal, A. and Klein, V. 1968. Women's Two Roles (2nd ed.). Routledge & Kegan Paul, London.
28. O'Connor, N. 1956. The evidence for the permanently disturbing effects of mother-child separation. *Acta Psychol.* 12:174–191.
29. Orlansky, H. 1949. Infant care and personality. *Psychol. Bull.* 46:1–48.
30. Pinneau, S. 1950. A critique on the articles by Margaret Ribble. *Child Developm.* 21:203–228.
31. Pinneau, S. 1955. The infantile disorders of hospitalism and anaclitic depression. *Psychol. Bull.* 52:429–452.
32. Pinneau, S. 1955. Reply to Dr. Spitz. *Psychol. Bull.* 52: 459–462.
33. Rapaport, R. and Rapaport, R. N. 1969. The dual career family: A variant pattern and social change. *Human Relations* 22:3–30.
34. Reich, W. 1962. The Sexual Revolution (3rd ed.). The Noonday Press (Farrar, Straus and Giroux), New York.
35. Schaffer, H. and Emerson, P. 1964. The development of social attachments in infancy. Monographs Soc. Res. Child Developm. 29(3):ser. #94.
36. Schneirla, T. 1956. Interrelationships of the 'innate' and the 'acquired' in instinctive behavior. *In* L'Instinct Dans le Comportement des Animaux et de l'Homme. P. Grasse, ed. Masson et Cie, Paris.
37. Spiro, M. 1965. Children of the Kibbutz. Schocken Books, New York. (First published by Harvard University Press, 1958).
38. Spitz, R. 1945. Hospitalism: An inquiry into the genesis of psychiatric conditions in early childhood. Part I. *Psychoanal. Stud. Child* 1:53–74.
39. Spitz, R. and Wolf, K. 1946. Anaclitic depression: an inquiry into the genesis of psychiatric conditions in early childhood (II). *Psychoanal. Stud. Child* 2:313–342.
40. Stannard, U. 1970. Adam's rib, or the woman within. *Transaction* 8:24–35.
41. Thomas, A. et al. 1963. Behavioral Individuality in Early Childhood. New York University Press, New York.
42. Tinbergen, N. 1951. The Study of Instinct. Clarendon Press, Oxford.
43. Wootten, B. 1959. Social Science and Social Pathology. Allen and Unwin, London.

44. Yarrow, L. 1961. Maternal deprivation: Toward an empirical and conceptual reevaluation. *Psychol. Bull.* 58: 459–490.
45. Yarrow, M. et al. 1962. Child-rearing in families of working and non-working mothers. *Sociometry* 25:122–140.
46. Yudkin, S. and Holme, A. 1969. Working Mothers and Their Children. Sphere Books, London. (First published by Michael Joseph, London, 1963).

23

A Cultural Anthropologist's Approach to Maternal Deprivation

MARGARET MEAD

* * *

COMPARATIVE STUDIES PROVIDE CORRECTIONS TO SIMPLISTIC FORMULATIONS

Comparative studies, especially of primitive peoples living under simple conditions of food gathering, hunting and horticulture, provide suggestive materials on the biological potentialities of such practices as the suckling of the child by several women or the use of the dry breasts of young girls, old women or men as comforters; and of situations which would seem to do various types of violence to the organism of mother or child, such as: the effort necessary to evoke milk from a non-lactating woman by keeping an adopted child persistently hungry so that enough suckling pressure is applied to the breast; the suckling of the neonate by a woman who has been suckling her own child for two or three years, with resulting change in the protein content of the breast milk; methods of binding and purposeful deformation of the child's head or whole body; permanent encasement of the child in some cradling device so that there is no contact between the body of the child and that of the mother,

SOURCE: "A Cultural Anthropologist's Approach to Maternal Deprivation" by Margaret Mead, in *Deprivation of Maternal Care: A Reassessment of Its Effects* (Geneva, World Health Organization, 1962), Public Health Papers no. 14, pp. 45–62. Reprinted by permission of the World Health Organization. References have been renumbered.

except between nipple and mouth; use of extreme methods of weaning including the smearing of the breasts with
mud, which is represented to the child as excrement, or
banishment of the child to the care of a stranger; the
simultaneous suckling of siblings with purposeful stimulation of jealousy in both, etc. There are a great variety of
such practices, both briefly reported[19] and in some cases
discussed in connexion with detailed studies of "culture
and personality," which it would be impossible to set up
experimentally today for paediatric and ethical reasons,
but which may be observed in a context of completely
responsible execution where the primitive people in question believe they are doing the best they can for their
children.

The cultural anthropologist deals with whole cultures
—under the greatly simplified conditions of absence of a
written language and a numerically small society—and is
therefore equipped to consider the way in which the
whole mesh of human behaviour characteristic of a particular society is reflected in the behaviour of any given
individual. This recognition of the complexity of the conditions within which an infant grows, or a given adult-
child relationship exists, can be used as a corrective to
the present tendency to over-attribute certain consequences to single causes or sequences of events, such as
breast-feeding or its absence, separation from a mother-
figure, institutionalization, early or late toilet training,
swaddling, etc., which has been characteristic of attempts
to apply clinical insight to the establishment of viable
theory and to the development of comprehensive recom-
mendations for changes in social practice. . . .

In order that anthropological contributions, both explicit and potential, may be brought to bear on the problem of maternal care and mental health in those respects
specifically outlined in Bowlby's monograph,[3] it will be
useful to break down his original discussion and that of
his commentators into a new set of categories. I should
like to distinguish among the following issues:

1. The removal of children from the care of familiar people, close relatives, members of the greater families, neighbours, godparents, etc., to impersonal institutions where they are cared for by strangers in a way which prevents the establishment of reliable personal ties.

2. Problems arising from breaks in the relationship of a child to its biological mother and father and siblings.

3. Problems of the very early hours and days of life and the establishment in the parturient woman, the neonate and the other members of the family of new patterns of relationship resulting from that particular birth.

4. Problems of the patterns of relationships over the entire life-span of the individual, in which early patterns of continuity, separation, concentration or diffusion of emotional ties, etc., are reflected in the responses of younger to older, older to younger, and equal to equal.

5. Problems attendant upon the attempt to apply the findings of the human sciences, both at the observational and at the clinical level, to preventive mental health practices in the various societies of the world, by altering patterns of hospitalization, by introducing mass measures of other sorts, and by advocating changes in the individual practices of mothers, fathers, teachers, paediatricians, etc.

INSTANCES OF INSTITUTIONAL PRACTICES

It is particularly important to take the institutional questions separately, because there are no comparable situations within the primitive societies in which the cultural anthropologist collects his primary data. All the functions served by institutions—care of the orphan, care of the child of a sick mother, care of the handicapped or defective child, care of the illegitimate child—are dealt with in primitive societies either by care of the child within the greater family or neighbourhood group, on an individual basis which obviates the major trauma-inducing aspect of institutional care—the impersonality of an institution—, or, drastically, by the elimination of the child by such means as burying the newborn child with the dead mother, or exposing immediately or extinguishing by a process of slow, low-level care children who show extreme handicaps. The child who is chosen to live is cared for personally, not impersonally. Our institutions have resulted from a discrepancy between our social conscience—which demands *impersonal* efforts to be made to protect every individual, regardless of whether he be illegitimate, orphaned, a refugee from war or catastrophe whose parents are unknown, or defective, and which demands the construction of services, medical, nursing custodial, etc., to carry out our impersonal ethical intentions—and our ability to provide adequate, artificially created personal situations within which the children who are saved can be cared for. . . . We have become increasingly unwilling to accept the effects of famine, war, and catastrophe, either on individuals or on groups. This discrepancy has also been aggravated by our improved methods of medical care, which make it possible to save so many children who would have perished under earlier conditions. The hygienic impersonal orphanage described by Spitz,[27] in which children eventually die, might be regarded as the analogue of the primitive situation, within which children who are markedly defective also die, in the midst of what is apparently adequate human care. A very conspicuous example of the way in which a society selectively distinguishes between the more wanted and the less wanted child is the differential survival rate of boys and girls reported for parts of India.[25] It is worth noting that the whole ethical agitation which led first to the creation of institutions for the care of abandoned children of various sorts, and then to the movement to examine the consequences of such care, can be seen first as a social ethical reaction against processes equivalent to

immediate infanticide, accompanied by a willingness to
accept a very high infant death rate, and, secondly, as a
social reaction against the recognition that such children,
instead of dying, young and innocent, lived on as trauma-
tized and antisocial individuals to create new social problems. . . .

DIFFERENCES IN SURVIVAL CONDITIONS

A second set of differences between studies in modern
large societies and those in primitive societies lies in the
actual conditions of survival. Under primitive conditions
the infant is entirely dependent upon breast milk, whether
from its own mother alone or from a number of women,
and also, in the absence of medical care, its life is exceedingly precarious. As a result, there is usually a very high
death rate, and all studies of primitive methods of maternal care and their concomitants in cultural character deal
only with those individuals who have been so placed, in
terms of their own constitution, familial and tribal constellation and cultural practice, as to be able to survive.
In no discussion of the kind of cultural character that is
produced by keeping the infant close to the mother, by an
available set of alternative wet nurses, by sudden and
abrupt weaning, etc., are we dealing with the effects of
such methods of child-rearing on the total group of infants who are born, but only upon a very small percentage who survive. The statement that every primitive
mother breast-feeds her baby—and in many tribes this
feeding may be interrupted by illness and resumed after
weeks—is not a statement that *every* primitive mother
breast-feeds *every* baby adequately. It is simply a statement that all babies who survive are breast-fed, and all
women who survive child-bearing have a capacity to produce some breast milk. Where as many as five out of
ten children born may die, the selectivity for certain
characteristics can be very high.[23]

Two totally unjustified extrapolations from the conditions where all infants were breast-fed were made during the discussions of breast-feeding—and mother and child separation—of the 1940's. It was assumed that because in such situations all surviving babies were breast-fed, breast-feeding could be advised for all infants. And it was assumed that because all parturient women had some milk, this milk could be assumed to be capable—if only the proper psychological attitude and medical support were there—of nourishing the newborn.[18] Both assumptions were naïve extrapolations which failed to take into account the differences between societies where most infants die and there are no artificial feeding methods available, and societies where most infants live and artificial feeding methods are available. A careful comparison of these very different conditions leads to the conclusion that failure to produce milk to nourish an infant which is demonstrating its non-viability by failing to thrive on the breast milk its mother gives it is a biologically adequate response on the part of the primitive mother. The cycle— failure of the child to gain weight, failure of breast milk, increased failure of the child, mediated by the mother's perception of the situation, maternal anxiety—whether an example of maternal rejection or not, is biologically appropriate behaviour. The modern mother whose milk does not agree with her child is behaving with biological appropriateness when she responds with anxiety, and then uses the culturally available means to save her child, thus correcting for a type of behaviour developed through many thousands and possibly hundreds of thousands of years. The mother who stubbornly insists on attempting to breast-feed a child who does not thrive, and the physician who attributes the failure of the particular physicochemical biological combination of that mother and child to "maternal rejection" or even to "infantile rejection" is failing to take these factors into account.[20]

Having separated out the types of evidence available from primitive cultures, the particular extension of the question of the unwanted child in the institutions of the modern world (orphanages), the confusion between institutional practices which interrupt the continuity of person-to-person relationships for the unwanted child and for the wanted child temporarily hospitalized, and the confusions introduced by applying the "success" of breast-feeding at a primitive level to a modern level, we may now tackle the series of questions raised earlier in this chapter.

REMOVAL OF CHILDREN
TO IMPERSONAL INSTITUTIONS

We may first consider the removal of children from the care of familiar people to impersonal institutions where they are cared for impersonally. Here all the evidence must come from the study of such institutions, and the only addition that anthropological studies can make is the insistence that institutions in several different cultures must be scrutinized by the same methods and with equal care, taking all the socio-cultural factors into account, before we can be certain that the low survival rate is due to the lack of interpersonal continuity. . . . The evidence that has been gathered so far is quite strong enough to suggest that this is a hazardous method of attempting to care for infants and children, and one which no authority is justified in risking if any other means are available. The evidence is, in fact, quite strong enough to suggest that present institutional practices are only a prolonged, ritualized method of disposing of the infant for whom no one wishes to care. But the evidence is not complete enough to show that with a will to give such institutionalized infants the same level of attention and care as that given by individual parents, the survival rate under institutional care might not be as high or higher. The weight of evidence from the *Kibbutzim*, where group care for loved children, not unwanted, anonymous children, is practised, suggest that, whatever the other by-products in later character structure, group care with high degrees of discontinuity provides for survival under institutionalized conditions.[26] The lethal element in orphanages may be the cultural acceptance of the "unwanted" state of the infant, rather than any specific way in which this unwantedness is mediated to an infant. Similarly, a mother who knows her child is going to die will, as the child gradually fades away, mediate to it the knowledge of its approaching death.

The untoward effects of hospitalization, or temporary separation of wanted children from familiar adults, can then be interpreted as the condition within which the hospital set-up, rules about visiting, and anxieties of the parents themselves mediate to the young child a sense of break with the familiar tie, with consequent separation anxiety. Here again the data are sufficient to alert the medical world to the dangers involved, but are not sufficient to prove that this sense of break is unavoidable if the mother does not accompany the child; although often it cannot be prevented as easily in the absence of the mother, it can be prevented.

Here again the traditional mother-child tie based on breast-feeding is, of course, the easiest method to assure a child continuity of relationship—if we are willing to disregard the extent to which the mother's biologically adequate anxiety may also endanger the child's life, not only by a biologically adequate failure in breast milk, but also by mediating to the child her biological knowledge of how ill and vulnerable it is.

SUPPLEMENTING BIOLOGICAL
PARENTAL BEHAVIOUR

We may go on, in fact, to consider whether the discoveries which have transformed the capacity which we share with other mammals to accept or reject our young into a capacity to preserve the lives of an increasing number of human infants may not actually be discoveries of ways of overcoming the handicaps of the biologically given aspects of maternity. Biological mothering is heav-

ily susceptible to conditions of pregnancy, whether the
child was wanted or unwanted, its sex, the conditions of
the mother's own childhood, relationships to the father,
the nature of the delivery and the nature of the postnatal
contact between mother and child, and finally the fit between the structure and functioning of the mother's
breast and the infant's constitution.[10] The cultural invention—in contrast to the simple biological one—is that of
conscious nurturing. Biological motherhood is a routine
occurrence in the natural world; nursing—the responsible, devoted, conscious care of the young—is cultural
and human. We ought perhaps to be discussing not how
much should a nurse be like a mother, but how much can
a mother be like a good nurse.

The shift from the practice of burying the infant alive
if its mother dies to that of the shared breast-feeding of
other women was the beginning of this order of nurturing,
continued in various forms of artificial feeding until men,
as well as women, could share in the cultural nurturing of
an infant.

So when we consider the effects of separation, the
question may well be asked: What are the consequences
of separating the infant, or child, from that person, or
persons, who have given it good *nursing* care? The existence of a biological tie may be not only irrelevant but
actually lethal.

THE NEONATAL PERIOD

It is generally recognized that the biological specificity
of mother-child ties, and even father-child ties—inasmuch as expectant fathers often have certain biochemical
responses during their wives' pregnancies[22]—may be expected to be closest during pregnancy, delivery and the
immediate neonatal period, and that culturally diversified
conditions may be expected to exert more and more influence the greater the distance from birth. It might be

expected that under "primitive conditions" there would
be found a greater correspondence between culturally
patterned care and biologically given "instinctive behaviour" than in our more artificial modern cultures. Actually, with the exception of the dependence upon breast
milk and such "natural" conditions as arise from ignorance of modern obstetrical methods, we find in primitive societies a great deal of "artificial" or culturally
regulated behaviour surrounding gestation, delivery, and
postnatal care. Although a case can be made for the biological basis of any frequently occurring phenomenon,
such as morning sickness, maternal cravings, and transfer
to the father of a series of imputed attitudes of illness, fatigue, and debility, there are many other societies, equally
primitive, in which these biological possibilities have not
been institutionalized. Furthermore, the mother may be
required to do everything for herself—cut the cord and
bathe the baby—or everything may be done for her; the
father may be required to be present or rigorously ban-
ished; attendance at the birth may be limited to close
relatives or to women who have borne children, or birth
may take place in the midst of a chattering crowd. The
infant may be placed at the mother's dry breast, fed at
once by another woman, kept without food until the
mother has milk, or may not be allowed to feed from its
mother's breast until "true milk" has appeared. The infant may be kept completely covered up, protected from
light and all but a minimum of air; it may be held constantly by its mother or by some other woman, or hung in
a basket, or strapped to a cradle board.[17] In short, the
accumulated evidence from primitive societies suggests
that at a very early stage in human history, traditional
modes of behaviour were evolved which were related not
to any immediate instinctive pattern of neonatal mother-
child relationship—such as has been described, for example, for goats and sheep and reindeer and moose—but
rather to other parts of the learned behaviour of the par-

ticular people, their mode of life, means of transport,
type of shelter, system of kinship organization, methods
of economic exchange, and beliefs about the soul and the
cosmos. Within these extremely diverse systems, in those
tribes which have themselves survived, enough infants
have survived to perpetuate their cultures to the point of
record. . . .

Primitive materials, therefore, give no support to the
theory that there is a "natural" connexion between conditions of human gestation and delivery and appropriate
cultural practices. The tie between the mother and child
can be established by delivery practices which enjoin
Spartan behaviour, which permit the mother to writhe
and scream, or which combine the agonies of a prolonged
birth with accusations of infidelity or sin. The tie between
a man and his wife's child can be established by any
number of arrangements: he may not see the child for a
month after it is born;[15] it may be attributed to him
because he, among his brothers, several of whom share
the same wife, performed the paternity-acknowledging
ritual years ago and no other brother has performed it;[24]
he may claim it when it is born three months after he has
returned from a year's absence, on the theory that it
"hurried up to see its father's face";[17] or, in modern
rather than primitive terms, after agreeing to artificial
insemination, the mother's husband may insist "he really
looks like me."* Thus, fatherhood is a cultural construct
based upon a man's relationship to the children borne by
a woman with whom he has had sex relations.

We may thus say that the establishment of permanent
nurturing ties both between a woman and the child she
bears, and between a man and the child borne by a
woman with whom he has had sex relationships, is dependent upon cultural patterning in which the ideas about
what constitutes motherhood and fatherhood, and later

* Unpublished studies of attitudes of husbands of women who
have received artificial insemination.

sibling relations, are of overriding importance. Among some primitive peoples, habits of adoption before birth accentuate this dependence upon cultural arrangements, so that the adoptive parents take over the infant at birth, even to the point of the dry-breasted adoptive mother inducing milk in her own breast with which to feed the adoptive child.[16] In parts of the Middle East it is the milk tie which establishes a woman's relationship to a child, her own or a foster-child; gestation is not regarded as establishing the relationship between mother and child.[9]

PATTERNING OF
CHARACTER FORMATION

Such evidence does not suggest, however, that the patterns of relationship and the theory of how they originated and how they should affect the future life of the infant may not be significantly related to the kind of child care, the kind of parenthood, and the kind of character structure which is found in a given society. If all children are expected to live and every effort is made to keep the puny and the defective alive, this changes the position of all individuals in a given society. If the father is allowed, or required, to care for the young infant, a tie is established which is absent when such behaviour is not customary. Whether the mother's right to keep her child is dependent upon the decisions of her relatives, or upon those of her husband, or if she herself is given the cultural right to decide whether the child should live or die, this will also change the quality of parenthood, and the culturally determined character structure. But whether a biological parent does or does not provide the best care for a child is, in all known cultures, a function of how biological parenthood is phrased, not of the establishment of point-for-point "natural"—i.e., pre-human— conditions of delivery and child-rearing.

THE ASSUMED NEED
FOR A SINGLE
MOTHER-FIGURE

The Bowlby findings are not, however, primarily concerned with these early hours of birth, nor with the presence or absence of the "biological mother," but rather with an imputed need, in human infants, for a mothering-figure during the first years of life. The assumption is that there is a biologically given need for continuity in this mother-child relationship, that it is a pair relationship which cannot be safely distributed among several figures, and that all attempts to diffuse or divide it and all interruptions are necessarily harmful in character, emotionally damaging, if not completely lethal. Although, logically, continuous care by a foster-mother or nurse meets the Bowlby requirements as well as such care by the biological mother, there is a demand that this continuity be accorded to, and provided by, the biological mother—a demand which is based on a mixed and unexamined set of premises.

It might be claimed that the biological mother establishes a shared tie with her newborn infant owing to the establishment during and after birth of a series of biologically given responses, to the infant's cry, to the smell of the mother's body, to the shape of the mother's nipple, to the nature of the infant's sucking reflex, that is of such an order that it will assure the kind of continuity of later care that the infant requires. This argument would then read: infants need the continuous presence of a mother-figure and Nature has provided a set of mechanisms which if permitted full play will establish just these conditions. Other methods of establishing such a pair relationship are less reliable—especially under modern urban conditions, which are implicitly assumed throughout the Bowlby analysis. If this shared tie is to include breast-feeding, without supplementary feeding, which is the surest method of making the mother and child—the nursing couple[21]—into an exclusive pair relationship, then, as has been discussed above, only a limited number of infants will thrive and survive. An actual return, on the part of society, to such a demand would result in a tremendously increased infant death rate, a change in our medical values—where life is a value at all costs—and might, if widely enough propagated, present some answer to the population explosion.

Actually, such an exclusive and continuous relationship between mother and infant is only possible under highly artificial urban conditions, which combine the production of food outside the home and the practice of contraception. For under primitive conditions there are two situations which require a break in the continuity of mother-child care: (a) the need of the other children for care, and (b) the demands on the mother for food gathering, materials gathering, horticultural and other contributions to the food supply of the family group. The assumption that a mother-child pair relationship can be maintained without interruption until the child is two actually exposes the child to more traumata than if it is expected that several women can breast-feed and care for the child, that a young girl or a grandmother or even a father can give it a dry breast for comfort, and that supplementary—premasticated—food can be made available to it at any time. It is among those people who consider that only the mother can care for the child that the child must be taken to the fields—and may be carried off by wolves, as in parts of India[12]—or left hungry and miserable in the village, as in Alor, bereft because there is no mother-substitute, while the mother is away at work in the gardens. Studies of the character structure of the members of tribes among whom such exclusive relationships obtain—notably the Alorese[6] and the Dobuans[8]—as compared with that of the Samoans, support Bowlby's position that separation from an exclusive mother-figure has a negative effect on character, but also suggest that diffusion of breast-feeding, feeding and nurturing ties

among a number of females of all ages, as in the typical
Samoan large household, ensures the child greater continuity of human care and less liability to trauma. It is
significant that the Samoans, who are conspicuous in the
extent to which mother-child ties are diffused, also have
one of the highest birth rates in the world.*

The queston may still be raised, as it has been by
Konrad Lorenz,[28] whether the cultivation of more exclusive and more intense parent-child relationships is not a
pre-condition of the kind of character structure which is
necessary to maintain and develop our kind of civilization. Here the argument would centre, not on whether life
is more precarious for a child dependent only upon its
biological mother for care, but rather on whether individuals so reared do not show a different and more desirable
—in terms of the stated requirements of the modern
world—character structure. The most definitive materials
available, aside from the studies of primitive societies,
are those collected by Spiro on children of the *Kibbutzim*
system in Israel.[26] Although the single *Kibbutz* which
Spiro studied is too small to be definitive, the analysis
which he presents is persuasive. Children reared with age-
peers, with changing and over-burdened nurses, who see
parents, themselves reared in old-style small families, for
short intervals every day, combine excessive responsiveness to parental behaviour with excessive dependence
upon the peer group, and in youth become heavily dependent upon the members of the peer group with whom
they were reared. The Hutterite studies,[7] in which the
parents were reared within the same system as the children, with children isolated for most of the time from
association with their own parents, confirm the extent to
which children so reared are dependent upon the com-

* 38.0 °/oo for Western Samoa (1958), 39.4 °/oo for American
Samoa (1959) ; as compared with 24.1 °/oo for the USA (1959),
rates beneath 20.0 °/oo for the European countries and an estimate
for rural India of 39 °/oo (data obtained from the United Nations
Statistical Office).

munity and unfitted for venturing forth as individuals. Neither of these bodies of data suggests that children do not thrive and survive under conditions of group nurturing; they both suggest, however, that their mobility and flexibility are impaired.

Data on children within the extended family systems of China[4, 5] and India,[13, 14] which involve multiple nurturing figures, ranging from child nurses to the aged, would seem to confirm the impression from the primitive materials that there is security in a large number of nurturing figures, and that rearing in such a setting leads to fecundity. The question may still be raised as to the character structure of individuals so reared, as Kenneth Soddy has done,[25] but incomplete data on Chinese character structure suggest a range of subtlety and flexibility of personality far beyond that of Westerners, although less complex than that of the Japanese, among whom the child-rearing pattern involves discontinuity of style—early indulgence followed by rigorous discipline—rather than discontinuity of persons.[1, 2]

TASKS OF MODERN
HEALTH AGENCIES

. . . There is undoubtedly evidence enough to warrant the advocacy of such public measures as aid to dependent children, provision of day care rather than residential care for the children of working mothers, hospitalization where continuity with home figures, not necessarily the mother, unless she has had the sole care of the child, is possible, extreme caution in changes of foster-home, and precautions for the care of children from homes that are broken by divorce and death. The problem remains, however, of how to separate the necessary protection of a child who has been isolated in an exclusive pair relationship with the mother—of a type which cannot be said to be natural at a human level, because it actually does not permit participation by the father, care of the dependent

older siblings, and ties with the three-generation family,
all of which are human experiences—from advocacy of
the artificial perpetuation, intensification or creation of
such conditions of exclusive mother-child dependence.

The effects of Bowlby's original monograph were
highly beneficial to the degree that world-wide attention
was focused on the evils of impersonal institutional care
for infants and young children and on types of hospitalization of either mother or child which resulted in traumatic interruptions of a highly exclusive relationship.
These effects have been partially nullified, however, by
the reification into a set of universals of a set of ethno-
centric observations on our own society, combined with
assumptions of biological requirements which are incom-
patible with *Homo sapiens*, although possibly compatible
with an earlier stage when a two-year-old could fend for
himself, and the family did not exist. . . .

REFERENCES

1. Benedict, R. (1946) *The chrysanthemum and the sword*,
   Boston, Houghton Mifflin.
2. Benedict, R. (1949) Child rearing in certain European
   countries. *Amer. J. Orthopsychiat.*, **19**, 342.
3. Bowlby, J. (1952) *Maternal care and mental health*, 2nd
   ed., Geneva (*World Health Organization: Monograph
   Series*, No. 2).
4. Bunzel, R. (1950) *Explorations in Chinese culture*, New
   York (Columbia University Research in Contemporary
   Cultures) [Unpublished report filed with the Institute
   for Intercultural Studies, Inc., New York].
5. Chiang Yee (1940) *A Chinese childhood*, London,
   Methuen.
6. Dubois, C. (1944) *The people of Alor*, Minneapolis,
   University of Minnesota Press.
7. Eaton, J. W. & Weil, R. J. (1955) *Culture and mental
   disorders*, Glencoe, Ill., The Free Press.
8. Fortune, R. F. (1932) *Sorcerers of Dobu*, London, Routledge & Kegan Paul.
9. Granqvist, H. (1947) *Birth and childhood among the*

Arabs: studies in a Muhammadan village in Palestine, Helsingfors, Soderstron.

10. Gunther, M. (1955) Instinct and the nursing couple. *Lancet*, **1**, 575.

11. Lin, Tsung-Yi (1960) *Reality and vision: a report of the First Asian Seminar on Mental Health and Family Life, Baguio, Philippines, 6–20 December 1958, sponsored jointly by the Government of the Republic of the Philippines, the Asia Foundation, the World Federation for Mental Health, the World Health Organization*, Manila.

12. Mandelbaum, D. G. (1943) Wolf-child histories from India, *J. Soc. Psychol.*, **17**, 25.

13. Mandelbaum, D. G. (1959) *The family in India*. In: Anshen, R. N., ed., *The family: its function and destiny*, New York, Harper, p. 167.

14. Mayer, A. C. (1960) *Caste and kinship in central India*, Berkeley, University of California Press, p. 214.

15. Mead, M. (1930) *Growing up in New Guinea*, New York, Morrow.

16. Mead, M. (1935) *Sex and temperament in three primitive societies*, New York, Morrow, Part II.

17. Mead, M. (1949) *Male and female*, New York, Morrow.

18. Mead, M. (1954) Some theoretical considerations on the problem of mother-child separation. *Amer. J. Orthopsychiat.*, **24**, 471.

19. Mead, M. (1954) *Research on primitive children*. In: Carmichael, L., ed., *Manual of child psychology*, 2nd ed., New York, Wiley, p. 735.

20. Mead, M. (1957) Changing patterns of parent-child relations in an urban culture. *Int. J. Psycho-Anal.*, **38**, 1.

21. Middlemore, M. P. (1941) *The nursing couple*, London, Hamish Hamilton.

22. Mirsky, I. A. (1950) Pepsinogen excretion (uropepsin) as an index of the influence of various life situations on gastric secretion. *Ass. Res. Nerv. Dis. Proc.*, **29**, 628.

23. *Report of a conference organized by the World Federation for Mental Health on malnutrition and food habits, held in Cuernavaca, Mexico, September 9–14, 1960* [editor: A. Burgess].

24. Rivers, W. H. R. (1906) *The Todas*, London, Macmillan.

25. Soddy, K., ed. (1961) *Cross-cultural studies in mental*

health: Identity-mental health and value systems, London, Tavistock Publications.

26. Spiro, M. (1958) *Children of the Kibbutz*, Cambridge, Mass., Harvard University Press.

27. Spitz, R. (1945) *Hospitalism*. In: *The psychoanalytic study of the child*, New York, International Universities Press, Vol. 1, p. 53.

28. Tanner, J. M. & Inhelder, B., ed. (1956) *Discussions on child development*, London, Tavistock Publications, Vol. 2 [Proceedings of the Second Meeting of the WHO Study Group on the Psychobiological Development of the Child, London, 1954].

CONTRIBUTORS

GRETE L. BIBRING, M.D., is Psychiatrist-in-Chief Emerita, Beth Israel Hospital, Boston, and Clinical Professor of Psychiatry Emerita, Faculty of Medicine, Harvard University.

HELENE DEUTSCH is a psychoanalyst renowned for her work on the psychology of women; she lives and works in Boston.

CLELLAN S. FORD was Professor of Anthropology at Yale University; FRANK A. BEACH is Professor of Psychology at the University of California, Berkeley.

LOIS WLADIS HOFFMAN, Ph.D., is Associate Professor of Psychology at the University of Michigan and co-author, with I. F. Nye, of *Working Mothers* (1974).

KAREN HORNEY was a psychoanalyst who pioneered in work on female psychology and founded the Karen Horney Institute. She died in 1952.

ALFRED C. KINSEY was the founder of the Institute for Sex Research and author or co-author of numerous works on sexuality. WARDELL B. POMEROY, CLYDE E. MARTIN, and PAUL H. GEBHARD were his associates for many years. Dr. Gebhard is now Executive Director of the Institute; Dr. Martin is engaged in research; and Dr. Pomeroy has a private practice of marriage counseling and psychotherapy in New York City.

BETTY J. KRONSKY is a certified social worker and Gestalt therapist in private practice in New York City.

W. H. MASTERS, M.D., and VIRGINIA JOHNSON are well known as pioneers in the field of sex research and as the authors of numerous works on human sexuality.

JOYCE MCDOUGALL is a leading psychoanalyst in Paris, specializing in work with children.

MARGARET MEAD is Curator Emeritus of Ethnology at the American Museum of Natural History and a seminal writer in comparative anthropology.

JOHN MONEY is Professor of Medical Psychology and Pediatrics at the Johns Hopkins Hospital and a leading researcher in human sexuality.

RUTH MOULTON, M.D., is a psychoanalyst in private practice in New York City and is on the faculties of the William Alanson White Institute and Columbia University.

NILES NEWTON, Ph.D., is Professor in the Division of Psychology at Northwestern Medical School, specializing in the psychology of child-bearing.

MALKAH E. NOTMAN, M.D., is a psychiatrist in private practice in Boston and is on the faculties of Harvard Medical School and Boston University.

ANDREA OSTRUM, Ph.D., is a clinical psychologist in private practice in New York City and Chief Psychologist at Brooklyn Family Court.

KAREN E. PAIGE, Ph.D., is Assistant Professor of Psychology at the University of California, Davis, and Research Associate at the Survey Research Center, Berkeley.

EVELYN GOODENOUGH PITCHER, Ph.D., is Professor and Chairman of the Department of Child Study, Tufts University.

ISADORE RUBIN, Ph.D., was with the Sex Information and Education Council of the United States and engaged in marriage counseling and sex research.

NATALIE SHAINESS, M.D., is a psychiatrist and psychoanalyst who has written extensively on female identity and the mothering experience. She is in private practice in New York City.

MARY JANE SHERFEY, M.D., is a practicing psychiatrist in New York City and is at work on volume 2 of *The Nature and Evolution of Female Sexuality*.

RENÉ A. SPITZ, M.D., was an important contributor to theories of ego psychology. At his death in 1974 he was Visiting Professor of Psychiatry Emeritus, at the University of Colorado Medical School.

CLARA THOMPSON wrote extensively on female psychology and was a pioneer in the American psychoanalytic movement. She died in 1957.

ROCHELLE PAUL WORTIS, Ph.D., is with the Child Care Resource Center, Cambridge, Mass.

ADDITIONAL READING

Extensive bibliographies are attached to many of the articles in this anthology; the following list of books is intended as a modest supplement for the general reader. (P = paperback available)

Bardwick, Judith M. *Psychology of Women: A Study of Bio-Cultural Conflicts.* New York: Harper & Row, 1971. An extensive survey of research in female psychology, from hormones to sex roles, with the author's own views, not always pro-feminist, freely expressed. (P)

Boston Women's Health Book Collective. *Our Bodies, Ourselves.* New York: Simon and Schuster, 1973. An excellent basic guide to all aspects of women's sexuality and health, written by feminists, with a balanced view on controversial issues and good reference lists for further reading. (P)

Bowlby, John. *Attachment and Loss.* New York: Basic Books, 1969–. Vol. 1, *Attachment*, 1969. Vol. 2, *Separation: Anxiety and Anger*, 1973. Volume 1 is a classic statement on the importance of a single mothering figure to a developing child. Volume 2 is its equally important sequel.

Brecher, Edward M. *The Sex Researchers.* Boston: Little, Brown, 1969. Entertaining and valuable history of sex research, with particular attention to women.

Chesler, Phyllis. *Women and Madness.* New York: Doubleday, 1972. A badly written, disorganized presentation of the thesis that men drive women crazy. Provocative, although can't see beyond woman-as-victim. (P)

Dalton, Katherine. *The Menstrual Cycle.* New York: Pantheon, 1969.

The menstrual cycle explained, with emotional aspects attributed primarily to chemical and hormonal imbalance. A good presentation, and quite persuasive.

de Beauvoir, Simone. *The Second Sex*. New York: Modern Library, 1952.
The foundation work of modern feminism. (P)

Erikson, Erik H. *Childhood and Society*. New York: Norton, 1963.
Contains Erikson's famous theory of women's "inner space," a modification of the old idea that "anatomy is destiny." (P)

Firestone, Shulamith. *The Dialectic of Sex*. New York: Morrow, 1970.
A radical analysis of the sexual class system, advocating extra-biological methods of reproduction and the abolition of the family as the means of eliminating sexual inequality. (P)

Frankfort, Ellen. *Vaginal Politics*. New York: Quadrangle, 1972.
A shrewd look at the politics of women's health, with useful information for dealing with doctors. (P)

Friedan, Betty. *The Feminine Mystique*. New York: Norton, 1963.
The classic study of American women. (P)

Horney, Karen. *Feminine Psychology*. New York: Norton, 1967.
Collected essays on women by the psychoanalyst who began refuting Freud's theories on women fifty years ago. (P)

Mead, Margaret. *Male and Female*. New York: Morrow, 1949.
Another classic. How the sexes relate to each other in a variety of cultures, showing the interplay between biology and culture in developing identity. (P)

Miller, Jean Baker, ed. *Psychoanalysis and Women*. Baltimore, Penguin, 1973.
Essays on women by sixteen psychoanalysts. (P)

Millett, Kate. *Sexual Politics.* New York: Doubleday, 1970.
The politics of sex in history and literature. Another classic. (P)

Mitchell, Juliet. *Psychoanalysis and Feminism.* New York: Pantheon, 1974.
A fascinating book in which Mitchell proposes to reclaim Freudian theory on sexuality from the misinterpretations of post-Freudians and feminist critics, after which the same theory is to be transformed into an ideological weapon for the overthrow of the patriarchy, of which, she says, it provides the finest extant analysis.

Money, John, and Anke A. Ehrhardt. *Man and Woman, Boy and Girl.* Baltimore: Johns Hopkins University Press, 1972.
An important work on how sexual differentiation is accomplished. Money looks at hormones, genes, environment and a number of other factors and comes up with startling evidence of the overriding force of environment in molding identity. (P)

Neumann, Erich. *Amor and Psyche: The Psychic Development of the Feminine.* Princeton, N.J.: Princeton University Press, 1956.
A commentary on the story of Amor and Psyche by a Jungian who sees in it a paradigm of female psychic development. (P)

———. *The Great Mother: An Analysis of the Archetype.* Princeton, N.J.: Princeton University Press, 1963.
The image of the Great Mother in myth and art. (P)

Oakley, Ann. *Sex, Gender, and Society.* New York: Harper & Row, Harper Colophon Books, 1972.
A concise, useful investigation of the relationship between sex and identity in society. (P)

Seaman, Barbara. *The Doctor's Case against the Pill.* New York: Peter H. Wyden, 1969.
An analysis of the hazards of birth-control pills. (P)

———. *Free and Female.* New York: Coward, McCann & Geoghegan, 1972.

A free-wheeling look at women's sexuality, aimed at
puncturing myths and providing an easy-to-read interpretation of various areas of research. (P)

Tanzer, Deborah, with Jean Libman Block. *Why Natural
Childbirth?* New York: Doubleday, 1972.
The history, theory, and practice of natural childbirth,
with useful references.

Tiger, Lionel, and Robin Fox. *The Imperial Animal.* New
York: Holt, Rinehart and Winston, 1971.
An anthropologist and a sociologist present their view
of the animal basis for human behavior and society, at
the center of which they see the mother-child bond.
Feminism and the education of females are seen as
inherently destructive to society. A major opposition
view. (P)